CHANNEL

THE MAKING OF THE
SOUTH WALES LANDSCAPE

THE MAKING OF THE ENGLISH LANDSCAPE
Edited by W. G. Hoskins and Roy Millward

The Making of the South Wales Landscape

by

MOELWYN WILLIAMS

HODDER AND STOUGHTON
LONDON SYDNEY AUCKLAND TORONTO

To my parents
whose memory I dearly cherish

Preface

THIS BOOK IS an attempt to study the human landscape as it has evolved through the ages in the hills, valleys, and coastal areas of South Wales. We who have inherited the contemporary scene, may look upon it as a kind of palimpsest of successive generations who, by devising different kinds of techniques and social organisation, strove recurringly to come to terms with their natural environment. The physical realities of South Wales, its relief, soils, and climate, have imposed a variety of constraints on the rate and kind of progress our ancestors were able to make (Fig 2). For instance, the inhospitable windswept uplands (lying above the 600-foot contour line, and forming about two-thirds of its surface area), with their ill-drained and shallow soils, have been associated from time immemorial with a sparse population dwelling in scattered homesteads, and depending mainly on a pastoral economy. In marked contrast, the more hospitable and fertile lowlands, with their freely drained loams and clay loams on sandstone tracts, provided conditions suited to arable and mixed farming which supported a denser population living in nucleated settlements. The traditional social differences that marked these two principal geographical divisions, persisted fairly clearly until about a century and a half ago when the exploitation of the rich coal deposits that lay hidden in the bowels of parts of the uplands gave rise to a unique man-made industrial complex, which replaced pastoralism that had for centuries dominated life in those parts (Fig. 3). There emerged from these new conditions an entirely new social milieu with which much of South Wales has been identified ever since.

7

The South Wales landscape contains an enormous amount of observable evidence of the processes of transition from early forms of society to the relatively ordered society in which we live today. By summoning the aid of the techniques of aerial photography, the skills of the archaeologist and palaeobotanist, the story may be greatly expanded and enriched, but never exhausted.

The Local Government Act of 1972 has brought about changes in the names and boundaries of some of the counties formerly included in South Wales, and these have been officially recognised from April, 1974 (Fig. 1). Thus Cardiganshire, Carmarthenshire and Pembrokeshire now form the new County of Dyfed; Radnorshire and Breconshire form part of the new County of Powys; Monmouthshire becomes Gwent; and Glamorgan has been divided into West Glamorgan, Mid Glamorgan and South Glamorgan. Throughout this work, however, it will be more convenient to adhere to the names of the old administrative counties.

In a work of this nature I have not thought it necessary to quote every source in detail, nevertheless my indebtedness to both original and secondary sources has been acknowledged in the footnotes, and by way of the select bibliographies at the end of each chapter.

In writing this book I have, perforce, incurred many debts which I gratefully acknowledge. For numerous personal favours I wish to thank many of my colleagues at the National Library of Wales; the staffs of the Welsh Office, Cardiff; the National Museum of Wales; the Welsh Folk Museum; the Glamorgan County Record Office; the Cardiff Central Library; the Guild Hall, Swansea; the National Coal Board; the Welsh Forestry Commission; the City of Cardiff Parks and Allotments Department; the West Glamorgan Water Board; the Milford Haven Conservancy Board; the Cwmbran Development Corporation; and the

Rheidol Power Station. I wish to express my thanks to the Secretary of the Royal Commission on Ancient Monuments in Wales and his staff for their many courtesies, and in particular to Mr W. E. Griffiths, who not only enlightened me 'in the field', but also read parts of the text and drew my attention to errors of fact; to Mr Howard Thomas, who also accompanied me on field work in the Vale of Glamorgan, and supplied me with information and diagrams relating to deserted villages in Glamorgan; and to Mr Douglas R. Hague for providing me with certain data on some of the South Wales lighthouses. I am grateful to Professor Glanville R. Jones, Liverpool University, who placed at my disposal a number of diagrams relating to medieval Welsh settlements. Emeritus Professor E. G. Bowen, Aberystwyth, and Professor Glanmor Williams, Swansea, read the text, and made useful criticisms and suggestions which rescued me from many errors.

I am deeply indebted to my wife, not only for typing my manuscript, but also for her patience and help in so many other ways.

Finally, my special thanks are due to Professor W. G. Hoskins, the editor, for inviting me to contribute to this series, and for his kind encouragement, criticisms, and wise counsel at all times.

List of abbreviations

Arch. Camb.	*Archaeologia Cambrensis*
B.B.C.S.	*Bulletin of the Board of Celtic Studies*
C.S.P.	*Calendar of State Papers*
Cymmr.	*Y Cymmrodor*
J.H.S.C.W.	*Journal of the Historical Society of the Church in Wales*
R.C.A.M.	Royal Commission on Ancient Monuments
Trans. Hon. Soc. Cymmr.	*Transactions of the Honourable Society of Cymmrodorion*

Contents

List of Plates

ACKNOWLEDGMENTS

The author wishes to thank the following for permission to
use their photographs:
A. F. Kersting: Plates 1, 31
The Royal Commission on Ancient and Historical Monu-
ments: Plates 2, 28 (Crown Copyright)
The Committee for Aerial Photography, Cambridge:
Plates 3, 13
The National Library of Wales, Aberystwyth: Plates 6, 7, 8,
9, 11, 12, 16, 18, 19, 22, 25, 26, 27, 29, 30, 32, 34, 35, 36,
40, 43, 46, 47, 51, 52, 54, 56, 57, 59, 66, 67
Roger Worsley: Plates 17, 44, 48
Major Herbert Lloyd-Jones: Plate 29
Terence Soames: Plates 23, 63
H. Tempest Limited: Plate 24
Chief Executive Officer, Guildhall Swansea: Plates 26, 55
Hugh Daniels, Pontarddulais: Plate 34
Rev. Gomer M. Roberts, Llandybë: Plate 35
C. Batstone: Plates 33, 42, 65
Dr Leslie Wyn Evans: Plates 37, 38
The National Museum of Wales, Cardiff: Plates 39, 45
National Coal Board: Plate 41
Mr Hayden Holloway, L.R.P.S., University College,
Swansea: Plate 52
The Forestry Commission: Plates 53, 64
Raymond Hawkins: Plate 58
Aerofilms Limited: Plate 60
Hylton Warner and Company Limited: Plates 61, 62
Plates 4, 10, 14, 15, 16, 28, 54, 56, 66, 67 are the copyright
of the author

List of maps and drawings

Editor's Introduction

SOME TWENTY YEARS ago I wrote: "Despite the multitude of books about English landscape and scenery, and the flood of topographical books in general, there is not one book which deals with the historical evolution of the landscape as we know it. At the most we may be told that the English landscape is the man-made creation of the seventeenth and eighteenth centuries, which is not even a quarter-truth, for it refers only to country houses and their parks and to the parliamentary enclosures that gave us a good deal of our modern pattern of fields, hedges, and by-roads. It ignores the fact that more than a half of England never underwent this kind of enclosure, but evolved in an entirely different way, and that in some regions the landscape had been virtually completed by the eve of the Black Death. No book exists to describe the manner in which the various landscapes of this country came to assume the shape and appearance they now have, why the hedgebanks and lanes of Devon should be so totally different from those of the Midlands, why there are so many ruined churches in Norfolk or so many lost villages in Lincolnshire, or what history lies behind the winding ditches of the Somerset marshlands, the remote granite farmsteads of Cornwall, and the lonely pastures of upland Northamptonshire.

"There are indeed some good books on the geology that lies behind the English landscape, and these represent perhaps the best kind of writing on the subject we have yet had, for they deal with facts and are not given to the sentimental and formless slush which afflicts so many books concerned only with superficial appearances. But the geologist, good though he may be, is concerned with only one aspect of the subject, and beyond a certain point he is obliged to leave the historian and geographer to continue and complete it. He explains to us the bones of the landscape, the fundamental structure that gives form and colour to the scene and produces a certain kind of topography and natural vegetation. But the flesh that covers the bones, and the details of the features, are the concern of the historical geographer, whose task it is to show how man has clothed the geological skeleton during the comparative past—mostly within the last fifteen centuries, though in some regions much longer that this."

In 1955 I published *The Making of the English Landscape*. There I claimed that it was a pioneer study, and if only for that reason it could not supply the answer to every question. Four books, in a series published between 1954 and 1957, filled in more detail for the counties of Cornwall, Lancashire, Gloucestershire, and Leicestershire.

Much has been achieved since I wrote the words I have quoted. Landscape-history is now taught in some universities, and has been studied for many parts of England and Wales in university theses. Numerous articles have been written and a few books published, such as Alan Harris's *The Rural Landscape of the East Riding 1700–1850* (1961) and more recently Dorothy Sylvester's *The Rural Landscape of the Welsh Borderland* (1969).

Special mention should perhaps be made of a number of landscape-studies in the series of Occasional Papers published by the Department of English Local History at the University of Leicester. Above all in this series one might draw attention to *Laughton: a study in the Evolution of the Wealden Landscape* (1965) as a good example of a microscopic scrutiny of a single parish, and Margaret Spufford's *A Cambridgeshire Community* (*Chippenham*) published in the same year. Another masterly study of a single parish which should be cited particularly is Harry Thorpe's monograph entitled *The Lord and the Landscape*, dealing with the Warwickshire Parish of Wormleighton, which also appeared in 1965.[1] Geographers were quicker off the mark than historians in this new field, for it lies on the frontiers of both disciplines. And now botany has been recruited into the field, with the recent development of theories about the dating of hedges from an analysis of their vegetation.

But a vast amount still remains to be discovered about the man-made landscape. Some questions are answered, but new questions continually arise which can only be answered by a microscopic examination of small areas even within a county. My own perspective has enlarged greatly since I published my first book on the subject. I now believe that some features in our landscape today owe their origin to a much more distant past than I had formerly thought possible. I think it highly likely that in some favoured parts of England farming has gone on in an unbroken continuity since the Iron Age, perhaps even since the Bronze Age; and that many of our villages were first settled at the same time. In other words, that underneath our old villages, and underneath the older parts of these villages, there may well be evidence of habitation going back for some two or three thousand years. Conquests only meant in most places a change of landlord for better or for worse, but the farming life went on unbroken, for even conquerors would have starved without its continuous activity. We have so far failed to find this continuity of habitation because sites have been built upon over and over again and have never been wholly cleared and examined by trained archaeologists.

At the other end of the time-scale the field of industrial archaeology has come into being in the last few years, though I touched upon it years ago under the heading of Industrial Landscapes. Still, a vast amount more could now be said about this kind of landscape.

[1] *Transactions of the Birmingham Archaeological Society,* Vol. 80, 1965.

Purists might say that the county is not the proper unit for the study of landscape-history. They would say perhaps that we ought to choose individual and unified regions for such an exercise; but since most counties, however small, contain a wonderful diversity of landscape, each with its own special history, we get, I am sure, a far more appealing book than if we adopted the geographical region as our basis. On the other hand, Wales, for so long a poverty-stricken country, despite its magnificent scenery, is better treated in two large areas—North and South—and this approach has been adopted here.

The authors of these books are concerned with the ways in which men have cleared the natural woodlands, reclaimed marshland, fen, and moor, created fields out of a wilderness, made lanes, roads, and footpaths, laid out towns, built villages, hamlets, farmhouses and cottages, created country houses and their parks, dug mines and made canals and railways, in short with everything that has altered the natural landscape. One cannot understand the landscape and enjoy it to the full, apprehend all its wonderful variety from region to region (often within the space of a few miles), without going back to the history that lies behind it. A commonplace ditch may be the thousand-year-old boundary of a royal manor; a certain hedge-bank may be even more ancient, the boundary of a Celtic estate; a certain deep and winding lane may be the work of twelfth-century peasants, some of whose names may be made known to us if we search diligently enough. To discover these things, we have to go to the documents that are the historian's raw material, and find out what happened to produce these results and when, and precisely how they came about.

But it is not only the documents that are the historian's guide. One cannot write books like these by reading someone else's books, or even by studying records in a muniment room. The landscape itself, to those who know how to read it aright, is the richest historical record we possess. There are discoveries to be made in it for which no written documents exist, or have ever existed. To write the history of the landscape requires a combination of documentary research and of fieldwork, of laborious scrambling on foot wherever the trail may lead. The result is a new kind of history which it is hoped will appeal to all those who like to travel intelligently, to get away from the guide-book show-pieces now and then, and to know the reasons behind what they are looking at. There is no part, however unpromising it may appear at first sight, that is not full of questions for those who have a sense of the past. So much of Great Britain is still unknown and unexplored. Fuller enjoined us nearly three centuries ago

"Know most of the rooms of thy native country
before thou goest over the threshold thereof.
Especially seeing England presents thee with
so many observables."

These books on The Making of the English Landscape are concerned with the observables of England, and the secret history that lies behind them. It is a special pleasure to welcome the first of the two volumes covering the landscape-history of Wales.

Exeter, 1970   W. G. HOSKINS

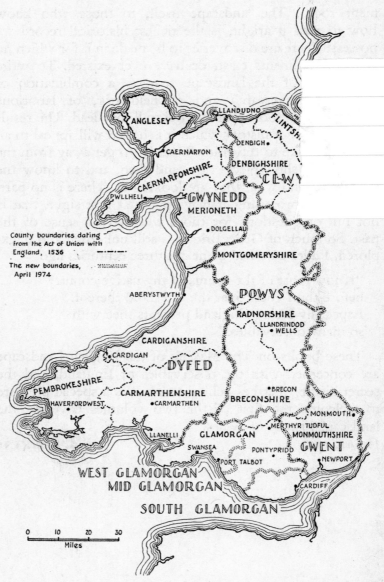

County boundaries dating from the Act of Union with England, 1536

The new boundaries, April 1974

ANGLESEY

LLANDUDNO

FLINTSH.

CAERNARFON

DENBIGH

DENBIGHSHIRE

CLWY

CAERNARFONSHIRE

PWLLHELI

GWYNEDD

MERIONETH

DOLGELLAU

MONTGOMERYSHIRE

ABERYSTWYTH

POWYS

RADNORSHIRE

LLANDRINDOD WELLS

CARDIGANSHIRE

CARDIGAN

DYFED

PEMBROKESHIRE

HAVERFORDWEST

CARMARTHENSHIRE

CARMARTHEN

BRECON

BRECONSHIRE

MONMOUTH

MERTHYR TUDFUL

MONMOUTHSHIRE

LLANELLI

GLAMORGAN

SWANSEA

PONTYPRIDD

GWENT

PORT TALBOT

NEWPORT

WEST GLAMORGAN

MID GLAMORGAN

CARDIFF

SOUTH GLAMORGAN

0   10   20   30
Miles

Fig. 1. The county boundary divisions. (Based on Welsh Office Circular 238/72.)

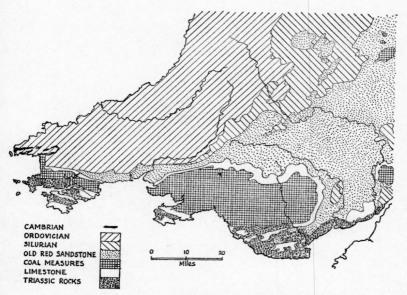

Fig. 2. The geology of South Wales.

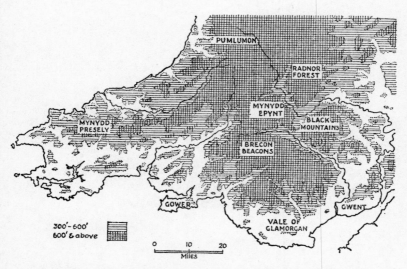

Fig. 3. South Wales: the distribution of uplands and lowlands.

1. South Wales before the coming of the Normans

The pre-Roman landscape. The Roman period. The coming of Christianity. Post-Roman landscape. Scandinavian influences

The pre-Roman landscape

THE TERRITORY TO which we now ascribe the title 'South Wales' has, since the Act of Union of 1536, included the counties of Cardigan, Pembroke, Carmarthen, Brecon, Radnor, Glamorgan and Monmouth,[1] and occupies an area of approximately 4,764 square miles, or about 3,000,000 acres, and has a population of over 2,100,000.[2] Today, the physical features of the area provide the spectator with a rich variety of natural beauty ranging from the fascinating, if sometimes forbidding, high ridges of Pumlumon and the Brecon Beacons with their wild shadowy moorlands, to the isolated valleys which fall away in a southerly direction, merging into rich meadowland and lush lowland pastures which are skirted by a rugged, yet picturesque, coastline extending from the Dyfi estuary to Chepstow on the Severn.

[1] It should be explained that although, ecclesiastically, Monmouthshire had always been a part of Wales, the Act of 1536 had made it subject to the Courts of Westminster, which, therefore, placed it in an anomalous position.

[2] It is of interest to note that this figure represents roughly seventy-six per cent of the total population of Wales, which stands at 2,730,000. The population of Glamorgan and Monmouthshire alone, however, is 1,800,000, which means that sixty-six per cent of the Welsh people are concentrated in the industrial south.

The landscape features, which we now take for granted, were not present when Palaeolithic (Old Stone Age) man first appeared in the area anything from 30,000 to 50,000 years ago. What was the precise nature of the landscape when man first stumbled into the region, we shall never know. But from our geological knowledge, we can safely assume that he would have found "no moled harbours—the coastline may not have assumed its present configuration until between 1750 and 250 B.C.—no roads, no fields to welcome him . . ." Instead, he would have encountered sub-arctic conditions, and an inhospitable landscape dominated by tundra and steppe, in which roamed long-haired and heavy-coated creatures such as the woolly rhinoceros, cave bear, reindeer, wild horse, mammoth and hyena.

The first people—they could not have been more than a handful—who encountered the primeval conditions in South Wales were Palaeolithic hunters and fishers who have left their traces in the form of roughly trimmed stone tools and weapons in the rock shelters or small caves in which they lived. The best-known examples of these are to be seen at Coygan Cave, near Laugharne, Carmarthenshire, King Arthur's Cave near Ross-on-Wye, and the so-called Goat's Hole cave, Paviland, in Gower. The last named gained fame in 1823 through the discovery by William Buckland, an Oxford geologist, of a human skeleton mistakenly referred to as the Red Lady of Paviland, which later expert examination proved to be that of a young man just over twenty-five years of age, 5 feet 6–8 inches tall, whose burial may have been accompanied by some kind of ritual involving a liberal use of red ochre, symbolising the blood that his fellow hunters thought he would need in the hereafter. These Early Stone Age men, armed simply with their rough stone tools and implements, could only have made a minimal impact on the landscape.

By about 10,000 B.C., climatic changes had brought about

warmer and wetter conditions which, in turn, affected local vegetation and animal life. A landscape that was once dominated by tundra and steppe now gave way to one dominated by forests. Groves of birch, aspen and willow, mixed oak, alders and beeches, in sequence, probably began to clothe the grassy plains and bare hills of South Wales. Despite the changing environmental conditions which characterised this so-called Mesolithic (8,000–2,500 B.C.) period, men continued to be food-gatherers, dependent on hunting, fishing, and the collecting of roots and berries. Their implements, however, became more refined under the influence of wood or bone as hafting materials. What traces have been found of Mesolithic man in South Wales in the form of tools, suggest that they were designed for use as borers, harpoon barbs, and knives by mounting in handles or shafts. Evidence of Mesolithic man has been found chiefly along the coasts on open sites such as on Tanybwlch beach, near Aberystwyth, and on the submerged land surface at Lydstep Bay, Pembrokeshire.

Although the impression made by the Stone Age culture on the South Wales landscape may have been small and of little importance, the archaeological evidence which has been assembled over the last century or so shows primeval man—dwarfed though he is by the remoteness of time—reacting to his natural environment for precisely the same reasons as historic man has done (and continues to do, but with more sophisticated 'tools'), namely, to secure the basic requirements of survival—food, clothing and shelter. Indeed, if there is an element of continuity in the history of man in South Wales, then it surely must be found in the way its inhabitants have, along the ages, endeavoured to get a living by utilising the resources of its highlands and lowlands, its coastline, and its lakes, rivers and streams. The pace of 'utilisation' has varied throughout the centuries according to the efficiency, or inefficiency, of man's equipment, or tools, with which he contrived to fish, hunt, build, mine, fell, clear, graze or crop.

About 5,000[3] years ago, the first farmers began to arrive in South Wales, and brought with them the Neolithic way of life. They probably came by sea from Western France and settled at various points along the coast between Pembrokeshire and Newport, in Monmouthshire, and in the Black Mountains of Breconshire. With the coming of Neolithic man, South Wales saw the beginnings of human settlement, and probably the beginning of the unbroken history of 'Wales', for it is now fairly established that the New Stone Age settlers who, in appearance, were generally short in stature, dark-haired and long-headed, were the ancestors of many groups of modern Welshmen to be found, more particularly, in South Wales. They brought with them techniques of cultivation and of the domestication of animals such as the Celtic ox, sheep, dog, horse, goat and pig. Their stone implements were now more highly polished, with a sharper edge, and more suited to the requirements of forest clearance, which became necessary, albeit in a small way, for arable farming. The increased demand for stone axes gave rise to stone-axe factories such as have been traced on the Presely[4] Hills and at Ramsey in Pembrokeshire. In this apparent stir in the production of stone axes, one might see the essential difference between the Mesolithic food gatherer and hunter, who accepted the dictates of their environment, and the Neolithic farmers who attacked it and started the long and erratic processes which have produced the landscape we observe today.

Although Neolithic man introduced revolutionary methods in the control of crops and animals (which must

[3] The conventional time scale must be used with reservation, as radiocarbon dating pushes this back about 1,000 years.

[4] Throughout this book the Welsh spelling of place-names has been preferred where the Welsh form is easily recognisable to the non-Welsh speaker.

have made for a higher and relatively more complicated standard of living) the landscape evidence of this culture survives almost entirely in a series of monuments in the form of communal tombs. These tombs, moreover, reveal on the landscape two techniques which they embody, namely, of transporting and erecting heavy unhewn stones, and of dry walling. They are known as *cromlechau* (or burial chambers), some bearing a close resemblance to the Cotswold-Severn long barrows, others to Irish tombs, and remain among the most mysterious and impressive features in many parts of the South Wales landscape (Plate 1). These mausoleums are well represented by the Pentre Ifan cromlech in Pembrokeshire; Tinkinswood cromlech near St Nicholas, in Glamorgan; Parc le Breos burial chamber, Gower, and at Pipton, about two miles north of Talgarth, in Breconshire. Distribution maps (Figs 4 & 5) of these tombs show the greatest concentration to be along the coastline of Pembrokeshire, with smaller groupings in the uplands of Carmarthenshire, and along the southern coastal region of Glamorgan and the Black Mountains of Breconshire. Unfortunately, there is no evidence to prove conclusively that the distribution pattern of the Neolithic houses of the dead bears any relationship to the distribution pattern of their houses of the living or settlement sites. Although the people who built the megalithic tombs laid the foundations of our modern agriculture, yet surprisingly few of their farmsteads have been found, simply because they were crudely built of perishable material such as wood, wattle and mud. Excavations of the tombs themselves have yielded substantial finds which indicate that the Neolithic settlers in South Wales had accomplished a limited clearance of forest in order to grow barley and corn. But here it should be borne in mind that forest clearance was not, of necessity, a prerequisite of settlement. Agricultural and pastoral activities were often parallel developments. For

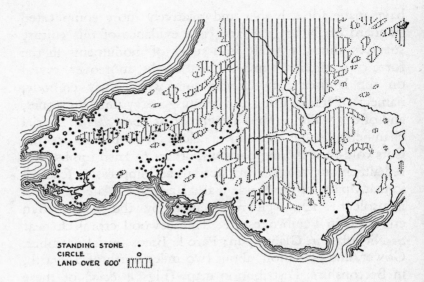

STANDING STONE •
CIRCLE ⊙
LAND OVER 600' ⨳⨳⨳⨳⨳

Fig. 4. Neolithic settlement in South Wales; distribution of standing stones and stone circles. (After W. F. Grimes.)

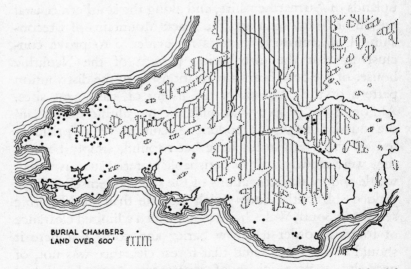

BURIAL CHAMBERS •
LAND OVER 600' ⨳⨳⨳⨳⨳

Fig. 5. Neolithic settlement in South Wales; distribution of burial chambers. (After W. F. Grimes.)

instance, until the development of fodder crops in the eighteenth century, the feeding of livestock in winter had, from time immemorial, presented a serious problem to man, and it was the forests, in fact, that served as the 'peasants' providence'. So that although crop husbandry required some degree of initial forest clearance, there were aspects of pastoral farming, browsing beasts, by thinning undergrowth and scrubs around tilled areas, which helped prepare the way for clearance of new forest zones. Grazing animals under the control of man must have exercised a considerable influence on the natural landscape. It has been suggested that "the contrast between the areas settled by pre-historic man, and those shunned by him, was not, of necessity, as between forested and open lands, or even between densely and lightly forested, so much as between those which he could and those which he could not culti-vate".[5] In the final analysis, however, it must be said that as yet we know almost nothing of the Neolithic settlements, and it remains a mystery that, so far as we know, people who could build the great megalithic tombs, did not build stone houses that have survived to the present day. It may have been that they depended on a semi-nomadic economy.[6]

The Neolithic culture was followed by the so-called Bronze Age, which was again fairly well represented throughout the South Wales region by a number of burial mounds, sometimes having been elaborately constructed with walls or kerbs of stone encompassing the burial area (Plate 2). The burials in most instances were now cremations, as distinct from the inhumation of the Neolithic peoples. The significance of these changes of burial practices on the landscape lies in the fact that the Megalithic chambered

[5] Graham Clark, 'Farmers and forests', *Antiquity*, XIX (1945); C. S. Orwin, *The Open Fields* (Oxford, 1938).
[6] Glyn Daniel, 'The first people' in *Wales Through the Ages*, Vol. I, p. 16.

tombs (*cromlechau*) gave way to round burial mounds appearing in the landscape as smooth earth mounds (barrows) in settlement areas in the lowlands and, predominantly so, as heaps of stone (cairns) in the hill country.

Again, little is known of the settlement sites of the Bronze Age peoples, but archaeological finds suggest that by about 1,000 B.C., implements and weapons in the form of axes, knives and spearheads "had reached a level of development which could not be surpassed except by some kind of revolutionary process" (Grimes). The appearance of new types of bronzes during the Late Bronze Age probably indicate that human needs, and the methods of satisfying them, were becoming a little more complicated. For instance, when Llyn Fawr (Great Lake), in Glamorgan, was drained in 1912, preparatory to being converted into a reservoir, in addition to "harness fittings, socketed sickles, razors, and two large sheet metal cauldrons", objects of iron, a new metal, were also found, including a fragment of a sword which was "an unmistakable product of the Hallstatt culture"—that is, the Early Iron Age.

Such finds as these must be interpreted in terms of a cultural development which, unfortunately, is not always traceable in the landscape in the form of settlement sites. As the *cromlechau* (round and long-chambered) serve as indicators to the pattern of Neolithic settlement, so do the pre-Roman hill forts provide guide-lines to Bronze Age as well as Iron Age settlements.[7] Although experts continue to argue about the precise function of the hill forts, it seems fairly clear that whether military in function or not, they provide landscape evidence of a way of life which probably depended on both agricultural and pastoral activities. The discovery of charred wheat grains in a Middle Bronze Age

[7] It is interesting to note that Wales contains more than a quarter of the hill forts in the whole of Great Britain including Scotland (*Arch. Camb.*, Vol. CXXII, p. 7).

(*c.* 1,000 B.C.) deposit at Pond Cairn, Coety, Glamorgan, suggests that there were cultivated tracts in the upper regions of the Vale of Glamorgan, whilst the economy suggested by the associated food refuse found under a round cairn at St-y-Nyll, St Brides-super-Ely, Glamorgan, was one based mainly on sheep and cattle rearing.

The Late Bronze Age (1,000–400 B.C.) and Early Iron Age were marked by the introduction of iron weapons and implements brought across from the Continent by a tall, fair-haired, Celtic people who probably spoke a Celtic language called Brythonic—the ancestor of modern Welsh. The Celts belonged to a military aristocracy who again have left their traces on the landscape in the form of hill forts and promontory forts. In South Wales they are to be found mainly along the coastland of Gwent, Glamorgan, Pembrokeshire, and the low coastal plateau of Cardiganshire, as well as in the valleys of Breconshire. In general, they lie between the densely wooded landscape of the valley basins and the bare summits of the hills—a fact which strongly suggests they were thus located in order to enable their builders to practise an economy which took full advantage of the open pastures and summer grazings of the uplands, together with the arable land on the lower contour lines. In other words, there is every likelihood that during the immediate pre-Roman period, the natives of South Wales had developed the technique of 'transhumance' that is, of moving their stock up to the moorland pastures in summer, and returning again to the lowlands in winter. It may well be that the Welsh '*hendre-hafod*'[8] system—still practised in some areas—had its roots as far back as the Bronze Age, and probably based on the hill forts, whether they were used as defences or refuges against periodic plunder.

[8] *Hendre* (*f*) = literally 'old dwelling', winter dwelling. *Hafod* = summer dwelling. See p. 91 *et seq.*, '*hafotai*', '*lluestai*'.

The Roman period

When the Romans arrived to 'raise the curtain on History' the people of South Wales were already versed in the art of agriculture and stock rearing, and were also practising some degree of commerce and trade. By this time, *c.* A.D. 50, man's achievement in modifying the landscape was visible to the Romans in the form of converted trackless forest areas into semi-civilised regions with, possibly, fields and villages in forest clearings connected by tracks which had been traversed for centuries before the Romans themselves constructed their military roads (Fig. 6).

Perhaps the expression 'Roman Wales' is misleading insofar as Wales, like Scotland, was too mountainous and, therefore, too costly in man-power and materials, to be overrun completely. Consequently it may be said that the Roman impact on the South Wales landscape was, in the main, limited to the construction of a strategic network of forts, fortlets, and roads that were essential to ensure a sound military control over the native Silures and Ordovices. Later, in those areas which became Romanised, more especially along the southern coastal plain, several villas were established, that is, country houses built in Roman style with estates surrounding them and occupied by Romanised Britons of wealth and social standing. Examples of Roman villas have been excavated at Llantwit Major and Ely.[9]

During the period of initial conquest numerous marching-camps were set up and these are still recognisable in many areas as fairly large and lightly embanked enclosures. It has been estimated that upwards of four hundred of these preliminary Roman camps could have been constructed and the largest that has been traced so far is located at Blaen Cwm-bach in Glamorgan.[10]

[9] See also, p. 48. For an account of the Roman villa at Llantwit Major see *Arch. Camb.*, Vol. CII (1953), pp. 89–163.

[10] A. H. Hogg, *Arch. Camb.*, Vol. XXII, p. 8.

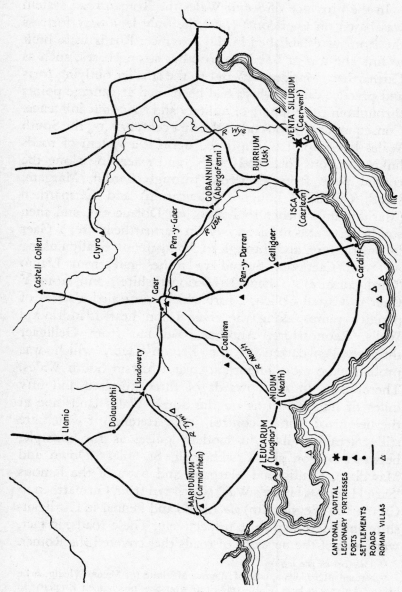

Fig. 6. General pattern of Roman roads, military and civil settlements in South Wales.

- ★ CANTONAL CAPITAL
- ■ LEGIONARY FORTRESSES
- ● FORTS
- ● SETTLEMENTS
- — ROADS
- △ ROMAN VILLAS

VENTA SILURUM (Caerwent)

BURRIUM (Usk)

GOBANNIUM (Abergavenni)

ISCA (Caerleon)

Pen-y-Gaer

Castell Collen

Clyro

R Wye

R Usk

Pen-y-Darran

Gelligaer

Cardiff

Y Gaer

Coelbren

R Neath

Llandovery

Llanio

Dolaucothi

R Tywi

NIDUM (Neath)

LEUCARUM (Loughor)

MARIDUNUM (Carmarthen)

In the province of South Wales the Roman road system was based on Caerleon[11] (*Isca*) the only legionary fortress the Romans established in the province. Roads were built to link the fort at Caerleon to other strong bases, such as Carmarthen (Maridunum) and to the smaller outlying forts and practice camps which had been sited at vantage points throughout their sphere of military and economic influence. Consequently, by the end of the first century A.D., the South Wales landscape had imprinted upon it a system of roads linking various forts and camps, and extending along the coastal plain from Caerleon, through Cardiff, Margam, Neath (Nidum), Loughor (Leucarum) and Carmarthen (Maridunum), thence to Llanio, *via* Dolaucothi, and then south-westwards to Llandovery in Carmarthenshire, Y Gaer in Breconshire, and through to Abergafenni, finally linking up with Caerleon. Subsidiary routes ran from Llanio (Cardiganshire) to Pennal (Merionethshire), and from Y Gaer to Castell Collen, a fort which controlled a series of practice camps along the river Ithon near Llandrindod Wells, Radnorshire. Another road ran from Gelligaer through Penydarren to the Brecon Gaer, which was probably the most important inland fort in South Wales. There were, in all, upwards of three hundred and fifty miles of military roads on the South Wales landscape at the height of Roman control, long stretches of which are still traceable, albeit in modern guise, as for example, between Brecon and Crickhowell, St Hilary Down and Mawdlam, Kenfig and Margam, and parts of the famous 'Sarn Helen'[12] (Helen's Way) which ran from Carmarthen to Caernarfon (Segontium) *via* Llanio and Pennal in Cardiganshire and Merionethshire respectively. These roads, in fact, were part of the network of roads that covered the Roman

[11] The fort of the legions.

[12] Named after Helena, wife of Magnus Maximus (or Maxen Wledig, as he became known in later Welsh tradition) who was proclaimed Emperor in A.D. 383.

world and remained for many centuries afterwards the chief means of communication within the province.[13]

As already stated, the Roman occupation of Wales was overwhelmingly military in character, and the landscape was, consequently, modified to meet the requirements of a military regime. There was, however, a human and social side to the legionaries' life. For instance, the fort sites were, in a sense, settlements, if only temporary in character. The only town founded by the Romans in South Wales was at Caerwent (Venta Silurum), a few miles from the hill fort at Llanmelin, from which the Silures, at one stage, had probably offered stern resistance to the initial onslaught of the Romans. The new town, which occupied about fifty acres, was sited in a fertile plain circled by hills where, it is thought possible, an earlier fortress had existed. We are not concerned here with the civil aspect of the Roman town of Caerwent, but rather with its impact on the landscape. It was built with emphasis on defensive features, like a fortress. It had four gateways, and the interior of the town was divided into twenty blocks, or *insulae*, by a roughly rectangular network of streets, divided centrally from east to west by the main road. Upon the north side of this road, in the centre, were the forum, or market place, and the basilica, or town hall, forming a single block. The market place was open to the sky, save that it was flanked on three sides by porticos, through which access was provided to rows of small apartments, probably shops or business offices. A temple stood near the forum, and other public buildings included an unfinished amphitheatre built, it appears, at a later stage over demolished dwelling houses and streets in the northern part of the town; and three blocks which were the social centres where people for-gathered in their leisure time. The typical Caerwent house consisted of a central courtyard, enclosed on four sides by

[13] Thomas Codrington, *Roman Roads in Britain* (London, 1903).

verandahs, from which opened four ranges of small rooms.

The decline of Caerwent was, in all probability, a symptom of the weakening influences of Roman power. The military importance of the town diminished, and as there was no economic base upon which it could thrive, this South Wales Roman town decayed and crumbled.

Although Caerwent is recognised as the only fully developed Romano-British town in South Wales, it should be noted that recent archaeological discoveries indicate that Carmarthen (Maridunum) has a 'history of Roman involvement on a scale not previously realised' and has been referred to in terms of a Venta Demetarum—a western pivot as big as Caerleon. Moreover, new excavations at Pumsaint and Dolaucothi (Carmarthenshire) confirm the existence there of a more substantial Roman settlement than hitherto assumed (Fig. 7). The gold-mines near by may have been first worked in pre-Roman period, but the Romans vigorously exploited the area from about A.D. 75. The scale of the mining operations may be gauged by the fact that two aqueducts were built, namely the Annell aqueduct, which was four miles long, and the Cothi aqueduct, which was no less than seven miles, and ran at a height of about 700 feet along the northern slope of Allt Cwmhenog. It was capable of carrying three million gallons of water a day to a series of reservoirs, tanks and sluices near the workings.[14] Such a major technical achievement points undoubtedly to the existence of a stable social organisation in this area from the first century A.D., and the element of continuity is thereby emphasised, despite the later decline of the gold-mines—the *raison d'être* of a once predominantly industrial settlement.

After the withdrawal of the Romans at the beginning of the fifth century, the South Wales landscape would

[14] G. D. B. Jones, I. J. Blakey and E. C. F. Macpherson, 'Dolaucothi: the Roman Aqueduct', *B.B.C.S.*, Vol. XIX (1960–2), pp. 71–84.

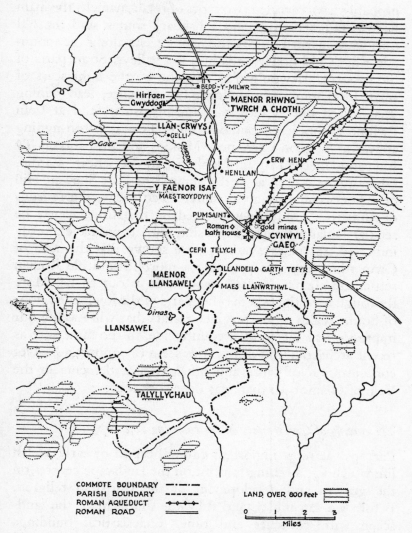

Fig. 7. An area of continuous settlement from Roman times around
Pumsaint. The names Hirfaen Gwyddog and Camddwr occur as early
as c. A.D. 850. (After Glanville R. Jones.)

probably have revealed two types of roads, namely, the main Roman military roads and subsidiary routes, and the old trackways marked out by the native Celts along the mountain ridges and downwards into the valleys. Some parts of the countryside would also have borne the light scars of small local mining operations. For instance, lead mining was carried out at Goginan, Cardiganshire, and at Cefn Pwll near Ruperra, Monmouthshire. Traces of iron-mining appear at Bolston Caer, near Miskin, and probably at Tŷ Isaf and Llechau near Llanhari, at Ely near Cardiff, Glamorgan, as well as at the summit of Port Skewett Hill near Caerwent, Monmouthshire. Even today, the remains of numerous gold mines worked by the Romans may be seen at Dolaucothi and Pumsaint, and, as we have already indicated, recent excavations have shown that this area of Carmarthenshire was probably a more formidable Roman settlement than historians have made it out to be. More thorough investigation in other parts of the lowland regions of South Wales might produce results that will modify our impression of the Roman countryside, in the same way as recent archaeological discoveries seem to support a heavier concentration of villas and other civil settlements in the Vale of Glamorgan than was once supposed.

The coming of Christianity in the changing landscape

Perhaps the most important cultural aspect of early Welsh life which left a lasting imprint on the landscape centres on the growth and development of the Christian religion. Before we can understand fully the filling in of the landscape with churches and other ecclesiastical buildings during the historic period, we must refer briefly to the evangelising work of the so-called Celtic Saints.[15]

[15] The term 'Saint' may be best understood in this context as a wandering monk. Canonisation was not involved.

There is little doubt now that Christianity had been introduced to South Wales—probably by merchants and traders—long before the Romans left, and small sections of the population had undoubtedly been won over to the Christian faith. But it was not until the fifth and sixth centuries that a systematic effort was made by the 'Saints' to convert the Welsh people to Christianity. Landscape evidence of this unprecedented missionary zeal may still be observed in the shape of numerous splendidly inscribed and decorated stone crosses. These early Christian inscribed and sculptured stone monuments provide the principal material remains of those centuries, extending from the withdrawal of the Romans to the coming of the Normans, which witnessed the conversion of Wales to Christianity and the development of the Celtic Church. The total number of known monuments belonging to various categories of inscription and design amounts to about 444, of which 328 are located in South Wales, including 117 in Pembrokeshire alone. The stones were generally erected as tombstones, and the evidence supplied by the inscriptions on these stones suggests the existence of an ordered and settled social life. Many of these monuments are to be found near the older churches where, probably, the earliest *llan* (cell or enclosure—church) may have been founded. But, like their huts and dwellings, Dark Age men built their churches of wood and, consequently, there is no part of any church in South Wales that is older than the Norman period.

Although we know the approximate site of the Celtic *llannau* (churches) in relation to the physical layout of the countryside, we know practically nothing of the layout or form of the original settlements as set up by the Celtic Saints. For instance, no trace has been found of the important monastic settlements established at Llanilltud Fawr (Llantwit Major) and Llancarfan, in Glamorgan. These are, indeed, representative of many other monastic cells which have completely vanished, leaving no trace at all in the landscape. Nevertheless, a considerable number of early dedications are well attested in modern place-names, many of which bear the prefix *Llan*. For example, in South West Wales, Dewi (St David), Teilo and Padarn were the chief saints, and are commemorated in such place-names as Llanddewi, Llandeilo (Carmarthenshire), Llanbadarn (Cardiganshire). In South East Wales, Dyfrig, Cadog and Illtud were chiefly culted, and are remembered in such place-names as Llanilltud Fawr (Llantwit Major), Llanilltud Nedd (Llantwit-juxta-Neath), Glamorgan; Llangattock-nigh-Usk, Monmouthshire. Brycheiniog (Breconshire), moreover, perpetuates the memory of Brychan.

The early Celtic monastic communities are difficult to visualise on the landscape. From the evidence available, it seems fairly certain that the monks did not inhabit a single building, but lived in separate huts or cells which were surrounded by a wall or rampart, after the pattern of that which girt the various buildings of a royal court or *llys*. This was the *llan* or enclosure; within it were also the church, the abbot's cell, the hospice for the entertainment of visitors, and such necessary outhouses as the kiln in which corn was dried for the mill. We are told that none of these buildings was of stone, but were of timber and wattle.

Evidence assembled from recent archaeological investigation supports the idea of continuity of settlement on the sites of many existing churches from the days of the Celtic Saints. Indeed, in passing, it is worth noting here the churches at Ysbyty Cynfyn, Cardiganshire (Plate 4), and possibly St Harmon, Radnorshire, where continuity is thought to have extended from Neolithic times down to the present day, that is, from being sites of megalithic tombs to being occupied by early Celtic cells, and later replaced by a modern church. In the case of Ysbyty Cynfyn, as its name suggests, it became an *ysbyty* (hospice) in the Middle Ages.

Such provable continuity of settlement, however, is extremely rare in South Wales.

More probable centres of continuity are those such as we find in 'Old Carmarthen'. It seems that a *llan*, or cell, was established by St Teulyddog—a disciple of St Teilo—at Carmarthen, and called Llandeulyddog after him. All visible traces of this settlement have long since disappeared, but it is strongly argued that here, as in other places where similar opportunities obtained, St Teulyddog's *llan* was located within the walls of the old Romano-British fort—Maridunum. His foundation became merged in the later Augustinian Priory of St John which, in full, is called the Priory of St John the Evangelist and St Theulacus—Theulacus being a Latinised form of Teulyddog. It would appear fairly certain that in pre-Norman times, the church at Carmarthen had become a foundation of special significance, ruled by an abbot-bishop "possessed of a considerable endowment of land".[16] Thus, as Professor Bowen has shown, we have at the eastern end of the present town of Carmarthen, the original Roman fort, the *llan* or *clas* of St Teulyddog and its successor, the Priory of St John, forming the nucleus of what has been known as Old Carmarthen.[17] The secularisation of early monastic communities and the increased endowments, such as had occurred at Llandeulyddog, had important effects on Welsh settlement. Such endowments from a wealthy prince or landowner, anxious to make atonement for misdeeds against the church, enabled the churches themselves to grow rich, and which, in the course of three or four centuries, had made "St David's . . . Llandaff . . . Llancarfan", and other churches, "the centres of groups of manors or hamlets of rent-paying serfs".[18]

An interesting feature of the Welsh landscape closely

[16] Baring-Gould and Fisher, *Lives of the British Saints*, Vol. IV (London, 1913).
[17] *Arch. Camb.*, Vol. CXVII (1968).
[18] J. E. Lloyd, *A History of Wales*, Vol. I (London, 1911), p. 214.

connected with the Celtic Church are the holy wells. Although their original significance may have now become blurred by the passage of time, many of the holy wells have survived as visible evidence perpetuating certain ancient beliefs and local folklore. Throughout the Middle Ages, and for some considerable time afterwards, wells featured prominently in the religion, song, folk tales and medicinal practices of the Welsh people. The close proximity of the wells to chapels, churches, and monuments of recognised pagan character, might indicate a greater degree of continuity of settlement within the vicinity of church sites than is realised, more especially as the Christian church had decreed that pagan sites were to be converted to 'Christian solemnities' by rededicating the well, megalith and tree, and by erecting churches or chapels near them. In South Wales alone, there are about 104 known examples of chapels and churches built at, or near, holy wells. They are distributed thus: Brecon 8, Cardigan 14, Carmarthen 14, Glamorgan 24, Monmouth 7, Radnor 4, Pembroke 33.[19] In certain instances it may have been that saints and hermits erected their cells near wells simply to ensure supplies of water for domestic purposes, or for Christian baptism. There were, also, many other factors which can only be conjectured. Archaeological evidence shows that at St David's in Pembrokeshire, human occupation goes back many centuries before the Christian era. We are told that traces have been found here of at least nine earth forts, the remains of six *cromlechau*, two tumuli, and at least four monoliths. There are also seven holy wells concentrated within the immediate vicinity of St David's, together with most of the *cromlechau*. It was on this remote promontory that St David, in turn, built his church.[20] Here, then, is surely an example of long continuity of local religious tradition which must pre-

[19] Francis Jones, *The Holy Wells of Wales* (Cardiff, 1954), p. 24.
[20] Francis Jones, *op. cit.*, pp. 23–6.

suppose some form of human organisation that developed and perpetuated it. Much work still remains to be done in archaeological investigation at other sites where the pre-historic and historic may be more fully correlated.

Most of the wells appear to have been formed in circular cavities in the ground, the water sometimes springing from the bottom of the cavity (Plate 5). Like domestic wells, many Christian wells were elaborated and embellished by building canopies or well-heads over them. Some wells were extended to facilitate bodily immersion. Many of the old well chapels have, by now, suffered the same fate as the *cromlechau* and monastic buildings, and have disappeared without trace, others fell into decay, became abandoned, or were deliberately destroyed during the Reformation.

There are, nevertheless, several ruined well-chapels still to be seen in the South Wales landscape, but it should be emphasised that none of these is older than the medieval period. At Llanddarog, Carmarthenshire, may be seen the little Capel Begedwin "twenty-eight feet by fifteen and a half feet . . . built over a well which still flows abundantly . . .". Earlier descriptions, however, help to show how the holy wells appeared to contemporary observers. At the beginning of this century, Oxwich churchyard well (Gower) was "roofed and there was a large flat stone on its edge in front of the well; it was large enough for immersion". Ffynnon Cybi (Cardiganshire) was "much resorted to for complaint" in 1913, and was "formerly roofed, and the water flowed into a bath which had seats around it to accommodate bathers". It was, however, only "in fair repair". St Anthony's well in Llanstephan (Carmarthenshire) "was walled and had a niche over it in 1811". The well, however, "has been much restored and contains an arched recess and a narrow stone ledge called 'the offering shelf' ".[21]

The holy wells that survive in the South Wales landscape

[21] Francis Jones, *op. cit.*, pp. 28, 163, 184.

throw into relief a religious phenomenon of attributing to them actual or assumed therapeutic qualities—an attribution which reaches back probably to pagan origins, and was perpetuated during the early Christian period, and even down to modern times, in the form of pilgrimages to their waters. However, scientific analyses of the medicinal mineral waters at Llandrindod[22] and other centres in South Wales eventually resulted in the growth of the South Wales spas, now perpetuated in the names Llandrindod Wells, Llanwrtyd Wells, Llandegley Wells, Builth Wells and Llangamarch Wells, to which places thousands of South Wales families formerly made annual pilgrimages, albeit in the form of holidays.

Post-Roman landscape

What, then, do we know about the South Wales landscape following the withdrawal of the Romans, and previous to the advent of the Normans—the period referred to as the Dark Ages? We shall probably never know precisely the mode of land occupation and utilisation during that period, but recent scholarly studies based on the 'alleged' Laws of Hywel Dda (Hywel the Good) (A.D. ?–950)—more especially those codes of law which related to North Wales—provide some basis for discussing the economic and social organisation of Welsh society in pre-Norman times. In this connection, however, we must avoid the temptation of projecting on to the South Wales canvas a picture of society which may have been peculiar to certain special conditions and circumstances obtaining only in North Wales. It is, perhaps, salutary to recall that there are about thirty Latin manuscript versions of the old Welsh laws, and we cannot be sure that any of these laws that have survived represents the 'law' as it existed in the time of Hywel Dda. Indeed, the

[22] For example, see Diederick Wessel Linden, *A Treatise on Three Medicinal Waters at Llandrindod in Radnorshire* . . . (London, 1756).

earliest of these manuscript copies are ascribed to the late eleventh century and may, therefore, contain rules of law which did not actually apply in Hywel Dda's day, but rather to a later period.[23]

The conventional model of early Welsh society was one in which the free tribesmen were originally semi-nomadic pastoralists who practised a kind of migratory tillage, sheltering in temporary dwellings, easily constructed and conveyed to new sites, as circumstances dictated. It has now been shown that arable farming played a more important role in the native economy than previously supposed, and that the 'bond' element was more extensive. It would seem, therefore, that previous to the coming of the Normans there were, in certain areas of South Wales, the so-called bond villages occupied by the local bondmen of the king or tribal chief who had jurisdiction over divisions of territory known as cantrefs (*cantrefi*) and commotes (*cymydau*). The bondmen, or *taeogion*, rendered services such as repairing the court house of the king, providing him with fuel and a proportion of food, and performing other menial tasks. In time the sites of the court houses grew into royal villages, or *maesdrefi*, where the bondmen worked on the king's home-farm. The king's villeins, or bondmen, seem to have lived grouped together in townships known as *trefydd*, comprising a number of homesteads so clustered together for the purpose of cultivating in common the adjacent land. Each man would have his own stock, house, and farm buildings, but such tasks as ploughing would be done in common. The *erwau* or strips of ploughed land lay in open fields, that is, undivided by ditches or hedges.

In contrast to the bond-unit of settlement, namely the bond-tref, was the free-tref where the inabitants, the free-

[23] Dafydd Jenkins, 'Legal and comparative aspects of Welsh laws', *Welsh History Review* (special number, 19163), pp. 51-4; J. G. Edwards, 'Hywel Dda and the Welsh law books' in *Celtic Law Papers: Introduction to Welsh Medieval Law and Government* . . . (Bruxelles, 1973).

men, dwelt in scattered holdings, of which a certain number were marked off to form a *tref*. This dichotomy between the nucleated bond village and the scattered village, the free-tref, has characterised the South Wales landscape even down to the present day, such a pattern being broken only where industry has intruded into these areas in the hills where the scattered villages were mainly located.

The results of recent documentary research again serve to correct a tendency to regard the traditional Welsh way of life as being exclusively nomadic and pastoral. There is growing evidence which points to the existence of well established permanent settlements from the ninth century. For instance, it has been shown that the words *Med diminih* which occur in the Book of St Chad, have been equated with the name Meddyfnych, which has been perpetuated in that of Myddynfych, a modern farm located in the parish of Llandybië, Carmarthenshire (Fig. 8). It is thought that, in medieval times, the parish of Llandybië was co-extensive with the old maenor, known as *Mainaur med diminih*, in which case we have an interesting example of continuity of human settlement from the ninth century to the present day.[24]

It is fairly certain that mixed farming was practised over a wider area of the Vale of Glamorgan in pre-Norman times than has been hitherto indicated. The area lying roughly between the rivers Thaw and Taff was probably intensively settled from quite early times. Indeed, recent excavations have revealed additional Roman sites, three of which— Whitton Cross, Moulton and Llanbethery—are thought to have been villas. Other known villas were the famous villas at Llantwit Major and at Ely. The villa system, as operated by the Romans, provided a basis for the growth of villages. The well-to-do lived in their villas, single-storeyed houses

[24] H. P. R. Finberg (ed.), *The Agrarian History of England and Wales* (Cambridge, 1972), p. 308.

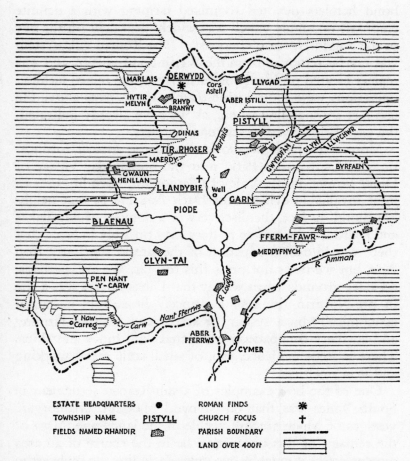

Fig. 8. The measure of Maenor Meddyfnych, Carmarthen, according to a marginal entry in the Book of St Chad *c.* A.D. 800. (After Glanville R. Jones.)

decorated with mosaic floors, with gardens and orchards, while the surrounding fields were cultivated by the *coloni*. After about 400, these became unoccupied, which probably marked the decay of the villa system—both in its agricultural and tenurial organisation—and inaugurated a system of bond hamlets devoted to mixed farming with a definite emphasis on arable which was widely prevalent on the eve of the Anglo-Norman conquest.[25] The Roman villa-system was not far removed from the Welsh bond-village, and was mainly located on low-lying territory where mixed farming operations were more viable than in those areas above the 600-feet contour line where, as we have already indicated, the population lived in scattered hamlets.

More recently, excavations around the ancient fortifications at Cwrt-yr-Ala Park, near the present-day village of Dinas Powys, in the Vale of Glamorgan, have brought to light invaluable evidence of Dark Age life in that neighbourhood. In fact, the discovery of a number of flint flakes and sherds of distinctive pottery may possibly indicate that there was human occupation of the site in the Early Iron Age, but we must not press this too far. We are, perhaps, on safer grounds when we say that Dinas Powys was a site in pre-Norman times of a princely household sustained economically by a system of arable and pastoral farming and ancillary occupations connected with hides and skins. There is some evidence, too, of small-scale metal working and iron smelting.

One of the best examples of a sub-Roman settlement in South Wales was that on Mynydd Margam, Glamorgan, vestiges of which are still visible in the landscape. Most of the remains of this occupation lie in the centre of an area measuring three miles by two miles, including the Bwlwarcau (the bulwarks) lying about a mile and a half west of the ancient parish of Llangynwyd (Plate 3). The situation of its main entrance indicates that the occupiers had interests 'down hill' rather than 'up hill', and the concentric features of the enclosures suggest that they can only have been needed by a community heavily dependent on stock raising.

[25] Glanville Jones, *Welsh History Review*, I (1960–1), pp. 111–32.

Within the neighbourhood of the bwlwarcau were several primitive farmsteads whose scattered distribution again suggests a pastoral economy, each farmer having a sufficient area for grazing, such as at Baiden and Ty-Talwyn farms. The late Sir Cyril Fox was of the opinion that the forts and farms on Margam mountain probably illustrate "a little known social, cultural and economic life in South Wales in the Dark Ages" and which had no "significant parallels in the British Isles . . .". The bwlwarcau, according to Fox, may have been a "belated expression in the Highlands of the country house tradition established by the Romans in Lowland Britain". The evidence, scanty though it is, suggests a continuity of settlement in these areas extending over several centuries—settlements which, in many cases, were later to be Normanised.

It seems fairly certain, therefore, that when the Normans arrived in South Wales at the end of the eleventh century, they found in the lowland landscapes evidence of the nucleated villages, occupied by mixed farmers, whose main preoccupation was probably with animal husbandry, producing, in open fields, just enough corn crops to feed a fairly stable human population. Probably the ox, sheep, pig and domestic fowl figured prominently in and around the pre-Norman settlements. The upland regions were scantily settled, but, as we have already seen, had interests 'down hill'. Pure nomadic pastoralism may have been practised in the hill districts, but with small woodland clearances increasingly brought about by their browsing stocks, the pastoralists were gradually able to apply themselves to small-scale arable farming in suitable areas, even in the hill districts, thereby initiating the *hendre-hafod* system, or transhumance. We shall see in a later chapter how this pattern of farming, and of land utilisation, became more conspicuous on the South Wales landscape.

Scandinavian influences

A phase in the Dark Age history to which a brief reference must be made is that marked by the Scandinavian raiders and traders who, from the last half of the ninth century to about the end of the eleventh century, made their incursions into South Wales from their settlements in Ireland and Scotland, and made their presence felt there, although their sporadic raids brought about the desecration of churches and Celtic monasteries, which must have resulted in considerable re-building. St David's Cathedral, for example, was sacked four times between 982 and 989, and as late as 1080 it was dismantled and its Bishop Abraham killed. In 1091 St David's was again ravaged. During the same period the church at St Gwynllyw (St Woollos), in Monmouthshire, also attracted the predatory attentions of the Norsemen.

The most lasting and positive evidence we have of Norse influences in South Wales is to be found in certain place-names. In Pembrokeshire, for instance, there are about seventeen place-names of 'well-attested' Norse origins among which are Caldey Island, Colby, Em-sger, Gateholm, Grassholm, Milford, Skokholm Island and Skomer Island. In Glamorgan, the ancient port of Swansea is probably of Norse origin, as are Burry Holms and Wormshead in Gower. Further east, the region around Pyle, Laleston and Newcastle, may have contained a fairly strong colony of Scandinavian settlers. This area is situated well inland, and within it occur such names as Laleston itself, Clakkston, nearby (long since lost), Vallis Danorum, situated near Stormy Down, and Gardinum Sweini (near Newcastle). Within the adjacent manor of Margam was a place called Meles (Grangia de Meles), and on the coastline, a few miles south of Pyle, are to be found Sker House (upon which is based Blackmore's *Maid of Sker*), and Tusker Rock, off the pleasure beach at Porthcawl, which presents as much of a hazard today as it did to the Norsemen a thousand years ago. In the parish of St Nicholas, near Cardiff, Homri is found as the name of a farm, whose earliest form was Horneby. It is probable, therefore, that the Norsemen had established themselves more successfully in the southern half of the country than written history records and, as in Ireland, fostered along the South Wales seaboard small marts and havens for the conduct of their "brisk trade in Welsh slaves, horses, honey, malt and wheat".[26]

In the Cardiff region itself, further place-name evidence of Norse settlement may be found. Womanby (Hundmanby) Street and Gollgate, both situated within a stone's throw of the now famous Cardiff Arms Park, are examples of Scandinavian influences within Cardiff, while names like Flatholm and Steepholm, two islands outside Cardiff, in the Bristol Channel, are of undoubted Scandinavian origin. The intensity of Norse settlement in and around Cardiff is illustrated by the personal names of the citizens of Dublin at the end of the twelfth century, when the Dublin roll of names included "forty to fifty burgesses from Cardiff", of which "nine of them probably bear Norse names".[27]

It has been shown, too, that the strength of Norse influence is revealed by the fact that in many instances, new Norse names supplanted old Welsh names along the coast. For example, Wormshead for Ynysweryn, Swansea for Abertawe, Laleston for Trelalas, Flat Holm for Echni, Caldey Island for Ynys Pyr, and Milford Haven for Aber-daugleddau—to mention only a few. But in general, the distribution of place-names containing Norse elements suggests that in Pembrokeshire, Scandinavian settlements were mainly coastal, and operated as centres of maritime

[26] Gwyn Jones, *A History of the Vikings* (Oxford University Press, 1968), p. 355.
[27] B. G. Charles, *Old Norse Relations with Wales* (Cardiff, 1934), pp. 158–9.

trade, whereas in the Vale of Glamorgan there were, probably, strong agricultural settlements which, indeed, may have encouraged the Normans to settle in South Wales.

In the final analysis, however, place-name evidence is "corroborative rather than primary". We know that the South Wales coast had been subject to sporadic Norse raids and incursions since the ninth century, and continued for at least two hundred years, yet the Norsemen left no identifiable landscape evidence. What impact the Norse settlements had on the actual landscape, we shall probably never know, but it should be remembered, when considering the history of the South Wales landscape, that beneath it lies a complexity of racial influences—Celtic, Roman, Norse, Norman, Saxon and Flemish—which contributed to the making of the landscape in ways that are no longer discernible.

Lack of evidence defies any complete description of the South Wales landscape on the eve of the Norman invasion. It is clear, however, that arable farming was a positive element in the local economy of the lowlands, but what field patterns emerged during pre-Norman times can only be conjectured. It seems fairly clear, too, that there were many areas sustaining small nucleated settlements which, undoubtedly, provided a basis upon which the Normans built up and extended the manorial system of cultivation. From what evidence we have, it was the Norman feudal lord and his Saxon peasant who really initiated the first notable advance in exploiting the arable potential of the South Wales coastal areas.

SELECT BIBLIOGRAPHY

Alcock, Leslie, *Dinas Powys* . . . (Cardiff, 1963).
Baring-Gould, S. and Fisher, John, *The Lives of the British Saints*, 4 vols. (London 1907–13).

Bowen, E. G., *The Settlements of the Celtic Saints in Wales* (Cardiff, 1965).

—— *Saints, Seaways and Settlements in the Celtic Lands* (Cardiff, 1969).

—— *Wales: a Physical, Historical, and Regional Geography* (London, 1957).

Cambrian Archaeological Association, *A Hundred Years of Welsh Archaeology*. Centenary Volume, 1846–1946 (Gloucester, 1946).

Charles, B. G., *Old Norse Relations with Wales* (Cardiff, 1934).

—— *Non-Celtic Place-Names in Wales* (London, 1938).

Finberg, H. P. R. (ed.), *The Agrarian History of England and Wales*. Vol. I. ii, A.D. 43–1042 (Cambridge, 1972).

Foster, Idris Ll. and Alcock, Leslie (eds), *Culture and Environment. Essays in Honour of Sir Cyril Fox* (London, 1963).

Foster, Idris Ll. and Daniel, Glyn (eds), *Prehistoric and Early Wales* (London, 1965).

Fox, Cyril, 'Forts and farms on Margam Mountain, Glamorgan', *Antiquity*, Vol. VIII (1934).

—— *Life and Death in the Bronze Age* (London, 1959).

—— *The Personality of Britain*. 4th ed. (Cardiff, 1943. New impression with amendments. Cardiff, 1959).

Grimes, W. F., *The Prehistory of Wales*. 2nd ed. (Cardiff, 1951).

Jones, Francis, *The Holy Wells of Wales* (Cardiff, 1954).

Jones, Glanville, 'The Tribal System in Wales: A Re-assessment in the Light of Settlement Studies', *Welsh History Review*, Vol. I, pp. 111–32.

Lloyd, J. E., *A History of Wales from the Earliest Times to the Edwardian Conquest*, 2 vols, 3rd ed. (London, 1939).

Lynch, Francis, and Burgess, Colin, *Prehistoric Man in Wales and the West* (Bath, 1972).

Margary, Ivan D., *Roman Roads in Britain*, 3rd ed. (London, 1973).

Nash-Williams, V. E., *The Early Christian Monuments of Wales* (Cardiff, 1950).

Powell, T. G. E., *Megalithic Enquiries in the West of Britain: A Liverpool Symposium*. Contributions by T. G. E. Powell and others (Liverpool, 1969).

Rees, William, *An Historical Atlas of Wales from Early to Modern Times* (Cardiff, 1972).

Roderick, A. J. (ed.), *Wales Through The Ages*, Vol. I: *From Earliest Times to 1485* (Llandybie, 1959).
Savory, H. N., 'Pre-Roman Brecknock' in *Brycheiniog*, Vol. I.
Turner, Judith, 'The Anthropogenic Factor in Vegetational History' in *New Phytologist*, Vol. 63 (1964).
Webley, D. P., 'Aspects of Neolithic and Bronze Age Agriculture in South Wales', *Bulletin Board Celtic Studies*, Vol. XXII (1970).
Wheeler, R. E. M., *Prehistoric and Roman Wales* (Oxford, 1925).

2. The Norman Conquest and the late medieval landscape

The Norman landscape—castles, manors and early mills. Monasteries and the landscape. Churches in the landscape. Towns, villages and fields. Deserted villages. 'Hafotaï' and 'lluestaï'

The Norman landscape—castles, manors and early mills

WE NEED SPEND very little time outlining the oft-recited details of the progress of the Norman invasion of South Wales; we are more concerned here with the results of the invasion as seen on the local landscape. But before we can understand fully the significance of these landscape changes, we must refer briefly to the pattern and extent of the Norman intrusion into South Wales.

The series of events which, together, constituted the Norman conquest of South Wales really started when William fitzOsbern (made Earl of Hereford in 108(?)7) and his knights crossed from Hereford into Gwent where the lordship of Strigoil was established with its castle founded at Chepstow. By 1085, the Normans had pushed forward along the old Roman road through southern Gwent to reach Caerleon where, to this day, may be seen the castle mound they built at that time. In 1090 Philip de Braose seized Radnor, and later moved on Buellt (Builth). Bernard de Newmarch, in turn, overran the kingdom of Brycheiniog in the face of fierce opposition. By 1091 Robert Fitzhamon

(Earl of Gloucester) had conquered Glamorgan, and had built his castle within the ancient Roman fort at Cardiff. The fertile Vale of Glamorgan (Bro Morgannwg) was quickly brought under direct Norman rule, and the land divided into estates granted by Fitzhamon to his loyal followers. By about 1100, the old Welsh commote of Gŵyr (Gower), lying to the west of Morgannwg, between the rivers Tawe and Loughor, was subjugated by Henry de Newburgh and his followers, who formed the Norman Lordship of Gower and Kilvey. From central Wales the family of Montgomery moved forward into west Wales and overran Ceredigion (Cardiganshire) before advancing into south-west Wales to establish itself in the lordship of Pembroke. A period of conflict between the Welsh rulers and the Normans followed, and it was not until the reign of Henry I (1100–35) that the Normans established a final balance of power and influence in South Wales.

In no part of South Wales was the Norman intrusion more complete than in the lowland areas of Glamorgan. Here, in the fertile Vale of Glamorgan, the land was sub-jugated to the manorial system of land cultivation, and the population, in turn, to the feudal relationships that were necessary to sustain it. Within this socio-economic frame-work many of the Glamorgan estates and villages we know today came into being, such as Dinas Powys, Wenvoe and Sully, St Fagans, Cogan, Wrinston and St Nicholas—all within the neighbourhood of Cardiff—to mention only a few.

The hill districts of Glamorgan (Blaenau Morgannwg), being more remote and less accessible, and consequently more difficult to bring under military control, remained in the hands of the local Welsh rulers who were apparently prepared to recognise the overlordship of the Norman rulers. In other words the subjugation of the lowlands was eco-nomic and political, that of the uplands primarily political. Consequently, certain areas became known as 'Englishries', and others as 'Welshries', according to the degree of Anglo-Norman control to which they were subjected. Such differences in governmental control were clearly mirrored on the landscape. The progress and reversals of the Norman Conquest of South Wales were, perhaps, the spectacular events of this period, marking a decisive turning point in the Principality, and bringing in their train innovations that were entirely new and revolutionary to the native population. These were the castles, the manorial system and its feudal methods of landownership and tenure, large-scale agriculture, the growth of towns, trade and commerce, a church reorganised on a diocesan basis, and, equally important, perhaps, in terms of the landscape, the introduction of Latin Monasticism.

The presence of the Norman settlers in South Wales was most conspicuously indicated on the landscape by their castles, which were built within the boundaries of each lordship, and may be regarded as visible evidence signifying the independence of each local Norman ruler—evidence of the sovereign rights they enjoyed over their subjects in return for a very shadowy allegiance to their overlord, the English King. The castle also signified the subjection of the native Welsh who had been replaced, temporarily at least, by an alien peasantry.

It is important to note also that the Normans normally built their castles at strategic points. For instance, the *caput*, or chief castle of Glamorgan, was built at Cardiff on the site of an old Roman fort, while others were founded at various bridgeheads such as Ogmore, Coety, Newcastle (Bridgend), Neath, Swansea, Oystermouth, Loughor. Some were also built at less vital sites to remind the native population of the power of the invader.

Structurally the castles were, at first, simple and unpretentious wooden motte-and-bailey type which were, in time, replaced by fairly elaborate stone structures, many of which still appear impressive and sometimes grandiloquent even in their ruinous condition. It has been suggested that the siting of motte-and-bailey castles calls for more careful study, as, apparently, many are anachronistic. But castles such as Y Gaer (the fort) near St Nicholas (not far from Tinkiswood) and Llangynwyd (a mile or so from Y Bwlwarcau) were carefully chosen on well-defended sites, and probably on, or near, well established sites of previous rulers. It is possible, too, that there was some continuity in the use of the Roman fort at Cardiff by post-Roman native rulers. The same might be true of the Roman station at Gelligaer and at Loughor—sites of Norman castles. It may be said, however, that castle building in South Wales culminated in the castle at Caerffili, which has been described as one of the most magnificent examples of the fully developed medieval castle in Europe.[1]

Like the prehistoric 'houses of the dead' (megalithic tombs), the castles were most densely distributed in the lowland regions. In Glamorgan, of some eighty castles, only six are set over 600 feet above sea level. But the predatory attacks launched by the native Welsh from the hills upon the invader in the lowlands compelled the Normans to build one or two castles at strategic points in the hills "to the end they might bridle the suddaine tumults of the Welshmen . . .".

The sites of the principal Norman castles, such as Chepstow (Plate 6) and Cardiff, were carefully chosen as centres intended for directing both military advance and long-term civil government. Thirteen Glamorgan castles were situated near the sea, but only Cardiff, Swansea, St Donat's, Ogmore, Loughor and Kenfig (Plate 7) were capable of being serviced by boat. The impact of castle building on the Glamorgan coastal regions may be assessed by the fact that in the sixteenth century there were twenty-seven castles

[1] William Rees, *Caerphilly Castle, a History and Description* (Cardiff, 1937).

bordering the sea coast, the greater number of these standing within about a mile of each other. The total number of castles built throughout the county was fifty-seven. In Pembrokeshire there were possibly fifty-three castles built, the remains of fifteen surviving to the present day. Indeed, it is true to say that right up to Tudor times the castles dominated not only Welsh life, but also the Welsh landscape.

One of the most striking castles which appeared on the South Wales landscape was St Donat's (Plate 8), and one of the very few which has remained in continuous occupation from its earliest years, and therefore preserved its living tradition. The various architectural modifications that have been made over the centuries are fairly easily recognised, but the general outline of the original plan has been substantially preserved. It stands on a magnificent point on the Glamorgan coast, having been built on the rocky east bank of a deep and wooded glen opening out into a full view of the sea. Tradition has it that an inlet leading up to the castle provided shelter for the small vessels, and an anchorage for the lords of the manor from which they sailed to the opposite coast of the Bristol channel.

Apart from its own dominating structural presence on the landscape, the castle effected landscape changes which are associated with the manorial system. For example, Cardiff castle had eventually developed into the administrative centre of the whole lordship of Glamorgan and, as such, served as an administrative centre and military headquarters of the lordship. In order to provide for the requirements of the castle household, numbering many hundreds, the local manor of the lord at Roath became vitally important, and in consequence a manor house was built with its adjacent farm buildings, the barton, and the stone-and-wattle ox houses. A mill was erected and powered by the waters of the adjacent Llechau stream (Nant Llechau). The customary tenants or serfs occupying their primitive farmsteads of wattle and daub, and grouped together in the village of Roath, shared collectively with the lord, the arable land which had been cleared from the surrounding waste in the open fields which made up numerous strips extending to the river Rhymney in the east, and to the town boundary in the west. In the fourteenth century the lord's demesne in arable in the open fields amounted to 288 acres. At the same time there were eighteen unfree tenants, each holding a dozen or so strips of about an acre in extent.

Moreover, in addition to Roath, the lords of Cardiff held the manor of Leckwith which included 150 acres on Leckwith moor, and was made up of 337 acres of arable in demesne, and 57 acres of meadow. Here a group of 29 bond tenants held 258 acres in open fields, holding about 12 acres each. In addition there were fourteen cottagers who held no land, but lived by day labour. Inland from these two manors of Roath[2] and Leckwith, the native Welsh freemen continued to occupy their former holdings, paying political homage to the lord of Cardiff, while those of unfree status lived in the villages of Llanishen, Lisvane and Llanedern.

The manor at Roath may be taken as an example of the kind of pattern that developed on the landscape in the neighbourhood of most of the Norman castles of South Wales. But it should be remembered that such generalisations are dangerous, for manorialism as such was, after all, merely an accretion around the village which, ideally, comprised a group of houses standing at the centre of its territory. The agrarian framework within which it operated was conditioned by the physical qualities of the land itself.

[2] Professor William Rees reminds us that the name Roath (*Rhath* in Welsh) is derived from *rath,* an ancient Irish term for a fortress or enclosure, with surrounding rampart. The present Roath Court, which marks the site of the old manor house is associated with a *fossatum* or ditch, and Rice Merrick's reference in 1579 to the existence of a mound here suggests that this may have been the royal centre of the former Welsh rulers in the Commote of Cibwr.

The feudal relationships which underpinned the manorial system merely restricted, or regulated, the rights and chances of various individuals in their use of the three main categories of land—arable, pasture, woodland and waste, and the resources of the rivers. The rivers and streams were a source of power exploited to the utmost within the manorial system.

Every manor contained one or more mills, either for grinding corn or the fulling of coarse cloth woven in the homes of the peasants. Most of the mills of South Wales were located near the river's edge. Windmills, however, were not uncommon in Wales in the thirteenth century, but their structures were not as imposing as those built in later centuries. The rivers and streams were so numerous in South Wales, that windmills appeared mainly in the dry southern limestone regions of the Vale of Glamorgan, and in certain areas of Pembrokeshire and Monmouthshire.

Power for the water-mills was made possible only by modifying the landscape. Weirs were constructed at a level above the water-line fixed by the custom of the lordship. Posts were driven into the bed of the river, and then fastened with heavy timber which provided a strong foundation for the weir. This was further strengthened with large boulders, and an additional framework of interwoven rods and branches, rendered more watertight with clay, sand and turf. The water was then diverted along a constructed water course leading direct to the mill, or to a mill-pond artificially constructed, being lined with turves and clay, enabling either an overflow or underflow to the water-wheel, according to whether it was supplied from a mill-pond or from the stream. Flood gates, too were erected at the weir to control the flow of water, and here were to be found fish-traps, so frequently associated with weirs.[3]

[3] William Rees, *South Wales and the March, 1284–1415* (Oxford, 1924), pp. 136–8.

Thus, an additional filling-in of the landscape was brought about by the building of new mills, but the harnessing of the water necessary to power the mills created a new landscape pattern in the immediate neighbourhood of each one. The appearance of additional sources of power generated by water and wind signified that the economy was expanding alongside an increasing population. At Llandyfai (Lamphey), in Pembrokeshire, there were at the beginning of the thirteenth century, two water-mills and a wind-mill, worth £4 yearly. There are many scattered references to corn and other mills in the Swansea area for 1449. Two corn mills were called Bryn Mills (which gave the name Brynmill) and another called Greenehill Mill. Besides these grist mills, there were also a number of fulling mills in the area. A mill at Brynmill was 'newly built' in the year 1428, and another was 'newly built' in 1443, in addition to which "vacant land at Brynmill had been let for twenty years . . . for building a new fulling mill". Such references must indicate that the fulling trade was quite important in the Borough of Swansea in the fifteenth century.[4]

The long lines of castles which the Normans had left along the South Wales coastal region were accompanied by even longer lines of mills, and it may be argued that the mills were, in a sense, more significant on the landscape than were the castles, and, as we shall show later, they were certainly more enduring. A development of great importance that took place under the shadow and protection of the Norman castle was the founding of the borough within which all trade in the lordship was to be confined in order to ensure an effective system of control over the collection of tolls payable to the lord. Within these towns the burgesses—mercers, haberdashers, coopers, etc.—had their own sites on which they built their houses (generally of wood), arranged in streets that were often occupied by

[4] W. R. B. Robinson, *B.B.C.S.*, Vol. XXII (1967), pp. 169–98.

Plate 1 The *cromlech* at Longhouse Farm, near Trefin, Pembrokeshire. The capstone resting on three of the six chamber stones measures about 16 feet by 9 feet, varying from 2½ feet to 5 feet thick.

Plate 2 Carn Llechart, Glamorgan; a striking example of a Bronze Age cairn-circle showing a ring of upright stone slabs and the central *cystfaen*. Note its situation on an upland ridge overlooking the lowlands. (Cf. Plate 44.)

Plate 3 Aerial view of the earthworks, Y Bwlwarcau, at Llangynwyd, Glamorganshire.

Plate 4   Ysbyty Cynfyn Church, Cardiganshire, showing the megalith as part of the present boundary wall.

Plate 5   St Trinity's Well, Cardigan, as seen by Thomas Dineley in 1684.

Plate 6   Chepstow Castle, by G. Childs, 1831. The Great Gate House is in the middle distance, and beyond it, the Great Tower, the lower part of which is the principal surviving structure of the original castle built by William FitzOsbern, Earl of Hereford, 1067–71.

Plate 7   Kenfig Castle in 1804, by E. Donovan. Built on the east bank of the Kenfig, near the coast, it was one of the few South Wales castles that could be serviced from the sea. It became submerged by moving sands in the sixteenth century. One tower, now barely visible, measured 46 feet by 44 feet, with walls 11 feet thick.

Plate 8 St Donat's Castle: showing the solid structure of the gatehouse and curtain wall rising from the moat.

Plate 9   Neath Abbey, *c.* 1849, by Newman & Co. John Leland (1506?–1552) saw Neath as 'the fairest abbey in Wales'.

Plate 10   Monknash: the grange of Neath Abbey as seen today. When the monks worked this grange, upwards of 1,000 acres were under the plough.

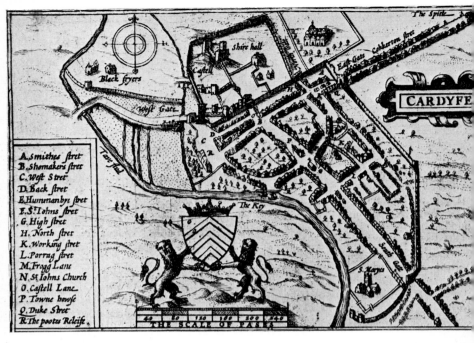

Plate 11   Speed's map of Cardiff, showing the defensive character of its plan as laid
out in Norman times.

Plate 12   Cardiff, c. 1838, showing the extension beyond the old town walls.

Plate 13 Open fields, half a mile south-west of Rhosili, Glamorgan.

Plate 14   An example of dry stone-walling at Rhosili, Glamorgan.

Plate 15   Stone and sod hedge previously planted with 'quick set' but now grown into trees and demarcating field boundaries at Ysbyty Cynfyn, Cardiganshire.

persons following the same trade. It was from these Norman boroughs that practically all the pre-industrial towns of South Wales emerged.

Monasteries and the landscape

Besides introducing a military aristocracy sustained by the castle and the manorial system of land cultivation, the Norman conquerors introduced the Latin monasteries which they endowed with lands and other forms of wealth for the supposed safety of their souls. For a period of three or four centuries after their foundation, the monastic houses were instrumental in changing the character of the landscape in many regions of South Wales, and for that reason, command some attention in this context.

The first Latin monasteries to be founded in South Wales were those of the Benedictine Order. At Ewenni, in Glamorganshire, the Norman Priory Church still stands on the landscape, reminding the observer of its dual purpose— a house of prayer and a fortress, and so symbolising, in much the same way as a castle, the social and cultural barrier that once existed between the foreign monks and the subjugated native Welsh, for the Benedictine monks were recruited almost exclusively for a non-Welsh population. Benedictine priories were much smaller in extent than the Cistercian monasteries which followed them, and from the point of the landscape it is, perhaps, worth noting that, without exception, they were located in the lowland regions in the shadow of the castle, which meant that their economy was based, in the main, on arable farming. Their income from sheep rearing was small in proportion to the whole.

Other important orders of monks who came to South Wales included the Augustinians whose three houses were centred at Haverfordwest, Carmarthen and Llanthony. The solitary Premonstratensian house founded by Lord Rhys of

E

Deheubarth at Talyllychau (Talley), *c.* 1196, was in fact "virtually indistinguishable in site, origin and patrimony from the Cistercian Abbeys".[5] The estates of the Abbey were extensive, and the substantial tower which still overlooks the ruins of the nave reminds us of the lands[6] which the old monks tilled, exercising "their beneficent influence in the lovely valleys of Carmarthenshire".

But of all the monastic orders introduced into South Wales, none had made a greater impact on the landscape than the Cistercians—the White Monks—whose abbeys may be divided into those of Anglo-Norman and those of Welsh foundations (Fig. 9). The first arrived in South Wales with the foundation of Tintern in 1131, followed in 1147 by Margam and then Neath which had been founded earlier as a Savignac monastery in 1130. The earliest of the Welsh Cistercian foundations arrived at Trefgarn, in West Wales, in 1140, and finally moving to a permanent home in Whitland—near the royal site of Hen Dŷ Gwyn ar Dâf—in 1151. Whitland, which had passed under the protection of a native Welsh dynasty, soon extended its influence into Cardiganshire, where it founded the so-called 'Westminster Abbey of Wales' at Strata Florida in 1164.

At first the monks were not always fortunate in their choice of site, and in many instances had to change their centres of settlement. Thus Whitland, after settling at Trefgarn in 1140, moved to its final site in 1151. Margam was probably founded at Pendâr in the Glamorgan hills in 1147 before moving to its marshland site at the foot of Margam mountain in 1151. Similarly Strata Florida, founded in 1164 by the Fflur stream, moved after thirty-six years, a distance of about two miles up stream, perhaps to ensure a more

[5] Glanmor Williams, *The Welsh Church from the Conquest to Reformation* (Cardiff, 1962), p. 21.
[6] See Melville Richards, 'The Carmarthenshire possessions of Talyllychau', *Carmarthenshire Studies* (1974), pp. 110–21.

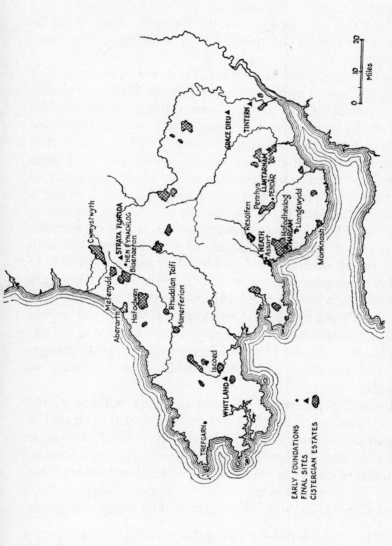

Fig. 9. Cistercian houses and their estates before the dissolution of the monasteries. (After D. H. Williams.)

EARLY FOUNDATIONS •
FINAL SITES ▲
CISTERCIAN ESTATES ▨

CWMYSTWYTH

STRATA FLORIDA ▲
HEN FYNACHLOG •
Blaenaeron

Aberarth •
Mefenydd
Hafodwen
Rhuddlan Teifi
Maenerfion

TREFGARN •
WHITLAND ▲
Iscoed

GRACE DIEU ▲
TINTERN ▲

Resolfen
Penrhys
LLANTARNAM
PENDÂR ▨
NEATH ▲
Assart
Hafodheulog
MARGAM
Llangewydd
Morknash

suitable site served with a better water supply, and it was after thirty-six years, in 1176, that the convent at Tyfaenor moved to Cwmhir, Radnorshire. In the final analysis it may be said that the location of the monastic lands is to be accounted for by the patronage of their respective benefactors.[7]

In taking account of monasticism in the development of the landscape, it must be stressed that the Cistercian monks were pioneer farmers—"the best farmers in the Middle Ages". In contrast to the Benedictines, their income was derived primarily from sheep rearing. The austerity of their discipline resulted in their abbeys being built in remote areas, and their endowments, on the whole, consisted of vast tracts of undeveloped, or partially developed, country. Indeed, Professor E. G. Bowen has argued that the monks at Strata Florida "identified themselves as closely with the economy of the Welsh peasants as we know they did with their social, historical and political background".[8] It would follow, therefore, that in *pura Wallia* the characteristically pastoral activities of the Cistercians would not only have fitted into the traditional economy of Wales, but would also have injected into it a new spirit of enterprise, resulting in some degree of expansion on their coastal granges for the wintering of sheep as well as the growing of cereals.

From the nature of the land normally granted to the Cistercians, much of it had to be assarted, that is cleared of woodland and waste and, if marshland, drained. The same was true also of Llanthony Prima, an Augustinian foundation described in the twelfth and thirteenth centuries as "an oasis in a wild barren valley". Again, Talley Abbey, according to Giraldus, was situated "in a rough and sterile

[7] William Rees, *An Historical Atlas of Wales* (London, 1972), p. 32.
[8] E. G. Bowen, 'Monastic economy of the Cistercians at Strata Florida', *Ceredigion,* Vol. I, p. 36.

spot surrounded by woods on every side and beyond measure inaccessible and sufficiently meanly endowed". Property exchanged by Neath Abbey (Plate 9) in the thirteenth century was, in fact, significantly referred to as the Assart. We shall never know the actual extent of land-scape changes brought about by monastic bodies, but some assessment of the range of territory within which they operated is possible by noting some of the grants made to them. For instance, the original grant given to the Abbey at Margam at its foundation appears to have been almost co-extensive with the old parish of Margam which covered an area of over 18,000 acres. So keenly did Norman and native Welsh families vie with each other in granting lands to Margam, that by the Dissolution it is estimated that the Abbey lands extended over 50,000 acres, most of which was in Glamorgan. Over such an extent of land, the attack on the landscape must have been quite spectacular, particularly in the upland reaches where the clearing of woodland was undertaken in order to bring additional tracts under cultivation. Lands so reclaimed were extensively enclosed, as is indicated in the lease of the Hafod-heulog Grange belonging to Margam in 1485, which stipulated that the lessees main-tained all buildings, ditches and fences. Similarly in Strata Florida where, in 1537, a lease to a Morris ap Ievan stated that he "must build, dig, and maintain in good order a hedge and a ditch between his land and the demesne of the Abbey".

The Cistercians, aided as they were by the lay brethren (*fratres conversi*) and hired labourers (*mercenarii*) were able to organise their lands into granges controlled and directed from the monastery. Some of these granges were, indeed, quite extensive. Two granges of Strata Florida (in Cardigan-shire), Pennard and Mevenydd, both exceeded 5,000 acres. Around Margam there were twelve granges. These were reasonably large; seven of them totalled 4,500 acres—that is, an average of about 651 acres per grange. They were as follows:[9]

Granges	Arable Carucates	(Acres)	Meadow Acres
Llangewy	8	(960)	83
Stormy	4	(480)	36
St Michael	7	(840)	29
'de Gardino'	7	(840)	70
Midd'	5	(600)	44
Meles	4	(480)	35
Terrys	3	(360)	—

In passing, it is interesting to note that there were at Margam in the year 1336, 38 monks and 40 *conversi*. Some indication of the landed strength of the South Wales monasteries may be given by the number of granges controlled by the various houses: Whitland had 17; Strata Florida 23; Margam 13; Caerleon 13; Tintern 8; and Grace Dieu, in Monmouthshire, 8.

It should be noted again that the Cistercian grange (*grangia*) was, in fact, a farm with its own necessary buildings for residence, barns for storage, etc. "It presented the appearance of a farmstead with hedges, ditches and walls to mark off the enclosure or several closes of the grange" (Donnelly). As we have seen, these granges were distributed over large stretches of upland and lowland territory of South Wales. Some of these have lived on in the Margam mountain areas in such names as Hafod Decca (fairest summer dwelling), Hafod Heulog (sunny summer dwelling), and Hafod-y-Porth (summer dwelling of the gateway). Neath had granges in Aissa (Monknash), Cwrt Sart (Court of the Assart) near Briton Ferry (but now built over by the railway station of Port Talbot), and Gelligarn and

9 Clark, *Cartae,* IV, p. 1197.

Paviland in Gower. Lowland granges are, perhaps, perpetuated in such place names as Mynachdy, a grange held
by the Abbey of Llantarnam in the manor of Llystalybont,
and Grangetown, Cardiff, which continued as the Grange
Farm; the remains of the house are still visible near the
library in Clive Street.

The increasing population at this time might easily have
encouraged an extension of arable cultivation. There is,
indeed, evidence which suggests that in the more favoured
lowland areas land was coming under the plough for the
first time. For instance, palaeobotanists have studied the
effects of monastic estate management around Strata
Florida Abbey, where pollen changes recorded in bog
profiles show that, in the twelfth century, arable farming
with barley and oats on the lowland granges "replaced
pastoralism of later pre-history and the Dark Ages".[10]
Again, at Stormy Down, a few years before 1170, Geoffrey
Sturmi had built a chapel "in his vill which he made in a
solitude and on land where no one had ever ploughed
before".[11]

The increase in the monastic population, too, as well as a
growing 'hospitality' bill, led abbeys to seek additional lands
in the coastal regions. An outstanding example of this trend
was the grange of Neath at Monknash (Plate 10) in the
Vale of Glamorgan where, in the thirteenth century, there
were more than 1,000 acres under the plough, besides its
granges at Sker and Newton Nottage, also in the Vale of
Glamorgan.

Despite their involvement in arable farming as, for instance, at Monknash and Sker, the Cistercian monks were
generally renowned for their sheep rearing. In 1291 the
Taxatio Ecclesiastica shows that Margam possessed at least

[10] H. N. Savory, 'Man and the Welsh countryside in the pre-industrial age'
in *Amgueddfa: Bulletin of the National Museum of Wales*, No. 5 (1970), p. 11.
[11] Clark, *Cartae*, I, p. 151.

5,285 sheep; Neath 4,897; Tintern 3,264; Strata Florida 1,327; and Whitland 1,100. The relative sheep population of the respective abbeys shows clearly the importance of pasture lands, and the mountain pastures were of paramount importance in South Wales. Between 1229 and 1336, Strata Florida held a considerable proportion of the pasture of Ceredigion (Cardiganshire).

The nature of the South Wales terrain probably led the Cistercians to continue the medieval Welsh custom of transhumance. Reference has already been made to the upland granges of Margam, but similar summer dwellings were evident on the mountain pastures belonging to Strata Florida. There were four in the Cwmystwyth grange alone —Hafod Gau, Hafod Uchtryd, Hafod Uchared, and Hafod-yr-Abad, and three in Pennard Grange—Hafod Odys, Hafod Rhydychen and Hafod Fraith.

The trade that followed the sale of wool from the monastic granges stimulated maritime activity in the small ports and creeks along the South Wales coast. In 1250 Margam was trading with Flanders, and in the same year sent forty-two and a half sacks of wool to Ghent. Strata Florida, too made use of the small port of Aberarth in Cardiganshire, where traces of the quay were still visible in the late nineteenth century.

The abbeys were also engaged in small-scale industrial activities, and although their impact on the landscape in this direction was, perhaps, minimal, nevertheless the consequences were characteristic of later industrial activity in the region. In 1249 Margam had been granted the right to work coal by Owein ab Alaythur who gave the monks "all the carbon stone" in his lands, along with the "ingress and egress" for "two-wheeled and four-wheeled" carts and other vehicles. The fouling of the landscape by mineral waste may be inferred from the undertaking entered into to pay compensation in the event of damage being done to crops.

The unprecedented building of parish churches and,

perhaps, to a lesser degree of monastic churches which took place at the end of the twelfth and beginning of the thirteenth centuries created a real demand, not only for local skilled and unskilled labour, but also for local stone taken from local quarries. Quarrying thus developed apace, and Margam and Ewenni drew their supplies of stone from the famous quarries at Sutton, near Southerndown. Tintern Abbey, too, worked quarries in the Wye valley.

The occupation of land in the low-lying regions of South Wales by the Benedictine monks, together with the later extension of grants to them or marginal lands along the coastline resulted in more land being brought under the plough. It has been estimated that at the end of the thirteenth century, monastic landowners in South Wales had well over 40,000 acres under the plough, much of which had had to be cleared. But low-lying marginal land held by Margam near the mouth of Afan and Ely, and by Neath near the estuary of the Loughor, required draining and embanking against the encroachment of the sea.

Many of the South Wales rivers, too, were subjected to the requirements of the monasteries. In the early days, the monks did not eat meat, and consequently the fish of adjacent rivers was at a premium. Fishing rights were granted them, and in consequence weirs were built. On the Wye, Tintern Abbey was granted three weirs, with a right to claim forest timber for their upkeep, which privilege was said to have reduced "the fern of the forest" in 1341.

It should be remembered that there were, in all, thirty-five religious houses[12] scattered throughout the South Wales

[12] *Black Monks:* Llanbadarn Fawr (Cardiganshire), Cardigan, St Dogmael's, Pill and Caldey (daughter outposts of St Dogmael's), Pembroke, St Clears, Carmarthen, Cydweli, Llangennith, Ewenni, Cardiff, Bassaleg, Goldcliff, Malpas, Chepstow, Monmouth, Abergafenni, Brecon, Llandovery.
Cistercians: Strata Florida, Talley, Whitland, Neath, Margam, Llantarnam, Tintern.
Augustinians: Haverfordwest, Carmarthen, Llanthony.
The Friars: Haverfordwest, Carmarthen, Cardiff (2), Newport, Brecon.

region, and these exerted their influence for the best part of four centuries. Their impact on the landscape through the daily labours of the monks and their *conversi* was, in a sense, more real and enduring than the conspicuous stone structures represented by the abbeys and their churches, and the military fortress of their Norman patrons in the form of castles.

Dove-houses and fishponds represent a form of development in the landscape which bears evidence, although not exclusively, to the diet of the monasteries in particular. In the late sixteenth century there were sixteen fishponds of varying sizes in Glamorgan, and at least ten dove-houses, or *columbaria*. The dove-cote (or pigeon loft as it is sometimes called) was a prominent feature on the larger estates, and sometimes housed hundreds of birds which provided a source of fresh meat throughout the winter.

In 1804 Malkin observed that in many places pigeon houses or dove-cotes were really ornamental: "their height, size, and circular construction, give them, at a distance, the effect of castellate towers". Some of them were of considerable antiquity and were particularly numerous at St Donat's, Monknash, and Llantwit Major in Glamorgan, and Slebech in Pembrokeshire. At Penrice Castle, for example, the building was about twenty feet high, and pierced with about five hundred pigeon holes. Oxwich Castle also had a similar one. An occasional dove-cote still stands on the landscape to remind us of the fact that pigeon meat was once a favourite item in the diet of certain sections of the native population. In feudal days the exclusive right to pigeon houses belonged to the territorial lord. When we remember, however, that some of these birds will eat their own bulk of food in a day, it will be seen what an impoverishment of surrounding crops the dove-houses must have created, not to mention the hatred of the local peasantry.

There is ample evidence to show that the monastic

settlements caused substantial displacement of local tenants within certain areas into which they expanded. For instance, the areas of original endowment of Margam contained a number of scattered settlements along the adjacent river valleys and the lower hill slopes, but within a generation of its foundation in November 1147, the abbey adopted a policy of clearing the tenantry from the lands within the area of original settlement. Original tenancies were shortened, and deeds of surrender made so rigid as to preclude future tenancies. One quit claim recited thus: "Moreover be it known that we have abjured the said land in such a way that never hereafter shall anyone of us or of our kin hold that land either from the king, the earls or any lord French, English or Welsh."[13] That the landscape was modified by such a policy is illustrated by the events which followed the grant made to Margam Abbey of a substantial holding in the knight's fee of Llangewydd. The abbey further came to an agreement with the holder of the fee, David Scurlage, by which the remainder of the fee was acquired for an annual rental.[14] The fee contained a castle which, according to Geraldis, was razed to the ground by monks who argued that a knight's fee without a castle would be of less value to the knight, and they might, therefore, hope to obtain the fee on better terms.

Churches in the landscape

The reorganisation of the Welsh church following the Norman incursion into Wales resulted in notable consequences for the landscape. The country was, in time, divided into dioceses and into parishes. The introduction of territorial bishoprics brought in the question of boundaries, and by about 1115, the territory of South Wales was

[13] Clark, *Cartae*, I, pp. 128–9.
[14] Clark, *Cartae*, II, pp. 169–70.

parcelled out between the diocese of St David's and Llandaff. The former included the greater part of Deheubarth, and included the Padarn churches of central Wales, while Llandaff was limited to the kingdom of Morgannwg and Gwent.

The basic unit in the reorganisation of the church was the parish, but this had no direct influence on the landscape. In each parish the tithes and offerings were assigned to the priest for his maintenance. The visual evidence for this were the tithe barns which served as collecting centres, and were distributed over extensive tracts of the countryside.

The landscape was, perhaps, more conspicuously affected by the buildings necessary to administer to the religious needs of the population within the reorganised administrative framework. Each parish was served by the parish church, and in the outlying parts 'chapels of ease' were established. The number of parishes in Glamorgan in the Middle Ages amounted to 121, but many of them varied considerably in size. It must be remembered that in the Middle Ages the demarcation of a parish was governed mainly by the economic capacity of a district to maintain a parish priest, and this accounts for the disparity in the areas of different parishes. In Glamorgan, an upland parish such as Merthyr Tudful covered 25,000 acres, whereas St Athan, in the Vale of Glamorgan, covered 1,531 acres, and Flemingston 701 acres. In Cardiganshire the disparity was even more striking. In mountain moorlands the parish of Llanbadarn Fawr comprised 52,700 acres; Caron Uwch Clawdd 39,138 acres, and Llanfihangel Genau'r Glyn 32,825 acres.[15] In more fertile areas of South Pembrokeshire there were thirty parishes of between 1,000 and 2,000 acres, and six of less than 1,000 acres. The distribution of churches on the landscape was, in a sense, determined by precisely the same

[15] W. T. Morgan, 'The diocese of St David's in the nineteenth century', *J.H.S.C.W.*, No. 27 (1972), p. 27.

physical and economic considerations as account for the distribution of the Norman castles and prehistoric remains. These factors are further highlighted in the nineteenth century when the exploitation of the mineral resources of the upland areas in Cardiganshire, and more particularly in Glamorgan, resulted in a redistribution of population. The impact of the growth of population on the religious life of the people as reflected on the landscape will be discussed in a later chapter. By the end of the thirteenth century, as a result of the parochial divisions introduced by the Normans, it is more than likely that within the archdeaconries of Llandaff, Monmouth, Carmarthen, St David's, Cardigan and Brecon (encompassing the greater part of the present-day South Wales), there stood in the landscape over 700 churches (including chapelries), as well as about 210 parsonage houses. The burial grounds, too, are to be remembered, with churchyard crosses, fonts and tombs— more economical than the chambered tombs of Neolithic times—all reflecting in the landscape many facets of the religious and social teachings of the time.

Apart from the cathedral churches of St David's and Llandaff, Welsh churches were of simple plan and construction (Plate 31). Built in the same way as Welsh houses, with local materials and local labour, they were unpretentious but homely. The churches which served the community were small, austere and primitive, exhibiting nothing of the scale and grandeur of the Gothic churches that were rising in England and Northern France. A large number of churches were probably still constructed of wood. The pre-Norman church of Llandaff was a mere twenty-eight feet long, fifteen feet wide, and twenty feet high.[16]

Perhaps the most distinctive physical characteristic of parochial churches in South Wales is that in the once thoroughly Normanised areas, such as Brecon, South

[16] *Book of Llandav*, p. 86.

Glamorgan, South Carmarthenshire and South Pembroke-shire, they have towers, whereas in the more historically Welsh upland regions they have none. In no district can this division be more clearly observed than in Pembroke-shire where, for centuries after the establishment of Christianity, the native churches developed from rude cells of the earliest Christian teachers and leaders into small buildings erected after a definite plan of single rectangular chamber and, later, of nave and separate chancel. Such simple structures were adequate to the requirements of a community hitherto little affected by the onward march of culture and the increasing sense of comfort and convenience. The stage of development reached in the majority of Welsh parochial edifices by the middle of the thirteenth century is probably represented in the structure of the small church of Llanwnda (Fig. 10). But with the Franco-Norman

Fig. 10. Sketch showing the typical Welsh church of Llanwnda, Pembrokeshire, which represents the stage the majority of Welsh parochial structures had attained by the middle of the thirteenth century. (R.C.A.M., Pembs., 1925.)

invasions of the region came more ornate and grandiose church buildings displaying towers similar to those visible in the Normandy landscape. The Norman lord, fortified as he was against worldly attacks behind the walls of his stone castle, built his church "with as strict an eye to business as his keep" for it was intended to become "the resting-place for the bones of himself and his successors".[17] Thus it was that the transeptal chapel was provided in the parish church. But the Norman lords wanted the best of both worlds, and built their churches with square battlemented towers. In many instances these were massive structures built for defensive purposes. The square-towered churches, which are to be seen today in the once Normanised regions of South Wales, represent on the landscape the subjugation of the early Celtic church by *force majeure* in the same way as the castles once represented the economic and political sub-jugation of the Welsh by the Norman invaders of the eleventh and twelfth centuries. We shall see later that a movement to re-assert the authority of indigenous religious feelings developed into open revolt when the Puritan upheaval reached Wales in the seventeenth century, and eventually gave rise to a powerful spiritual revival with far-reaching consequences, which became clearly expressed on the landscape.

By the end of the fifteenth century, all South Wales churches aspired to alterations in the Perpendicular style, with the result that most rural churches of Wales present "an early type of plan and elevation in outline with archi-tectural detail characteristic of the close of the fifteenth century, or the opening of the sixteenth".[18] Many parishes saw the complete reconstruction of their churches, while

[17] *R.C.A.M.*, an inventory of the ancient monuments in Wales and Mon. VII—County of Pembrokeshire (London, 1925), pp. xiix–li; Rev. E. Tyrrel-Green, 'The Ecclesiology of Pembrokeshire' in *Trans. Hon. Soc. Cymmr* (1921–2); Glanmor Williams, *The Welsh Church*, pp. 428–34.
[18] *Cymmr.*, xl, 73.

others were enlarged by building an additional nave or aisle. This was particularly the case in the diocese of St David's where there was "an almost universal reconstruction and enlargement of churches". Towers became one of the outstanding features of this period, in marked contrast to the square battlemented towers which characterised the churches located in areas with strong Norman influences. St John's, Cardiff, and St Woollos, Newport, are fine examples of the striking elegance of towers. Apart from the external structures of churches, finer craftsmanship was also applied to such details as stained glass windows. Screens and rood-lofts, too, were the crowning glory of Welsh medieval church architecture.[19]

Thus, with the coming of the Normans to South Wales, the landscape took on a new appearance over extensive areas of the countryside. The castle, the church, priory, and monastery—the outward symbols of militarism and religious piety—were all, nevertheless, underpinned by the economic achievement and potential of the native soil and population which was distributed within the towns and villages, probably in general accordance with the rest of the country, ranging from between five and ten persons per square mile, and rising to, perhaps, twenty in more favoured areas.

Towns, villages and fields

One of the privileges enjoyed by the Marcher lords was the right to create boroughs, and to establish markets and fairs, thereby exercising control over all trade within a lordship. In other words, no retail trade was permitted in the lordship except within the limits of the borough. Towns meant trade, and trade meant a greater circulation or distribution of goods and services.

In examining the growth of towns in South Wales, it

[19] Glanmor Williams, *loc. cit.*

should be remembered that an economy in which towns were needed was not, in fact, developed in South Wales until the advent of the Normans.[20] There were, of course, existing centres of administration in the area, despite the impression given by Giraldus when he wrote in 1188 saying that the Welsh "do not live together in towns or villages and fortresses. Rather after the manner of hermits, they cling to the edge of the forests where, instead of constructing permanent homes, they build cottages of woven twigs that last but for a year." The Welsh, however, had their 'royal' villages, or *maesdrefi*, which functioned as centres of local government before the Normans established their boroughs.

To some extent, the Normans utilised sites already settled, such as at Cardiff, Neath and Carmarthen. Later, with the development of the manorial economy, and an increasing population in the countryside, settlements which were not boroughs in origin, later acquired urban functions. The close connection between strategic sites of Norman castles and their boroughs is apparent in such places as Chepstow on the Wye, Newport on the Usk, Cardiff on the Taff (Plate 11), Bridgend on the Ogmore, Aberafan on the Afan, Neath on the river Neath, Swansea on the Tawe, and Loughor on the Loughor river. All these were, initially, fortified towns, that is, bastide towns, and have ever since the medieval period played a dominant part in the planning and siting of the Welsh urban scene.

The plan, or shape, of towns is almost exclusively man-made. Unlike the shapes of fields, which were largely determined by terrain, soil and vegetation, agricultural practice and legal restrictions, the town, especially the walled town, was planned initially according to the requirements of a defensive system within a definite site (Fig. 11).

The wall of the town, and the castle walls within it, were

[20] E. A. Lewis, *The Medieval Boroughs of Snowdonia* (London, 1912).

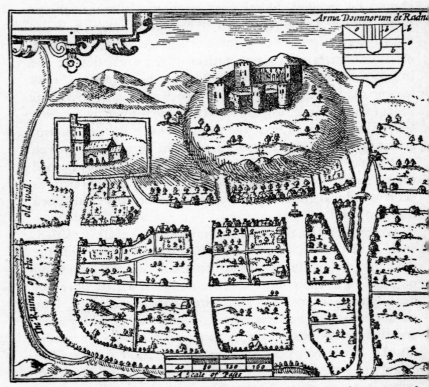

Fig. 11. The town of New Radnor was a walled town and represented an advanced outlook in town planning. The walls may be seen to this day. The castle guarded one of the most important gateways between England and mid-Wales. The western gateway, the High Gate on the Llanfihangel Nant Melan–Knighton road, gave its name to an existing house called 'Porth'. (From a plan by Speed, A.D. 1610.)

the chief factors in shaping medieval Welsh towns, and, whilst the castle remained an essential institution in the government of the country, so the market place, which marked the hub of the economic life of the surrounding countryside remained the focal point of town life. Once the importance of the castle waned, the focal centre of towns very often changed because of new economic factors and considerations of accessibility. How these developments affected South Wales towns will be discussed in Chapter 7. Meanwhile, it could be said that the growth of towns and their market places encouraged foreign trade, and during the thirteenth and fourteenth centuries, alien vessels from French and Spanish ports, from Cornwall and Devon, and particularly from Bristol, arrived frequently at Carmarthen, Haverfordwest and Milford with salt and wine. The nature of the shipping found in the early medieval ports of South Wales may be assessed from the fact that occasionally certain merchant ships in Carmarthen, Swansea, Tenby and Milford were arrested and converted into men-of-war. This meant that such ships were of sixty, eighty and, sometimes, two hundred tons burthen.

In Wales, as in England, the village was an expression on the landscape of a mode of life. All villages, although different in form, are an expression of the need to organise agricultural activity within a particular neighbourhood. In its simplest form, the village may be seen as a single cluster of houses—sometimes two and more—standing in the middle of its territory. The rights of the villagers within this territory amounted to an intricate mixture of claims requiring constant co-operation between neighbours. This co-operation revolved around the convenient principle of sharing the local land resources—the arable fields, the use of meadow and pasture, and the exploitation of the miscellaneous resources of wood, fen and river, not least the regulation of the commons, both upland and lowland. The sharing of the arable land was most important, and the practical application of the ancient rules and methods of cultivation gave to the landscape the appearance of an intermixture of strips separated from each other by fringes of unploughed turf or unsown furrows.

The majority of the lowland villages we know today in South Wales were probably established by the twelfth

83

century, and lie below the 100-metre contour (roughly 300 feet). Many of the villages took their names from the surnames or forenames of their Norman, or earlier, founders, such as Colwinston, Laleston, Bonvilston, Flemingston, in Glamorgan, and Wiston, after Wizo (a prominent Flemish leader) and Rudbaxton, after Alexander Rudepac, in Pembrokeshire. Others retained their ancient church-name, with the addition of the suffix *ton*, as in Cadoxton.

We know very little about the settlement of South Wales before the coming of the Normans. It is true that the 'nucleated' or 'compact' village became more conspicuous on the landscape after the Norman settlement, but it is fairly certain that the Normans did not introduce the 'nucleated' settlement pattern. Wales has no Domesday Survey upon which to discuss earlier settlement, but the oldest extant documentary evidence which cannot be ascribed to a period earlier than the twelfth century must, surely, mirror events which go back to a much earlier period. Place-names, for instance, must hold some clues. Bonvilston, situated on the main road leading from Cardiff to Bridgend—formerly the 'portway'—was probably a nucleated settlement with a church and fortified dwelling whose lands had already been intensely exploited before the Norman conquest as a "*tref* belonging to the *clas* of Llancarfan" (Cowley).

In the 'Englishries', the areas dominated by the Normans, the buildings were, according to George Owen's *Description of Penbrokeshire*, 'English like in townreddes and villages, and not in several and lone houses'. The implication being that the compact village is 'English like', and that the pattern of 'several and lone houses' was characteristically Welsh. The scattered landscapes of the Rheidol Valley in North Cardiganshire, the upper Wye valley beyond Rhayader in Radnorshire, and the Talgarth area of Breconshire provide excellent examples of the Welsh pastoral scene which is in complete contrast and, in general, reflects the differences between everything the 'Englishries' and 'Welshries' stood for in history.

A more specific example of these differences may be seen to this day (although now dulled by recent building works) in the lordship of Coety where, as in the adjacent lordships of Llanbleddian and Talyfan, the Englishry (Coety Anglia) and the Welshry (Coety Wallia) impinge upon each other without any clearly defined geographical boundary. Within the Englishry, however, may be seen the pattern of two nucleated villages and a hamlet, Coety, Coychurch, and Nolton. In the Welshry, however, the human landscape is completely scattered, with no semblance of a village within it. It is significant, too, that the Welshry was thickly wooded in Norman times, for the lordship was held on a tenure of 'sergeanty of hunting'. Even today such names as Allt-y-rhiw, Coed-y-mwstwr, Pencoed, and Cefn Hirgoed, respectively mirror the ancient wooded character of this Welshry. Nevertheless, there are one or two exceptions where a nucleated village developed in the hill districts. For instance, Llangynwyd, in the Llynfi Valley, was in the Welshry of Tir Iarll (Earl's Land). But here the soil will be seen to have favoured the practice of arable farming, and consequently its development as a compact village occurred for precisely the same reasons as the nucleated villages of the lowland areas.

There are numerous instances which support the theory that the compact village was of Saxon origin, but there are instances, such as Llysworney, Llancarfan, having Welsh names that probably go back to the Celtic era. Indeed, the Welsh Laws tell us that the bondmen of the Uchelwr were grouped together in *trefydd* originally signifying houses or dwelling-places; a secondary meaning signified a hamlet, village, that is a group of villein homesteads clustered together for the purposes of common cultivation of the surrounding land.

Villages, although nucleated, reveal a variety of shapes, such as the ribbon village where the houses elongate along a roadway instead of in a cluster around a green or pond. Such villages are Coychurch, Laleston and Marcross, in Glamorgan.

Because of the lack of reliable knowledge concerning the evolution of the rural settlement in Wales, it would be pointless to emphasise the differences between types of villages. The reasons for the compact village and the elongated village are sometimes plain for all to see. But one cannot generalise in the sphere of original causes. The important fact that should be remembered is that the village was an essential social unit for the admistration and control of the rural economy—the cultivation of the soil, and the rearing of animals, etc.—upon which whole communities depended for their daily sustenance.

The agricultural economy of the lowland regions was based mainly on arable farming, and consequently the methods employed in the process of cultivation called for a method of land distribution suited to the agricultural methods of the time. For instance, in Wales, as in England, the plough became "the measuring rod controlling men's lives". Land measures, such as the *erw* (acre) and furlong were derived directly from it, and consequently the size of holdings was measured by its work load—the ox-gang or bovate, the hide, and later, the carucate (Lat. *caruca*, a plough). The equal distribution of land was ensured by what is called the open-field system. So far as we know, this was never developed on an extensive scale in Wales,[21] and today only limited areas carry traces of open fields such as will be found at Laugharne, in Carmarthenshire; Rhosili (Plate 13), Nottage, Llanbethery in Glamorgan; Llyswen

[21] Margaret Davies, 'Field systems in South Wales' in *Studies of Field Systems in the British Isles*, ed. by A. R. H. Baker and R. A. Butlin (Cambridge, 1973).

in Breconshire (Fig. 12); Llannon in Cardiganshire; and Caldicot in Monmouthshire. Remains of field systems are rare, but may still be identified by the aid of air photography.

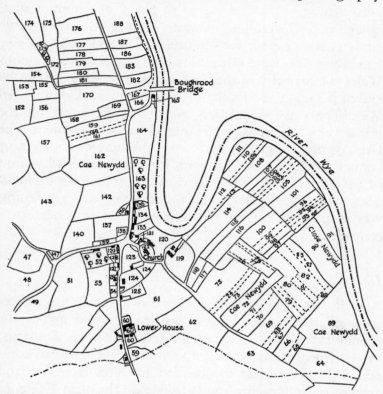

Fig. 12. The common fields of Llyswen (Brecs.) as shown on a tithe map of 1840 when seven tenants farmed upwards of fifty strips or slangs. The enclosure of several groups of strips had already created new field units referred to as *cae newydd* (new field) nos. 72, 89, 162 and *close newydd* (new close) no. 90. After an Enclosure Award in 1856 a further fifty acres of strips were transformed into a new pattern of fields.

A rare example of Celtic Fields in South Wales is visible around the old fort near Llanbleddian, Glamorgan.

Throughout the early part of the medieval period, therefore, the South Wales landscape probably revealed extensive

areas in the arable regions marked off by narrow strip fields
or quillets, unhedged, upon which men laboured to follow
a rotation of crops on a subsistence level of farming.

Enclosure, or the fencing in of pieces of common land,
as well as the hedging-in of waste lands and strips of arable
land, went on quietly for centuries before the Parliamentary
Enclosure Acts were introduced, and it seems that in South
Wales the majority of the open fields were enclosed by the
end of the reign of Elizabeth I and the outbreak of the Civil
War. The early enclosures were generally made on the
initiative of large and small landowners by agreement. The
large owners frequently enclosed commons, waste lands, or
common fields or part of them, for the sake of cultivation
or pasture farming, while the smaller proprietors enclosed
a few acres into one farm. This suggests that active enclosing
was in progress in the late fifteenth and early sixteenth
centuries.

Deserted villages

Apart from the physical factors of erosion and the advancement of sand-dunes, villages became deserted mainly for
economic reasons. The causes for deserted medieval villages,
or settlements, are basically the same as those which compelled primitive man to abandon his sites from lowland
areas to upland pastures, and vice versa. The main difference
lies in the factors which brought them about. In Glamorgan
there are instances, such as at Kenfig, where villages have
been submerged by sand, and new situations adopted at
higher levels. When Leland visited Kenfig he saw the
process in operation, for he observed "a little village on
the east side of Kenfig, and a Castel, booth in ruine and
almost shoked and devoured with the sandes that the
Severne Se there casteth up". In Gower, because of coastal
erosion, new settlements were established at Penmaen,

Penard, Rhosili, and possibly Nicholaston. In 1478 on the north-eastern portion of Oxwich Bay on the Gower coast, moving sand was so damaging that rents were caused to be reduced, while by 1528, the church vicarage, all the glebe lands and the land of many other tenants within the parish had been "utterly and clearly destroyed and overdone with drift sands of the sea". A survey of the manor in 1650 says of the castle erected about 1270: "scarcely there remayneth one whole wall, and it is now compassed with much sand". Lavernock, too, stands on its present eminence, on the coast near Barry, having moved to a safer site. These 'desertions' were the result of an 'act of God'.

Many other medieval villages became deserted for quite different reasons which, in the main, were economic. There are numerous examples of deserted medieval villages in South Wales, such as Runston, a derelict village in the wood north of St Pierre in Monmouthshire, Peterston-super-Ely, Barry, Cwmcidy and Uchelolau (Highlight) in Glamorgan. Runston was once a place of some magnitude and antiquity. The site occupies an eminence on the side of the road leading to Shirenewton. When Archdeacon Coxe visited the site at the end of the eighteenth century he found that "the place may be traced to a considerable distance by numerous foundations". But not a single building now remains except a dilapidated chapel which may still be seen today.

Cwmcidy was a small parish of 280 acres situated within the manor of Penmark. In the early fourteenth century, there were probably nine or ten houses, of which five were clustered along a village street. There was a parish church *c.* 1348, but at some time previous to 1622 it had become defunct, the parish having been absorbed into the neighbouring parish of Porthkerry. In 1622 the village of Cwmcidy still contained seven houses, including the parish church which was, by that time, used as a dwelling. By about 1800, however, the number of houses had been reduced to two, a farm and a small freehold.

Uchelolau, near Barry, was a parish of 405 acres and a sub-manor of Dinas Powys. In 1300 there were probably between six and eight houses standing together, with a parish church, a manor, and a water grist mill. The village had become depopulated before the end of the first half of the sixteenth century when there were only two houses. The parish church, the ruins of which still stand, seems to have continued, probably as a private chapel for the occupants of the manor house, but it was abandoned *c.* 1570. Recent excavations suggest that there may have been two manor houses here, the earliest (thirteenth to fourteenth century) consisting of a moated homestead sited in an isolated position at the junction of two small streams. This was replaced in the fifteenth century by a new manor house built adjacent to the road. At the time of writing, the remains of these small human settlements are visible, but the inevitable modern development plans threaten even the foundations of these ancient settlements.

Some villages have disappeared without leaving any visible remains of their existence, while others are accounted for only in documentary evidence. Such is the case with regard to a village called Stedworlango, with its church and arable lands which once stood, during the early part of the fourteenth century, on the site of the present Penmaen Burrows.[22] Much work remains to be done in South Wales in promoting archaeological excavation in order to confirm field scrutiny and what flimsy documentary material remains extant.[23]

We should not overlook in this context those early medieval Welsh homesteads whose sites are now marked in

[22] *Arch. Camb.* (1871, 1898).
[23] See W. S. G. Thomas, 'Lost villages in South Carmarthenshire' in *Trans. Inst. British Geographers*, Vol. XLVII (1969), pp. 191–203.

the landscape only by their characteristic platforms, levelled into the hillsides in many parts of South and Mid-Wales, and referred to as 'platform houses'. In 1939 Aileen Fox[24] described the landscape evidence on the Gelligaer Common, Glamorgan, of an early medieval settlement made up of five or six farmsteads within an area of a third of a mile, and a maximum distance of 250 yards at elevations varying between 700 feet and 1,300 feet, but within sight of each other. The remains in each case consisted of rectangular platforms levelled into the hillside. It was suggested that these platform houses were deserted sometime in the four-teenth century mainly because of a succession of bad seasons and cattle disease.

Again, at Dyrysol in Radnorshire, the site of a settlement was discovered consisting of platform houses similar to those in Glamorgan but at an elevation of 1,300 feet. These houses were thought to be distinctly Welsh having their origins perhaps before the Norman conquest.[25]

'Hafotai' (*summer dwellings*) *and* 'lluestai' (*shepherds' huts*)

It has been said that the stimulus to enclose arable land for the production of wool after about 1450 did not affect Wales as much as it did certain parts of England. Indeed, the tendency in Wales may have been to over-stock pastures, and to insist on 'exclusive grazing rights'. But besides sheep, the South Wales hills were grazed by goats, and cattle grazed the middle pastures. The need to milk the cattle, as well as the ewes and goats, on the summer pastures brought about the establishment of small units of temporary settlements in the form of *hafotai* (summer dwellings) and *lluestai* (huts or sheds) to sustain the practice of trans-humance. Some of these temporary dwellings developed

[24] 'Early Welsh homesteads on Gelligaer Common' in *Arch. Camb.* (1939), pp. 163–99.
[25] *Arch. Camb.* (1948).

into more permanent farmsteads, and sometimes hamlets. The general decline of the practice of transhumance at the end of the eighteenth and beginning of the nineteenth centuries resulted in the abandonment and decay of numerous summer dwellings which now strew the landscape in many areas of Cardiganshire and in the hills of Glamorgan. These 'deserted' summer dwellings are as historically significant on the landscape as the more conspicuous deserted villages, and deserve equal consideration.

It was not until the early part of the sixteenth century when, with the rise to power of the new landed gentry, a premium was placed on land-ownership. The dissolution of the monasteries and manipulation of monastic finances ushered in an era in which the landscape was re-drawn. How this occurred will be discussed in the following chapter.

SELECT BIBLIOGRAPHY

Baker, Alan R. H. and Butlin, Robin A. (eds.), *Studies of Field Systems in the British Isles* (Cambridge, 1973).

Birch, W. de G., *A History of Margam Abbey* (London, 1897).
—— *A History of Neath Abbey* (London, 1902).

Cowley, Frederick George, 'The Monastic Order in South Wales from the Norman Conquest to the Black Death' (University of Wales unpublished Ph.D. thesis, 1965).

Davies, Margaret, 'Field systems in South Wales' in *Studies of Field Systems in the British Isles*, ed. by A. R. H. Baker and R. A. Butlin (Cambridge, 1973).

Evans, A. Leslie, *Margam Abbey* (Port Talbot, 1958).

Glamorgan County History (Gen. ed. Glanmor Williams), Vol. III, *The Middle Ages*, ed. by T. B. Pugh (Cardiff, 1971).

Gray, Thomas, *Notes On the Granges of Margam Abbey* (London, 1963).

Green, E. Tyrrel, 'The ecclesiology of Pembrokeshire' in *Transactions Hon. Society Cymmrodorion* (1921–22).

Jones, T. I. Jeffreys, 'The enclosure movement in South Wales during the Tudor and early Stuart periods' (University of Wales unpublished M.A. thesis, 1936).

Lewis, E. A., *The Medieval Boroughs of Snowdonia* (London, 1912).

Orwin, D. S. and C. S., *The Open Fields*, 2nd edition (Oxford, 1954)

Pierce, T. Jones, *Medieval Welsh Society* (selected essays ed. by J. Beverley Smith (Cardiff, 1972).

Rees, William, *An Historical Atlas of Wales from Early to Modern Times* (Cardiff, 1972).

—— *Industry before the Industrial Revolution*, 2 vols. (Cardiff, 1968).

—— *South Wales and the March, 1282–1415* (Oxford, 1924).

Royal Commission on the Ancient and Historical Monuments and Constructions in Wales and Monmouth. An inventory of the ancient monuments in Wales and Monmouthshire VII— County of Pembroke (H.M.S.O., 1925).

Thomas, W. S. G., 'Lost villages in South Carmarthenshire' in *Transactions Institute British Geographers*, Vol. XLVII (1969).

Williams, David H., 'The Cistercians in Wales: some aspects of their economy' in *Arch. Camb.*, Vol. CXIV (1965).

Williams, Glanmor, *The Welsh Church from Conquest to Reformation* (Cardiff, 1962).

3. Tudor and Stuart landscapes

The Act of Union of 1536 and the changing landscape. Hedges in the landscape. Cattle trade and drove-roads. Ports and creeks. Parks. The dissolution of the monasteries and the rise of country houses. Early grammar schools and almshouses in the landscape

The Act of Union of 1536 and the changing landscape

IT HAS BEEN said that the foundations of modern Wales were firmly laid in the early sixteenth century. The policy of centralisation adopted by the English kings during the period from 1485 to 1603 meant that in its local application, at least, military gave way to civil power. Consequently the freedom enjoyed, hitherto, by the Marcher lords in South Wales was an anomaly which was finally abolished by the Act of Union, 1536. One important result of this Act was to introduce into Wales and the March, a public system of government in place of the private rule of the feudal lords which, in effect, raised the political status of the people from being simply tenants of a lord, to being subjects of the king. Moreover, the geographical boundaries which were henceforth to separate Wales from England were legally defined, and the limits of the Welsh shires were established, and were to be recognised until our own day. More important, perhaps, in respect of the landscape, were the changes brought about in the Welsh legal system through its fusion with that of England, by which the

94

principles of land tenure were remoulded, with primo-geniture legally supplanting gavelkind as the general rule of succession. Under the latter inherited land succeeded equally to all sons, and this led to excessive subdivision of estates. The effect of minute subdivision of land that had occurred under gavelkind did not disappear for generations, however, although George Owen was able to write (*c.* 1600) that as a result of its abolition in Pembrokeshire, "in many partes the grounde is brought together by purchase and exchanges and headging and enclosures much increased, and now they fall to the tillinge of this wynter corne in greater abundance than before".

We have seen in a previous chapter how the conquest of Welsh territory by the Anglo-Norman lords of the Marches in the eleventh and twelfth centuries resulted in the intro-duction of the manorial system of cultivation into extensive areas along the littoral of South Wales. These events were represented on the landscape mainly by numerous castles, nucleated villages, ecclesiastical buildings, and the compli-cated network of roads. By the beginning of the Tudor period, many of those buildings were to lose their signifi-cance.

The social relations that evolved in South Wales in the sixteenth and seventeenth centuries mirrored the trans-formation that had taken place from the purely feudal relations of the medieval system of cultivation to the system by which the landowners exploited their ownership of the land to secure greater economic advantages as well as greater political control of the country. Further, with the growth and expansion of commercialism, land had become an economic commodity, and the landlords seized every opportunity to push their claims, and to manœuvre their rights, at the expense of their tenantry. These developments resulted in a considerable modification of the landscape, not least because of the spirit of commercialism which characterised the Tudor period, and the premium that was set on the ownership of land and its economic exploitation.

Thomas Churchyard, travelling through Wales in 1587, saw obvious signs of a progressive attitude towards agriculture in the Welsh countryside

> They have begun of late to lime their land
> And plowes the ground where sturdie okes did stand,
> Converts and meares and marrish everywhere . . .
> They teare up trees and takes the rootes away,
> Makes stonie fieldes smooth fertile fallowe ground,
> Brings pastures bare to bear good grasse for hay . . .
> Wales is this day (behold throughout the sheeres)
> In better state than twas these hundred yeeres.

A Glamorgan bard of the seventeenth century confirms Churchyard's testimony when he records that in the parish of Ystradyfodwg, in the hill regions of Glamorgan, a certain Hopkin Thomas Philip had grown "strong robust wheat" where deer once roamed in the woods.

In 1677 Andrew Yarranton, in his *England's Improvement by Sea and Land*, observed that the corn market along the English border, particularly at Hereford, had suffered because "formerly Wales took away their corn when plentiful, but since the Welsh took to break up their mountains and sow with corn, they have corn sufficient for themselves and much to spare".

This is testimony of the manner in which the Welsh hillsides were now being modified to meet the new demand for agricultural produce. But we must not, however, be misled into thinking that agrarian changes in South Wales matched those on the England landscape. For instance, the Tudor enclosures did not affect Wales to the same extent as England, but proceeded along similar lines, if less spectacular. That is to say, open field husbandry was beginning to disappear from the landscape by the intrusion of hedges and other man-made boundaries such as mounds of earth, walls and ditches, and scattered strips of land in many areas were consolidated into compact holdings, again marked off by hedges, fences and ditches. Arable was sometimes converted into pasture, tenements engrossed, and vast areas of waste and common land were enclosed, with consequent deleterious effects on the ancient rights of the tenantry. The fusion of scattered holdings into compact holdings must have gone on surreptitiously in many areas, but in Carmarthenshire the freeholders of the royal manors in the north of the county were allowed to have their holdings divided from one another and their boundaries permanently established.

In the Vale of Glamorgan a great re-drawing of the landscape had taken place in the early part of the sixteenth century. Leland found, *c.* 1536, the ground by the shore at West-Aberthaw, in Glamorgan, had good corn and grass, little wood, but was 'much inclosed'. Writing in 1578, Rice Merrick (d. 1586/7), the oft-quoted gentleman and antiquary of Cottrell, St Nicholas, observed: "This part of the country . . . was a Champyon and open country, without great store of inclosures; for in my time old men reported that they remembered in their youth, that Cattell in some time for want of shade, to have from the 'port-way' [i.e. the main road from Ewenni to Cardiff] runne to Barry which is 4 miles distant, whose ffore-fathers told them that great part of the inclosures was made in their dayes" (Plates 23 and 24). So that by the seventeenth century the open fields in the Vale had disappeared, and the manorial system of cultivation which had given rise to its nucleated villages and its complicated network of roads, had long since decayed.

In many areas where pastoral farming predominated, it was necessary to hedge the meadows. In Pembrokeshire, leaseholders were forced to repair hedges and fences on their tenements, and were "threatened with eviction if they tried to evade this obligation". Likewise, in Glamorgan, in Tudor and Stuart times, leaseholders on the Margam estates were forced "yearley to digg or cause to be digged" specified lengths of ditches "in the meeres of Margam". Similar obligations attended leaseholders on the Briton Ferry estates, and in the Vale of Glamorgan.

The conversion of arable into pasture land did not proceed to any significant degree in South Wales; it was not imperative, for the rich hill pastures were fairly extensive, and carried heavy stocks of sheep. A large proportion of the mountainous pasture lands remained unenclosed until the nineteenth century; tenants of neighbouring farms enjoyed the right of common to most of these without any limitation as to the stock they might send to them. The sheep that grazed these mountain tops could "vie both as to form and quality with the best English breeds, and afford wool of excellent texture". It may be argued that the enclosure movement in Wales during the Tudor and Stuart periods was not inspired by the demands to convert arable to pasture, but rather by the need for more enlightened husbandry. Yet it should be noted that Elizabeth's Act of 1598 for the maintenance of husbandry ordered that land formerly used for tillage but converted to pasture had to be restored to its former use by May 1599, and Pembroke, in South Wales, was singled out.[1]

But many hundreds of acres of common land had been 'grabbed' by the squires of the lordship of Gower in 1590, and in the lordship of Cydweli "it appeareth that anciently there were large and great Commons and Waste within the sayde lordship out of which it should seeme greate Inclosures and Incroachments have byne made by Tenants borderinge uppon them . . .".[2]

[1] David Williams, *A History of Modern Wales* (London, 1950), p. 83.
[2] Geraint Dyfnallt Owen, *Elizabethan Wales* (Cardiff, 1962), p. 88.

It may be said, therefore, that the South Wales landscape in the sixteenth and seventeenth centuries generally revealed a fairly intricate field pattern, within which could be discerned the evolution of the chequered field that is so familiar a feature on the modern rural landscape. In many lowland areas modern fields had emerged by the end of the sixteenth century, while in the upland regions the transformation was not completed until the nineteenth century. As a result of Tudor policy in Wales, the familiar medieval symmetry of open fields surrounded by the waste land with a few holdings, was being disturbed, and it probably took about two centuries of modification and adjustment before the symmetry of the modern rural landscape of patchwork-quilt fields was finally established.

Hedges in the landscape

Hedges are taken so much for granted that there has been a tendency to overlook their importance in the making of the modern landscape. They have, undoubtedly, been a feature of the landscape since pre-Norman times, but most of the hedges visible today are probably of more recent origin, and date from the enclosures which took place between the sixteenth and nineteenth centuries. Indeed, it has been said that upwards of 180,000 miles of hedges were planted in the last two hundred years of this period. In South Wales, hedgerows and trees have been the outstanding feature of the countryside (Plate 15), demarcating farm boundaries and field boundaries, thus producing a distinctive man-made patchwork-quilt appearance on the landscape. The importance attributed to hedging in the agrarian economy of South Wales in the second half of the eighteenth century is indicated in the list of premiums offered by the early Agricultural Societies, and these contributed immensely to the development of the art of hedging in rural communities.

Three types of hedges may still be seen in almost any South Wales parish where arable farming predominates, namely, 'quick' hedges, stone walls, and naked sod-hedges, or stones and sods in alternate layers. All three types required a special skill in their construction, and the growing demand for hedges in the enclosure of common lands in the eighteenth and nineteenth centuries gave rise to a new class of rural craftsman in Wales.

The hedges in Gower and the Vale of Glamorgan, as in many other parts of the region, still exhibit the skilful, and often artistic, work that went into dry-walling. At the 'Vile'[3] in Rhosili, Gower, the many miles of walls which divide the arable fields from the common grazing land bear testimony to the skill of the stone-masons who constructed them from the stones dug from the neighbouring cliffs some centuries ago. The stones are mainly rectangular in shape, because of the natural 'jointing' and 'fissuring' of the local limestone, and are built up, not only to divide the arable from the open fields, but to protect the whole from the strong prevailing winds. Many of these walls curve outwards at the top in order to break the wind force, and so preserve the stability of the wall structure (Plate 14).

Most living hedges came into existence because of the economic requirements of farming, and although they have acquired a characteristic beauty of their own they are, nevertheless, still functional in the eyes of the farmer, but are often grubbed up because the requirements of modern farming make them no longer necessary. In the countryside of South Wales, hedges still fulfil their original function as living stock-proof barriers, and in those areas where sheep and cattle grazing form the principal farming activity, hedges will continue because they are necessary.[4]

[3] 'Vile' is the Gower dialect word for 'field'. I am grateful to Professor Glanmor Williams for this information.

[4] The age of a hedge can be estimated by applying the technique developed by Dr Max Hooper of counting the number of shrubby species it contains.

Cattle trade and drove-roads

The growth and expansion of London and Bristol during the sixteenth and seventeenth centuries created an increasing demand for agricultural produce, more particularly meat and butter. South Wales was still a preponderantly pastoral region, producing considerable numbers of cattle and sheep, and, consequently, a brisk trade in livestock developed between South Wales and the south-eastern and south-western counties of England. Although there is evidence of Welsh cattle being sold to English dealers in the thirteenth century, and possibly earlier, it was during the period from the fifteenth to the nineteenth century that the cattle trade assumed significant proportions, with the cattle drovers, as we shall see, occupying a key position in the economic and social life of Wales.

At the beginning of the eighteenth century, Daniel Defoe observed that from Brecon and Radnor "they send yearly great herds of black cattle to England, and which are known to fill our fairs and markets, even of Smithfield itself", while Cardiganshire was "so full of cattle, that 'tis said to be the nursery, or breeding place, for the whole kingdom of England S[outh] by Trent . . .".

After the summer and early autumn fairs, the drovers of Cardiganshire, Carmarthenshire and Pembrokeshire arranged the assembling of their cattle at given points, such as Abergwili (Carmarthenshire), Llanddulas (Breconshire), Eglwyswrw (Pembrokeshire), and Tregaron (Cardiganshire), where they were shod for the long trek to the English markets (Plate 16). The South Wales drovers' tracks along which the cattle were driven converged in a west to east direction, on the main gateways into England—the Powys way opening to the English lowlands by way of the Severn, and the Gwent way in the south, giving access to Herefordshire. Their extension into English territory is still in

evidence in such names as the 'Welsh road' across southern Warwickshire and beyond, and the 'Welsh way' near the old Droitwich Salt way. Part of the ancient road near Barnsley and Bagendon, in Gloucestershire, is known as the 'Welsh way', and on the Heath, north of Farnborough in Hampshire, there is a tract called the 'Welsh Ride or Drive, a grassy road between gorse and heather'.

The various routes followed by the drovers and their droves (Fig. 13)—many of which are still visible—led into the heart of the English countryside and on to the cattle fairs of Barnet and Smithfield. Glamorgan cattle were either driven on the hoof from local fairs to the English markets, or to the local ports such as Cardiff and Aberthaw, whence they were shipped to Bristol and Minehead, or to Sully, from where they were conveyed by boat to Uphill, near Weston-super-Mare, and then driven overland to Bristol, Bath, Exeter, and sometimes as far south as Plymouth and Portsmouth. It is not without real significance that on the outside wall of a private house in Stockbridge, Hampshire, formerly the 'Drover's Inn', is the following Welsh inscription: 'GWAIR-TYMHERUS-PORFA-FLASUS-CWRW-DA-A-GWAL-CYSURUS' (seasoned hay, tasty pasture, good beer and a comfortable bed). It seems that the old inn was a resting place for the weary Welsh drovers and their cattle on their way to supply the naval yards at Portsmouth.[5] Cattle were also conveyed by sea from Tenby and Haverfordwest to Watchet and Minehead.

The Welsh drovers who acted as the middlemen in the vast cattle trade with England had to be licensed annually, and had to be able to give adequate financial guarantees before a licence could be granted. As a class, they provided one of the main links between South Wales and the English world of commerce in pre-industrial times. Indeed, it was a drover, named David Jones, who founded, in 1799, one

[5] *Arch. Camb.*, Vol. CVII, 1958, p. 125.

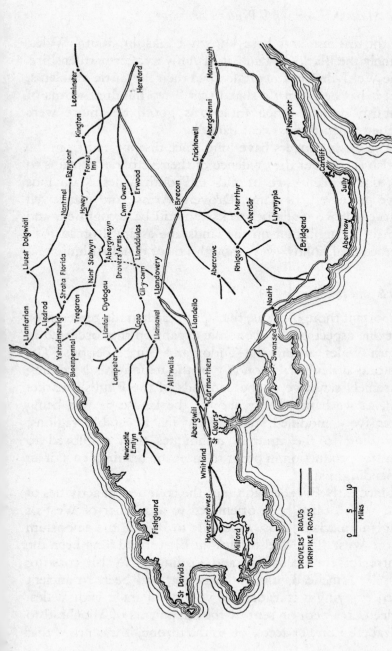

Fig. 13. The main drovers' and early turnpike roads. (After William Rees and Margaret Davies.)

DROVERS' ROADS ——————
TURNPIKE ROADS ════════

0   5   10
    Miles

103

of the earliest and best known banks in South Wales, namely the Black Ox Bank at Llandovery, Carmarthenshire. The Welsh drovers, naturally, had their linguistic problems, and it has been wittily stated that "two hundred words of English sufficed when trade was good, but more were needed when things went badly".

The cattle drovers have long since disappeared from the Welsh scene, but the evidence of their activities remains to this day in many parts of mid- and south Wales. Many inns have preserved the name 'Drovers' Arms', and many well marked drove-roads or tracks can still be recognised, and remain as significant on the landscape as any Roman road or medieval hollow-way, though not of equal antiquity.

Ports and creeks

Important though it was, the Welsh cattle trade represented but one aspect of the economic expansion that occurred in South Wales during the Tudor and Stuart periods. The pastoral-agricultural economy of the region was becoming extremely sensitive to the demands of the English market and, as we have already shown, the landscape was being extensively modified, particularly in the arable regions, according to the agrarian techniques then employed to increase production in order to meet the requirements of an expanding market.

Since early Elizabethan times the commercial activities of South Wales had been orientated to a number of West of England markets, more especially to Bristol, the emporium of the West. The 'Welsh Back' at Bristol had long been the centre for the unloading and loading of Welsh coasting vessels. Minehead, too, in Somerset, had been an ancient port, enjoying a considerable volume of trade with Wales. Indeed, in a petition sent by the inhabitants of Minehead to Elizabeth I on her accession to the throne, it was urged that unless financial aid was forthcoming for the repair of the pier, serious losses would follow, including "the decay of an ancient and daily passage from the partys of Glamorgan in Wales to your saide Piere, by mene of which the fairs and markets of your Countie (Somersetshire) aforesaid have ever been furnished with no small number of cattle, sheepe, woole, yarne, clothe, butter . . . and other sundre kindes of fish and flesh, to the losses of Your Majesty's Customs there . . .".

Agricultural commodities and the products of the domestic industries of South Wales were exported from the natural ports and creeks—the river- and sea-ports—that dotted the coastline. An Elizabethan document, dated 1562, indicated that there were twenty-five havens, pills and creeks, between Chepstow and Newport (Pembrokeshire), and of these, thirteen were located at various points along the more limited stretch of coastline between Cardiff and Loughor. At a time when road-transport would have been difficult and highly hazardous, the ancient sea-routes—some possibly established since Neolithic times—were of vital importance to the economic welfare of the South Wales region, enabling the coastal trade with the West of England to flourish over many centuries (Plate 17).

Many of the ports that prospered in the Elizabethan and Stuart periods have long since declined into disuse. In Monmouthshire, for example, Magor was described in 1561 as a 'pill' (i.e. a tidal creek) "where is grete ladying of small boates with butter, chese and other kyndes of vitalles to shippes", whilst Goldcliff was another 'pill', "where is also mouche ladying of thynges to convey to the shippes of Bristol". The site of Goldcliff, a once flourishing priory, became a farmhouse and a barn, and the monks had probably drained Caldicot Level, and constructed sea walls or dykes around Goldcliff, stretching along the shore for several miles from Caldicot to Goldcliff. No one today, however, would attribute maritime activities to either Magor or Goldcliff.

Carmarthen in the west, a staple river port, remained an important trading centre so long as the cloth trade prospered. In 1548, when the cloth trade was at its zenith, Carmarthen was described as "a fair market town, having a fair haven, and the fairest town in all South Wales and of most civility".[6] But during the sixteenth and seventeenth centuries, coal increasingly usurped the place of cloth among the exports of South Wales, which led to the decline of the trade from Carmarthen. Also, as piracy was brought under more effective control, its distance from the sea ceased to be an advantage, and the silting up of the river Towy finally contributed to its decline as a port. Camden described Carmarthen in 1610 as a "town where before-times was a convenient haven for ships arrivage, but now is sore pestered with sands and shelves; notwithstanding, some small vessels ascend up the river, even unto the bridge of this town". Supporting Carmarthen were several smaller ports and creeks such as Laugharne (with a population of 90 households in 1566), and Gwendraeth Fychan (upon which stood Cydweli) which, by 1566, had declined into a "scant landing place".

We have shown elsewhere how the Cistercian monks had used the small creeks of Cardiganshire, Glamorgan and Monmouthshire for the export of their wool, and these continued to be used well into the eighteenth century for the export of a wider variety of goods. Perhaps the most active ports and creeks of South Wales in Elizabethan and Stuart times were those which skirted the coastal regions of the Vale of Glamorgan—Penarth (Ely), Barry, Aberthaw, Ogmore and Newton. "In all this coaste of Kardyff and Glamorganshier," states an Elizabethan document, "is grete ladying of butter and cheese and other provysion partely

6 J. R. Daniel Tyssen, *Royal Charters of Carmarthen* . . . (Carmarthen, 1876).

into other shiers of Wales where lacke is thereof, and partely into Devon and Cornewall and other places. And here goeth awaye much lether and tallowe to the shoppes of Bristoll and so fourthe over seas . . .". When Defoe visited Glamorgan almost 150 years later, he observed that "the low ground is so well cover'd with grass and stock'd with cattle that they supply the City of Bristol with butter in very great quantities salted and barrell'd up just as Suffolk does the City of London".

The small sea ports of Penarth, Sully, Barry, Porthkerry, Colhugh, Ogmore and Newton in Glamorgan had, in turn, provided facilities for small scale coastal traffic from quite early times. Penarth was frequented by vessels during the Norman Conquest, while Colhugh, situated below Llantwit Major, and described by Leland as a place where "hither cummith symtyme Bootes and Shipplettes for socour", was probably used as a 'port' in pre-Norman times. Recently an old oak breakwater located well out on the beach at Colhugh was subjected to a Carbon 14 dating, which yielded a date between A.D. 1305 and 1495, and, together with other evidence, makes 'more plausible' the 'port' or anchorage of Illtud mentioned in his *Vita*.[7] It seems highly probable that the 'port' of Colhugh was abandoned soon after 1590, when the pier was said to have been in a state of 'decaye and utter ruin', where formerly 'ships loaded with wheat' had been anchored.

Newton, standing farther west, was, in turn, described by Leland in 1542 as a "Station or Haven for Shippes", and three hundred years later it was still a sea-port "whence shippes of small burthen carry on a coasting trade with Bristol and other parts of England".

But, undoubtedly, the most important and interesting port along the whole coastline between Neath and Cardiff

[7] M. W. Barley and R. P. C. Hanson (eds), *Christianity in Britain* (Leicester Univ. Press, 1968), pp. 130, 143, n. 5.

in pre-industrial times was Aberthaw. An examination of a map of the Vale of Glamorgan will show one river more strongly delineated than the others. This river, the Thaw, once referred to as the 'Cowbridge Brook' rises at Breigam, about two miles north of Llansannor, and then flows past the old market town of Cowbridge, meanders beneath the ruin of Llanblethian Castle onwards through the lush meadows of Beaupré, and near Llancadle, is reinforced by the waters of the Kenson before it reaches the sea at Aberthaw. Ships of upwards of 200 tons once sailed from this small port to St Kitt's and St Christopher's in the West Indies, and French wines and salt were imported direct from La Rochelle and Bordeaux. Yet most of the trade from Aberthaw was directed to Minehead, Bristol, Ilfracombe, Bridgwater and other western and southern English ports.

Aberthaw had its own customs house, which was still visible some years ago. Although many of the ships that sailed from Aberthaw were built by English boat-builders, a small boat-yard was established at Aberthaw itself where local carpenters and shipwrights were employed by local merchants such as the Hollands, the Cottons, the Spencers and Walters of west Aberthaw.

Time and tide have left no evidence of the maritime activities that once characterised the mouth of the river Thaw, and it is impossible for the modern observer to realise that Aberthaw was once the 'port of the Vale'. Today the site of the old port is overshadowed by a gigantic power station which bestraddles the landscape, marking the requirements of a new age, and at the same time obscuring, for all time, the ancient setting of Aberthaw, and the sea walls and harbour which Sir Edward Stradling (1547) had built to meet the requirements of a distant age. But Aberthaw merely represents a large number of ancient river and sea-ports in South Wales which failed because the facilities they afforded in an industrial age could not compete with the more successful ports such as Cardiff, Barry, Penarth, Swansea, Neath, etc., which we shall discuss in Chapter 7.

Parks

The parks, which we have come to regard as a natural part of the rural landscape are in fact man-made, some more so than others, and fall into the same category as enclosed fields, though not generally as old (Fig. 14). Park-making goes back to the eleventh century, and perhaps one of the most conspicuous of the early deer parks in South Wales was at Parc le Breos, in Gower, where at the end of the thirteenth century William de Breos, one of the Marcher lords, enclosed an area of 500 acres for deer. The park included a thickly wooded valley, with a wall enclosure four miles square. By 1650, however, it had "a long time been disparked" and divided into three farms—Long Oaks, Park and Llethrid. Yet, parts of the park may still be identified on the landscape. But by Elizabethan times in South Wales, as in England, even the smaller gentry, "the one manored men", could hope "to achieve in miniature what kings, lords and bishops had achieved much earlier at Windsor, Warwick and Devizes".[8] Many of the South Wales gentry had resided in Norman castles and fortified manor houses previous to Elizabethan times, and many of the castles were later modified in accordance with accepted standards of the times, in much the same way as the monastic buildings.

In the sixteenth century, the Welsh gentry were always ready to identify themselves with new ideas in domestic architecture and to impose these on the landscape as an expression of their social standing. They were, in this respect, merely following their English counterparts in

[8] Maurice Beresford, *History on the Ground* (London, 1971).

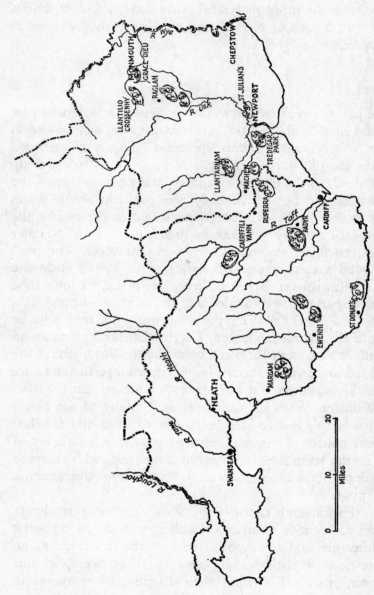

Fig. 14. Glamorgan and Monmouthshire parkland, as recorded by John Speed in 1610.

placing a premium on conspicuous wealth and the various manifestations of opulence and social ambition. Sir Rice Mansell is, perhaps, a good example of the trend. As we shall see, after acquiring the site and buildings of the Margam monastery, he converted the monastery itself into an elegant mansion with an extensive deer park, fishponds, and a dove-house. Some of the deer from the park were hunted during a visit by the first Duke of Beaufort in 1684, and it is recorded that one was killed "weighing fifteen and a half stone".

Edward Carne of Ewenni, like Rice Mansell at Margam, had built for himself, within the confines of the old Priory, "an imposing house" as the chief family residence where there were again two parks, one for red deer and one for fallow deer.

St Donat's Castle, the ancient home of the Stradling family, was extended by Sir Edward Stradling, and in Leland's time there stood "betwixt the castelle and the Severn . . . a parke of falow dere". There was also another park of "redde deere more by northe west of the castelle". These parks aroused great interest outside the boundaries of Wales, for their produce was in general demand, and sheriffs of all counties around were not slow when the visit of the assize judge was expected, to pray him to "bestowe a bucke" or "healpe them to a piece of fleash".

At Radyr, the seat of the Mathew family, Leland found "a park not quite finished and another park with Deere newly made 2 miles above Radar by north west". Further north, at Caerffili "within half a mile by Est" there was a "fair place caulled Vanne wher Mr Edward Lewys dwellith" where, in 1578, there was a "newly enclosed" park.

In Pembrokeshire, Sir John Perrot had spared no expense in erecting a wall around his park at Carew Castle (Plate 18), where he had a good stock of fallow deer.

In 1578, there were, in Glamorgan, upwards of thirteen

parks, some having been in the process of completion for a considerable time. Many of these parks were in the middle of woodland and heath, and so far as we know, the process of emparking proceeded without encroaching on agricultural land, although when, in 1578, Cefn Hirgoed Park, in Coety Wallia, was finally enclosed, it was 'in strife'. It should be pointed out, however, that by the last quarter of the sixteenth century, there was evidence of a process of disparking, and about five parks had disappeared by 1580. They included the parks at Clun of red and fallow deer, Coety and Talyfan. This process of disparking was probably due to pressure of population making it necessary to increase the area of farmland. But, on the other hand, the heavy outlay involved in building and maintaining the surrounding walls and hedges, so essential to prevent the deer from wandering, may have become prohibitive, resulting in the more economic use being made of the disparked land. Thus it was that emparking for showing off the new country houses involved the conversion of agricultural land into another form of man-made landscape, while the later disparking meant the reversion to the original man-made landscape, perhaps with newly settled farmsteads.

The dissolution of the monasteries and rise of country houses

The dissolution of the monasteries was a disruptive process which had far-reaching results, not only on the history of Wales, but also on its landscape. It should be remembered in this context that the monastic houses were dissolved "because the king coveted their wealth", and monastic lands, in consequence, were either leased or sold at competitive prices, which only the very rich and ambitious could hope to pay. Many buildings were consequently released and sold to speculators who despoiled them, selling their lead, glass, timber and iron to sundry buyers. In this way

Plate 16 An old drovers' route leading from Tregaron to Abergwesyn. Droves of cattle were assembled at Tregaron and then taken on the hoof along this route to Rhydspence and beyond.

Plate 17 Porthgain, Pembrokeshire: slate, granite and bricks were sailed from here at the turn of the century.

Plate 18 Carew Castle, Pembrokeshire, in 1810. Built originally *tempore* Henry II, it is considered to be an admirable example of the development over 400 years of the domestic ideal imposed on military architecture. Its extensive deer park was subdivided into many enclosures by 1800.

Plate 19 Margam Castle, *c.* 1860: built between 1827 and 1830 in Tudor style, it replaced the original stately building erected by Sir Rice Mansell (d. 1559) out of the ruins of the Abbey in 1552 and which continued for two centuries to be the family seat.

Plate 20 Treowen, the ancient seat of the Jones family of Lanarth, descendants of Henry Fitzherbert. By the nineteenth century, this magnificent mansion, built by Inigo Jones, with its porch in anglo-greco style, had become a farmhouse.

Plate 21 Werndee, the ancient seat of the Herbert family once dominated the rich plain near the south-west extremity of the Great Skyrrid. By the nineteenth century it had decayed and was converted into a farmhouse.

Plate 22 Clytha Castle: a folly near Clytha House, Monmouthshire.

Plate 23 *Bro Morgannwg* (The Vale of Glamorgan), described by Rice Merrick in 1578 as being 'a champyon and open country without great store of inclosure'.

Plate 24 The coastal area of the Vale of Glamorgan looking south towards the Bristol Channel.

Plate 25   Swansea Town Hill in 1846 occupied by farms.

Plate 26   Swansea Town Hill in 1930 from a plan at Swansea Guildhall. Note the rows of houses following fairly closely the previous boundary lines of farms and fields.

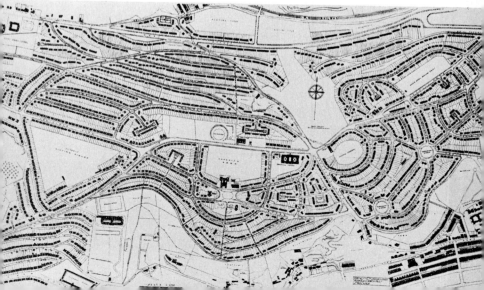

Plate 27 A windmill near St Donat's *c.* 1815, drawn by Samuel Prout.

NEAR ST DONATS

Plate 29 Hafod Mansion, Cardiganshire, where lived Thomas Johnes, author, agriculturalist, and founder of the Cardiganshire Agricultural Society (painting by F. Nash).

Plate 30 The Manor House and church at Gileston, Glamorgan, by J. Lavars, *c.* 1830. The manor house was probably built in the sixteenth century. The church is, significantly, situated in the grounds of the manor.

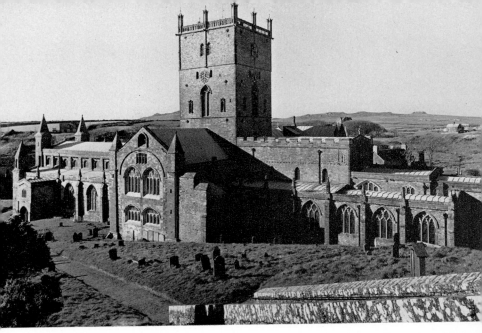

Plate 31   The Cathedral Church of St David's, from the south-east. Begun in 1180, it succeeded the old Church of Menevia destroyed in the same year. The present structure has been described as the noblest example of architecture in Wales.

Plate 32   The Calvinistic Methodist College, Trefeca, formerly Howel Harris's 'Family' centre. Today it is used as a centre for religious group meetings for young people.

most of the once majestic edifices such as Neath, Strata
Florida, Ewenni and Tintern, were either savagely dis-
figured, or reduced to utter ruin, only to survive into the
present day as monuments to ancient Welsh culture. The
ruined monastic buildings marked the end of an era in
which monasticism had stood for much that had been held
in high esteem by the native Welsh. The Welsh bards, in
particular, sorely lamented the passing of the monasteries,
for within their stout walls they had for so long found warm
patronage, and enjoyed generous hospitality. 'Cambro-
Briton' saw Tintern Abbey

> . . . spoil'd of all her pride
> Whose mournful ruins fill the soul with awe,
> Where once was taught God's holy saving law,
> Where mitred abbots fann'd the heavenly fire,
> And shook, with hymns divine, the heav'nly choir.
> Though now her fallen roof admits the day,
> She claims our veneration in decay;
> Looks like a goodly matron, drown'd in tears,
> By friends forsaken, and broke down with years,
> Her fine old windows, arches, walls, unite
> To fill the mind with pity and delight;
> For from her splendid ruins may be seen
> How beautiful this desecrated place has been.[9]

Indeed, it has been stated that 'every monastery was a
museum stored with priceless treasures of Welsh poetry
and romance'.[10]

Although most of the monastic buildings, following the
policy of dissolution, were eventually to appear on the
landscape as plundered and roofless objects, many of the

[9] Edward Davies (1719–89) *Chepstow . . . a poem in six cantos* (Bristol, 1786).

[10] W. Llewelyn Williams, *The Making of Modern Wales* (London, 1919), p. 198.

H

monastic churches such as Margam, Ewenni, and the church at Llanthony, continued to be used for worship, while a number of monastic buildings lost their identity as they became modified and transformed into country mansions for those families who profited most from the dissolution, and were to dominate Welsh life for centuries to come. However, most of the Benedictine churches remained.

In 1540 Sir Rice Mansell, for instance, succeeded in acquiring the house and site of the monastery at Margam, together with most of the lands which included "the church, the steeple and churchyard thereof; with a water-mill and fishery in the water of Avon . . .". By adapting the structure of the monastery, and by additional building, it was eventually converted into a large and stately mansion with its park, dove-house and fishpond. Later, in 1557, Mansell bought the manor of Laleston, and in 1558 he and his heirs were granted free warren in certain lands "with permission to make a park of one hundred acres". Sir Edward Carne, in turn, "the last British ambassador to the Holy See" acquired Ewenni Priory, where he built an imposing house which was to become the family seat for several centuries. Neath Abbey went to Richard Williams, Cromwell's nephew, and the cousin of Sir John Price (1502?–1555), a Welsh notary, who acquired Brecon priory. Other major families, such as Sir Edward Stradling of St Donat's, and Sir George and Sir William Herbert all became consolidated, consequent on the chances and opportunities for economic and personal aggrandisement which followed in the trail of the Act of Union and the dissolution of the monasteries.

In Cardiganshire we see the same trend in the history of the Crosswood Estate, near Aberystwyth. Although its early history goes back to the beginning of the thirteenth century, it was in the sixteenth century that expansion and consolidation occurred. A judicious settlement which Richard ap Moris Vaughan made on his son Moris, on the occasion of his marriage to Elliw verch Howell in 1547, laid the foundations of one of the largest estates in Cardiganshire, for Elliw, the only child of "Howell ap Jankyn ap Ieuan ap Rees", brought with her "a large amount of land" near Crosswood. Soon, more land was acquired, and by 1585, a great number of tenements in the parishes of Llanfihangel-y-Creuddyn, Llanafan and Llanfihangel Gelynod were acquired, to be followed soon by purchasing the dwindling resources of less opulent and less fortunate neighbours. In 1630, about 13,000 additional acres were acquired, made up, in the main, of the former monastic granges belonging to Strata Florida.

The house at Llantarnam, Monmouthshire, was described as having formed part of the ancient Abbey, if not, indeed, constructed "from its immediate ruins". It was here that William Morgan, to whom the manor of Magna Porta, in the lordship of Netherwent, was conveyed on 24 July, 1558, in consideration of a sum of £1,613 6s. 3d., finally established himself in 1561 when he purchased, from William, the first earl of Pembroke, "all the town of Mynyddislwyn . . . also lands etc. known as Wentsland and Bryngwyn . . .", and then succeeded in purchasing the whole of the property of the Abbey of Llantarnam. Morgan was the eldest son of John Morgan of Caerleon (M.P. for Monmouthshire 1553–4), and was himself M.P. from 1555 to 1571. Archdeacon Coxe referred to the house, as he saw it, at the end of the eighteenth century as, "The only remains of the ancient structure are the stone cells, converted into stables, the walls of the garden, and a beautiful gothic gateway which is still called Magna Porta, and was the grand entrance." In 1836 the whole premises and house were practically rebuilt. About the same time, the main road to Newport was being altered and made to run direct from the inn called Ty-gwyrdd to Croes-y-mwyalch instead of in a winding fashion through the park. It was at this time that the park wall was built, and the original road, up to recent years, could be traced inside the wall.

Worthy of note in this context, too, is the extensive building undertaken by William Morgan on the site of the grange called Cefn-y-mynach (Monk's Ridge). The building was on such a scale that the place was called Pentrebach (little village), and had a hall fifty feet long, fifteen feet wide, and twenty feet high. For many years afterwards it was used as a barn and other farm buildings.

Besides the new country buildings that grew on the landscape out of the ruins of the monasteries and monastic granges were the still more numerous country houses built by the minor gentry who were gaining social power through the magistracy, and who thus subdivided, and participated in, the administration of law in the country. We saw at the Conquest that the lords lived in formidable, stately, but inconvenient strongholds, whereas the lords of smaller estates inhabited 'embattled mansions', and these were succeeded, in more peaceful times, by those inhabiting convenient and elegant homes.

Houses reflect not only ideas of the standard of living of its inhabitants, but of the 'police of the country' at particular periods. In the buildings which immediately succeeded the ancient castles, rooms were not generally disposed to much comfort, "provision being made on one floor for the great object of the possessor, a display of hospitality—all those admitted as in castles dined in the grand halls". This custom seems to have continued until the reign of Henry VIII, for parlours were not in vogue until the reign of Elizabeth.

The castle of Raglan, in Monmouthshire, was probably a truly singular edifice at the time of its construction, and might more properly be termed a castellated house, combining the requirements of a fortress with the convenience and comfort of a magnificent and elegant place of residence. Its foundation was laid in the reign of Henry VII, and additions made to it at various times until 1646. The castle has been fully described elsewhere[11] and therefore we need only refer here to those features in the construction which would have dominated the landscape of the day. The castle was approached by three gates in direct line; the first was of brick, and at a distance of 180 feet stood the white gate, of square stone, situated 150 feet from the castle. Its tower (Twr Melyn Gwent) was, for sheer height and stoutness, superior to most "if not every other tower in England and Wales". It was hexagonal in shape, standing sixty feet high, each side being thirty-two feet broad, with walls ten feet thick, all made of square stone. Its battlements were, however, but eight inches thick. The towers were joined to the castle by an arched bridge surrounded by an outer wall with six arched turrets, all of square stone, adjoining a deep moat thirty feet broad. Thomas Churchyard (1520?–1604) wrote:

That Raglan hight, stands moted almost round,
Made of freestone . . .
Whose workmanship in beauty doth abound.
The stately tower that looks o'er pond and poole:
The fountain trim that runs both day and night,
Doth yield in showe, a rare and noble sight.

It had three parks planted thick with oak and large beech, and well stocked with deer. The surrounding estates were so fertile that the castle could garrison 800 men. But like so many other stately edifices, it was plundered after the Civil War. After surrendering to Sir Thomas Fairfax on 19th August, 1646, the woods in the parks were destroyed, its lead and timber were carried to Monmouth, and thence by water to rebuild Bristol bridge after the last fire.

Perhaps the oldest inhabited castle in Wales is Fonmon

[11] David Williams, *A History of Monmouth*, Appendix No. LIV, p. 132 *et seq.*

(Glamorgan). It was a possession of the St Johns from the century following the Norman Conquest until the Commonwealth, when it was acquired by Colonel Philip Jones. When Leland undertook his antiquarian itinerary shortly after the Dissolution, many of the South Wales castles were already in ruins, but "the castelle of Fonmon", as he recorded, "yet stondith and longith to Sir John St John". In the early-seventeenth century its condition was described as being no better than a good farmhouse.[12] But apart from later modifications to its fabric, it remains substantially the same medieval building referred to by Leland more than four centuries ago.

After the accession of James I (1603), the country had enjoyed a period of comparative peace, during which industry and the useful arts were developed and encouraged. Such conditions probably influenced the domestic and social requirements of the gentry, whose homes no longer assumed the appearance of a fortified stronghold. Their interiors, too, became more ostentatious with lavish furnishings and fittings hitherto undreamed of. Rooms were wainscoted in full and half panels, and increasing demand was made on local timber in providing additional tables, chairs and cupboards for the comfort and convenience of their residents.

The filling in of the rural landscape with human habitations after the Civil War went on apace, but it is an aspect of our history which has been neglected, mainly on account of the lack of evidence available. The men who transformed the medieval open fields into a patchwork of enclosed fields further modified the landscape by their domestic buildings. The country houses of the gentry, the farmhouses of the yeomen, and the cottages of craftsmen and labourers of the pre-industrial era, may be looked upon as visible facets of native life and culture, exhibiting

[12] *Glamorgan County History*, Vol. IV (Cardiff, 1974), p. 123.

the methods by which the inhabitants of the upland and lowland regions of South Wales collectively utilised and adapted local building materials to provide themselves and their families with shelter and other physical comforts. The interiors of most of these dwellings were adapted, and sometimes modified, to facilitate the performance of those domestic tasks which were ancillary to agriculture, namely spinning, weaving, malting, brewing and dairying. It is fairly clear that although local climatic, geographic and social conditions play an important rôle in varying folk dwellings, the traditional requirements of local farming have been equally influential in the evolution of local houses. And as the peasantry modified the interiors of their houses to meet the requirements of the daily chores, so did the gentry modify and adapt their habitats to conform to the requirements of new social tastes and architectural styles (Plates 20 & 21).

The landscape of South Wales in the sixteenth and seventeenth centuries clearly reflected the kind of social stratification that emerged out of the economic and social developments of Elizabethan-Stuart times.[13] England's trade increased, and her merchants became peers, building themselves great houses, as did every 'prosperous man of that age. Wales shared in this prosperity, and Welshmen exhibited the same tendencies to build, or re-build, houses to match, and so mirror, their social standing. Houses and their interiors became the status symbols of an agrarian society which was gradually becoming involved in industry and commerce. By about 1690, there were in Glamorgan about 220 gentlemen with country seats, and throughout the whole extent of South Wales there were upwards of 610 gentlemen whose houses heightened the rural scene in almost every parish, though externally the white-washed peasant houses and cottages were not indifferent to the eye.

[13] Cf. W. G. Hoskins, *Provincial England* (London, 1963), pp. 131–48.

In Glamorgan, gentlemen's homes appeared in the landscape in the proportion of two to every hundred households. In other words, almost every South Wales parish had its 'gentleman', and in the richer agricultural areas many parishes had more than one gentleman, with their appropriate residences (Plate 30).

The Hearth Tax Returns of 1670 for the county of Glamorgan provide an interesting picture of the relative size of houses that dotted the landscape at that time. From the assessments made, it would appear that about sixty out of every hundred households in the county lived in houses with only one hearth; twenty households out of every hundred had two hearths, and about one per cent lived in houses with seven and more hearths. The gulf that existed between those who occupied houses with the greatest and those with the lowest number of hearths was thrown into high relief by the distribution of personal wealth, and it was probably this distinction that the gentry strove to emphasise visibly in their houses, gardens, and parks. The Glamorgan Hearth Tax Returns for 1670 show that Sir Edward Mansell, of Margam, was taxed on thirty-two hearths; Sir John Aubrey of Llantrithyd was taxed on twenty hearths; Bussy Mansell of Briton Ferry on twenty-two, and Lady Stradling of St Donat's Castle on thirty hearths. Those who occupied the large houses also exercised almost complete control over the fortunes of the county. In Glamorgan, for instance, the county seat in parliament had been occupied directly, or indirectly, by Mansells, Talbots, Tyntes, Beauforts or Windsors from about 1700 to 1832. In the boroughs, too, the same group of families exercised control. Throughout the eighteenth century the Windsors controlled Cardiff, Cowbridge and Llantrisant; the Mansells of Margam controlled Kenfig; the Mackworths, Aberafan and Neath, while Swansea and Loughor "were firmly in the pockets of the Beauforts". It has been shown that of the twenty-eight parliaments between 1710 and 1832, only five families shared the representation.[14] It was the social status and economic wealth of this class that we find being represented most conspicuously on the landscape by the building and re-building of bigger and better houses of the late sixteenth and early seventeenth centuries.

The evidence concerning the state of peasant houses during Tudor and Stuart times is painfully scanty, and what information we have is based mainly on probate material and archaeological discoveries. Topographical works of the late eighteenth century reveal that in Glamorgan "the antiquity of the cottages is a strongly marked feature in the appearance of the county", and it was thought that many of them were "as ancient as the castles to which they were attached", and that numerous Gothic cottages "carry with them the recommendation of a venerable exterior and a portion of internal room, comfort and security from the elements rarely enjoyed by their fellows in any part of the world . . .". Another astute observer, the celebrated Iolo Morganwg (Edward Williams, 1747–1826), himself a stone mason by trade, was of the opinion that on the whole, from the style of their building, probably nine out of every ten houses in the Glamorgan countryside in the eighteenth century were at least three hundred to four hundred years old.

Although a great deal of building and re-building of splendid houses and mansions had taken place in the countryside and towns of South Wales by the seventeenth century, a large section of the population continued to live in "miserable one-roomed hovels with earthen floors and open hearths, built by their own efforts"—a situation which almost certainly obtained in Glamorgan.[15] Many people,

[14] Ieuan Gwynnedd Jones, *Morgannwg*, Vol. VI (1962), p. 52.
[15] *Glamorgan County History*, Vol. IV (Cardiff, 1974), p. 130.

too, lived in equally squalid two- and three-roomed cottages with no upper floor, but where an upper room was formed by loose boards covering the lower rooms. The single-roomed cottage with a loft over all its area was not uncommon, and sometimes portable screens were used to divide the single room for more comfort or privacy. Indeed, as late as 1893, the cottages in the coastal areas around Lantwit Major were generally single-roomed with a room above to which access was gained by means of a wooden ladder. But despite their primitive interiors, these small cottages were regularly white-washed, giving them an outward appearance which added immensely to the richness and charm of the Welsh rural scene.

On the whole, the houses of the gentry were much more varied in plan, and show "no obvious sign of descent from a common ancestry" as is typified in most peasant houses. In Breconshire, for instance, the dissimilarity between the houses of the gentry and those of the 'long-house' tradition is so striking as to "indicate that there were social implications of house plans" and that those who built 'country houses' moved in wider circles, and brought into their building activities considerations of design which hardly affected those whose way of life was expressed in the 'long-house'.[16] Here, indeed, we have the landscape evidence of the dichotomy that existed between the peasantry and the gentry in general. The same picture presented itself throughout the South Wales region. In Monmouthshire, the pre-industrial scene was made up of innumerable sites "nestling in the midst of unsurpassed natural beauty" with whited peasant dwellings dotting the hills and vales under the long shadows of the country mansions of the temporal lords and masters.

A study of Monmouthshire houses[17] has shown that

[16] *Brycheiniog,* Vol. I.
[17] Fox and Raglan, *Monmouthshire Houses: A Study of Building Techniques and Small House Plans in the Fifteenth to Seventeenth Centuries* . . . (Cardiff, 1951–4).

between *c.* 1550 and 1610 the old medieval timber houses with one or more ground-floor rooms 'open to the roof' were generally giving way to two-floored houses, stone walled, with a loft or bedrooms over the ceiled living and inner rooms, with a stairway leading to them—a development in house construction which probably illustrated the contemporary 'social movement towards privacy'. This period saw a degree of building and re-building with new materials which must have transformed, not only the Monmouthshire landscape, but, in varying degrees, the greater part of the lowland regions of South Wales.[18] Here, then we had on the landscape some of those novel ideas which accompanied a new individualistic outlook expressed in terms of a craft of vernacular building designed to afford better protection from the weather, more warmth than an open hall could provide, and, above all, more privacy. A countryside steeped in the 'medieval tradition' which had lasted for hundreds of years, was now in decay, and a new rural landscape was beginning to blossom.

In trying to visualise the proportion of stately homes to the number of lowly dwellings that occupied the landscape in the seventeenth century, it should be emphasised that probably not more than about five persons out of every hundred belonged to the gentry or above in the social hierarchy. Moreover, if the classification of households in the hearth tax returns for Glamorgan in 1670 can be taken as a general indicator, then about twenty-five to thirty per cent of households were probably paupers. Although these figures must be used with the utmost caution, nevertheless they serve to emphasise the marked variations in wealth and social standing that divided the respective social classes, and

[18] For a discussion on the differences between rural housing in north and south Wales see Peter Smith, 'Rural housing in Wales' in *The Agrarian History of England and Wales* (ed. by Joan Thirsk), Vol. IV, 1500–1640 (Cambridge, 1967).

the relative numerical distribution of their houses in the countryside, and in the towns, merely provided part of the visible evidence of those inequalities.

Early grammar schools and almshouses in the landscape

We have seen that the general agricultural and commercial prosperity that marked the Tudor period led to what has been described as the "great amendment of lodging" whereby stately and elegant houses were built for greater comfort and "the pleasure of living" as provided, in part at least, by extensive private parks and ornamental gardens.[19] The agricultural prosperity which formed the basis for these landscape changes in South Wales was, however, partly the result of the consolidation of estates made possible to a greater degree than ever before by the introduction of primogeniture in place of gavelkind through the Act of Union 1536. Younger sons were now forced to seek their livelihood away from home—a venture which, to be successful, required a good standard of education. The disappearance of the monastic schools following the Dissolution, and the growing realisation on the part of the gentry of the importance of education led to the foundation and, sometimes, the re-foundation of grammar schools modelled on those of England, wherein would be taught the classical languages, and other subjects, considered necessary to equip a young man to carve out for himself a career in the church, or in the legal and administrative professions which, previous to the Act of Union 1536, had received but few Welshmen.

Consequently, one of the first grammar schools to appear on the South Wales landscape was Christ College, Brecon, founded in 1541 for "the Glory of God, the edifying of the

[19] W. G. Hoskins, *The Making of the English Landscape* (Hodder and Stoughton, 1955), p. 126.

people and the good education of youth". Thomas Church-yard, the English poet, described the school, as it appeared *c.* 1587:

A free house once, where many a rotten beame
Hath here of late, through age and trackt of tyme,
Which bishop now refourmes with stone and lyme:
Had it not bene with charge repayred in haste,
That house and seate, had surely gone to waste.

Later, other South Wales grammar schools were founded at Abergafenni, Carmarthen and Cowbridge—all towns of some importance at that time.

The free grammar school at Abergafenni was founded by Henry VIII, by letters patent dated 24th July, 1543, and endowed in trust to the Corporation, with great tithes of several properties formerly belonging to the priory at Abergafenni for the maintenance of a master, an usher, and a number of scholars.

The credit for establishing a grammar school at Cow-bridge (Plate 36) is given to Sir Edward Stradling, of St Donat's, but it was Sir John Stradling who, in fact, built the first school and school-house in 1609. One of the most illustrious old boys of the school was Sir Leoline Jenkins, the ardent Royalist and learned Judge, and former Principal of Jesus College, Oxford. Indeed, in the seventeenth century the administration of the school was transferred from the Stradling family to the Principal and Fellows of Jesus College, Oxford.

This was strictly in line with what was happening in England, where the mercantile aristocracy and the gentry were at pains in "linking schools which they had founded to the Universities by rich and elaborate scholarship endowments . . .". But although Humphrey Llwyd had made the exaggerated claim in his *Breviary of Britayne* (1568) "that no Welshman is so poor, but for some space he setteth forth his children to school, and such as profit in study, sendeth them to the Universities . . ." it was, in fact, during the Commonwealth period that popular state education received any serious attention. Between 1630 and 1730, a large number of Nonconformist schools and academies came into existence, but their impact on the landscape was not commensurate with their contribution to Welsh social life and culture.

Although the agricultural and commercial prosperity of the Tudor period led to the building of elegant houses by the more affluent members of society, yet a large section of the landless classes lived in poverty. Under the Elizabethan poor laws each parish appointed overseers whose responsibilities included the building of houses in order to provide for the 'necessitous poor'. From the end of the sixteenth century, almshouses and poor-houses appeared in almost every parish, and these represented not only the growing concern of the State for the poor, but also the massive voluntary charitable gifts that were made by private individuals in order to alleviate the economic and physical distress of the more unfortunate members of the community. One is reminded, in this sphere, of innumerable bequests, both modest and noble, made by testators during this century. For instance, in 1658, Evan Trehearne, of Llanwonno, Glamorgan, bequeathed to five poor persons of the almshouse at Llangeinor, six pence a piece, and "sixpence a piece to eight poor persons at the almshouse at Llantrisant, four poore persons at the almshouse at Llantwitvayrdre, to nine poore persons at the almshouse at Llandaff, and to sixteene poore persons at the almshouse at Cardiff". Again, Eleanor Mathew, of Aberafan, had built an almshouse for four poor persons of the village of Aberdâr, and then, in 1727, bequeathed the income from certain lands towards the maintenance of the persons settled in the

almshouse. Many of the early almshouses were unpretentious, but nevertheless provided visible evidence of the
early attempts made to deal with the problem of the poor.

SELECT BIBLIOGRAPHY

Bradney, Joseph Alfred, *A History of Monmouthshire*, 4 vols.
(London, 1904–33).

Charles, B. G., *George Owen of Henllys: a Welsh Elizabethan* (Aberystwyth, 1973).

Churchyard, Thomas, *The Worthines of Wales* (London, 1587).

Coxe, William, *A Historical Tour Through Monmouthshire* (Brecon,
1901).

Dodd, A. H., *Studies in Stuart Wales*, 2nd ed. (Cardiff, 1971).

Emery, Frank V., *The World's Landscapes: Wales* (London, 1969).

Fenton, Richard, *A Historical Tour Through Pembrokeshire* (Brecknock, 1903).

Fox and Raglan, *Monmouthshire Houses . . .* (Cardiff, 1951–4).

Hoskins, W. G., *The Making of the English Landscape* (Hodder and
Stoughton Ltd, 1955).

Howells, Brian E., *Studies in the Social and Agrarian History of
Medieval and Early Modern Pembrokeshire*, 2 vols (University
of Wales, unpublished M.A. thesis, 1956).

Hughes, P. G., *Wales and the Drovers* (London, *c.* 1944).

Jenkins, R. T., *Y Ffordd yng Nghymru* (Wrecsam, 1933).

Leland, John, *Itinerary* (ed. Toulmin Smith) (London, 1906).

Lewis, E. A., *The Welsh Port-books, 1560–1603* (Cymmrodorion
Record Series, No. 12) (London, 1927).

Merrick, Rice, *A Booke of Glamorganshire's Antiquities*, 2nd ed. by
J. A. Corbett (London, 1887).

Owen, George, *The Description of Penbrokeshire* (ed. by Henry
Owen), 4 vols (London, 1902–36). *See also* Charles, B. G.

Owen, Geraint Dyfnallt, *Elizabethan Wales: The Social Scene*
(Cardiff, 1962).

Peat, Iorwerth C., *The Welsh House: a Study in Folk Culture* (Liverpool, 1946).

Pollard, E., Hooper, M. D. and Moore, N. W., *Hedges* (London,
1974).

Rees, William, 'The Union of England and Wales', *Trans. Hon. Soc. Cymmr.* (1937).

Standing Conference for Local History, *Hedges and Local History* (London, 1971).

Stradling, Sir John, *The Storie of the Lower Borowes of Merthyr-Maure* (ed. H. J. Randall and W. Rees), South Wales and Monmouthshire Record Society, No. 1 (Cardiff, 1932).

Thirsk, Joan (ed.), *The Agrarian History of England and Wales*, Vol. IV, 1500–1640 (Cambridge, 1967).

Williams, David, *A History of Monmouthshire* (London, 1796).

Williams, Glanmor (ed.), *Glamorgan County History*, Vol. IV (Cardiff, 1974).

Williams, Moelwyn I., 'Agriculture and Society in Glamorgan, 1660–1760' (University of Leicester, unpublished Ph.D. thesis, 1968).

Williams, W. Llewellyn, *The Making of Modern Wales* (London, 1919).

4. The landscape of agricultural progress

Enclosures—early and parliamentary.   Agricultural Societies and the landscape.   New roads in the landscape.   Mills and lime-kilns

THE ADVANCEMENT MADE in agriculture during the Tudor and Stuart periods was the primary force in changing the general face of the South Wales landscape before the spectacular growth of large-scale industrial complexes after 1760. The progress made in both arable and pastoral farming during the sixteenth and seventeenth centuries may be attributed mainly to the increasing local demands for agricultural produce following the development of small-scale non-agricultural industries and the singular expansion of trade and commerce, not to mention a probable marked increase in population. In a sense, these developments reflected the triumph of individualism that followed the decline of the old feudal relationships of medieval society.

Enclosures—early and parliamentary

The landscape changes of the sixteenth and seventeenth centuries were marked mainly by an extension of various forms of enclosures. Earlier centuries had witnessed the enclosing of land for varying reasons. We have already seen, for example, how deer parks were impaled and set aside by the great lords to preserve animals for hunting, and large areas were again afforested for the sole purpose of the lord's pleasure. The most spectacular example of this practice was the Great Forest (Fforest Fawr), a tract of mountain and moorland covering an area of fifty square miles of country, extending over the major part of the south-west of the county of Brecon, which was created a 'Forest', and was maintained by the Norman lords (for the sake of sport), and deer in the 'Forest' were protected by the most stringent laws. Emparking was not carried out on an extensive scale in South Wales, though it does appear that some townships such as Clemenston (Glamorgan), St Pierre (Monmouthshire), and Maesllwch and Llangoed (Breconshire) were, in fact, engulfed.

The more conventional of the early forms of enclosures were seen on the landscape in the form of areas of land varying in shape and size, separated by hedges or ditches, and sometimes referred to as closes or arable pasture, and such modifications of the landscape as these effected had been going on from the fourteenth century when escheated lands were sometimes enclosed. The demesne of the abbey of Tewkesbury in Cardiff, Llandough and Llantwit Major were, by 1393, rented, and consisted of many closes of arable pasture.

The term curtilage (of Anglo-French origin), used frequently in early Welsh documents, was also an area of land enclosed by a ditch, hedge, or palings, and served as a garden or paddock used either for grazing or the cultivation of fruit trees and vegetables. In the fourteenth century, these were often identified with the burgages in the English boroughs such as Carmarthen, and by the reign of Henry VI (1422–1461) we find, in the manor of Ogmore, a class of "tenants of cottages and curtilages at will" where many of the curtilages had been carved out of the waste land.[1]

[1] T. I. Jeffreys-Jones, *The Enclosure Movement in South Wales* . . . (Univ. Wales, unpublished M.A. thesis, 1936).

From the studies already carried out on the subject of
enclosures in South Wales, it is impossible to estimate
precisely the extent of the early enclosures, but, from the
evidence available, it is fairly clear that enclosure was steady,
albeit slow, in the common fields. Enclosures were probably
more pronounced on the landscape of the more accessible
tracts of the country such as north Pembrokeshire, Carmarthen and Glamorgan, where the proximity to the Welsh
markets via the sea-ports had resulted in considerable
progress in dairy farming during the sixteenth and seventeenth centuries, and had probably resulted in more selective
breeding of battle.

In the sixteenth century there must have been widespread
encroachment, without authority, on common pasture by
the more powerful landlords, often at the expense of tenants
with rights to co-pasturing, as in the lordship of Mylwood.
Records of the *Court of Augmentations* are full of references
to improvement of lands by houses, hedges and ditches,
and to the destruction of ditches and hedges by neighbouring objectors. For instance, in the early sixteenth
century, a widow "Anne verch John Duy of Neath",
complained that Morgan Gwillim Morgan, and thirteen
others, had "enclosed a piece of void ground leased to
her . . ." which was claimed "as a common of the town of
Nethe". In the manor of Talyfan, of a parcel of 240 acres
of pasture, 70 acres were enclosed by a certain David
William Gronow, claiming it as his own inheritance.[2]

The progress of enclosure, therefore, was by no means
uniform throughout the South Wales region, and consequently some landscapes were more modified by enclosures
than others. In Maelienydd (Radnorshire) for instance, lands
called Coedswydd, in the parish of Llandegley, contained
2,223 acres of pasture which, in 1548 were "in dyvers parts

[2] E. A. Lewis and J. Conway Davies (eds), *Records of the Court of Augmentations Relating to Wales and Monmouthshire* (Cardiff, 1954), pp. 110, 116.

severed with hedges, ditches and rivers . . .". In Elfael we find that the free tenants of lands adjacent to the Forest of Colwyn held messuages and tenements "containing ten thousand acres of enclosed lands". Contemporary documents indicate that in Breconshire, too, enclosure proceeded fairly steadily throughout the sixteenth century.

Enclosed fields in Monmouthshire had increased considerably by the seventeenth century, and in some parishes we find fifty per cent of the land had been enclosed. In Glamorgan, according to an extant manorial survey of 1622, about seventy-five per cent of holdings in the manor of Llancadle had been enclosed, whilst in the manor of Fonmon, the proportion was ninety-two per cent, and as high as ninety-nine per cent in the manor of Barry.

It is now fairly clear that the monks had practised enclosure long before the Dissolution, and even if Giraldus Cambrensis exaggerated when he accused them of adding 'field to field', it is highly significant that at the end of the fifteenth century, their leases invariably stipulated that all ditches and closes had to be kept in good repair.

Contemporary wills offer us some clues to the progress of the enclosure of open fields in various parts of the country in the seventeenth century. For instance, the will of John Thomas, the elder, of Peterston-super-Ely, in the Vale of Glamorgan, who died in 1674, refers to "my several closes, or parcells, of landes with their several appurtenances called . . . *kae'r glegeren* latelie divided into two parcells, *kae gwyn* (white field) latelie divided into five parcells, and the houses thereupon built; *y deg-erw-gwair-y-mynydd-ucha* (ten acre hay field in the upper mountain), *kae bach* (little field), *kae mawr kenol* (large middle field), *kae mawr ycha* (large higher field) . . ." containing in all about fifty-two acres.

In the manor of Clase, Llangyfelach, in 1670, William Vaughan, the elder, bequeathed his lands "with customary closes or parcels of lands lately by me enclosed". In the parish of Llansannor, Glamorgan, Rees Estance, yeoman, who died in 1709, bequeathed certain lands including "certain parcells of lands about twenty acres which heretofore were severed and inclosed under hedge and ditch from the common or downe of St Mary Hill". From the information gleaned from contemporary wills, we find the same tendency continued to operate in the eighteenth century.

The progress of dairy farming during the sixteenth and seventeenth centuries, more particularly in those areas most accessible and contiguous to the English markets, probably resulted in more selective breeding and a corresponding increase in enclosure. In the rougher pastures of less accessible areas, such as the mountain regions of Cardiganshire, cattle were herded in the traditional manner and, consequently, there was little incentive given to agriculture. There is considerable evidence to be found in seventeenth-century wills which suggests that there was more experimentation in improving breeds than we have hitherto imagined. For example, numerous references to 'spotted' cattle must, undoubtedly, testify to a widespread practice of cross-breeding or, indeed, of some degree of experimentation in inbreeding local types or other breeds, as in fact Robert Bakewell and his colleagues did in England, in leading the way to producing finer meat-yielding animals. Owain John, for instance, yeoman of the parish of Coy-church, Glamorgan, who died in 1672, was probably one of many yeomen in the pastoral regions of South Wales who endeavoured from time to time to improve their herds, and in his will he was careful to divide his cattle thus—to Evan Owain "one red cow wth caulf . . . and one yeolow steere by me formerlie bought from a place called Cwm Carne", and to his daughter "one heiffer of my owne breed y^t now is in my dayrie". The Llanwonno mountain pastures in the lower upland areas of Glamorgan also

133

sustained a fine breed of horned cattle, supposed and found to be preferable to those crossed with any other.[3] These long forgotten efforts were reflected on the landscape by 'newly' enclosed fields, which, in time, became an established feature on the landscape.

Despite the evidence of enclosures and consolidation, it should be stated in passing that private estates were, on the whole, relatively small in annual value, if not in extent. When James I offered the title of Baronet to all knights and squires possessed of £1,000 a year "with a virtual command that the title should be purchased" only twelve out of the 200 baronetcies so created were Welsh. In 1660 South Wales could claim only eighteen—five in Glamorgan and Carmarthen, three in Pembrokeshire, three in Monmouthshire, two in Breconshire, and none in Cardiganshire and Radnorshire.

It is fairly clear that pressures on the waste would have been more acute in the low-lying coastal regions, and this tendency is, perhaps, explained in part by the efforts made by the monks to improve marshy ground in the Margam area. Similarly, in the early seventeenth century we have evidence that "divers marches in Carmarthen, Pembrokeshire and Glamorgan were drained by a partnership made up of Endymion Porter, William Ward and William Wright, who divided the land, so gained, between them". Laugharne Marsh, a considerable tract of land lying near Laugharne, was embanked from the sea, and a regular course of husbandry had been established here long before the eighteenth century. The land was built up in ridges about twenty feet wide, and "as high as the soil will bear".

It is impossible to state with any degree of accuracy the extent of enclosure which had been carried out in South Wales by the middle of the seventeenth century. Some estimate that twenty to thirty per cent of the whole area of

---

[3] *Glamorgan County History*, Vol. IV (Cardiff, 1974), pp. 327–8.

South Wales, and at least half of the open field acres were enclosed, but these figures must be accepted with the utmost caution.

By the end of the seventeenth century we may visualise extensive areas of the South Wales landscape as having already assumed the appearance of a patchwork of enclosed fields and commons, but mainly in the lowlands and in parts of the lower upland regions. The multiplicity of field shapes brought about by pre-parliamentary enclosures is reflected in the field names mentioned in early documents relating to various parts of the region. For instance, in the seventeenth century we find names such as cae bach (little field), cae mawr (big field), tir-y-berth-gron (the land of the circular hedge) in the Peterston-super-Ely and Llanfaban areas, whilst in Dinas Powys we have such names as erw'r delyn (harp shaped acre), erw bengam (the crooked acre), cae main (narrow field), erw fain (narrow acre), and cwarter pica (a small field shaped like an isosceles triangle).[4]

In the upland areas, we would find that by this time many shacks for temporary use under the seasonal custom of transhumance (*hafotai* and *lluestai*) had been converted into permanent settlements, a process in which one might "detect the beginnings of that breach between lowland and upland farmstead which as time proceeded, produced the modern social dichotomy between valley and mountain communities".

By the middle of the eighteenth century it is fairly certain that a rapidly growing population was exerting an increasing pressure on the resources of the land, and it is significant to find small enclosures of commons being made in order to grow potatoes, which became very popular in South Wales during the second half of the eighteenth century. Examples of these were recorded at Mynydd Cadley in

[4] Gwynnedd O. Pearce, *The Place-Names of Dinas Powys Hundred* (Cardiff, 1968). Badminton MSS. (N.L.W.), First Series 2737.

Gower where, in 1752, a piece of ground had been enclosed
by one Hopkin David 'for a potato garden'. The lord's
waste was encroached upon at a place called *Llwyn-Evan-Ddu,*
in Llandeilo-talybont, where a croft and potato garden were
made thereof. During the same period, in the Llangyfelach
area near Swansea, 'potato gardens' were becoming fairly
numerous. These 'gardens', which were later to become
quite commonplace, were in the early stages, significant
features on the landscape.[5]

Another century or so had to pass before we come to the
parliamentary enclosure movement, which was mainly
operative between 1760 and 1900—a period when many
areas of the landscape were re-shaped and completely transformed by a systematic and well-organised policy creating
'a memorable rural revolution' in England and Wales. The
lands usually ordered to be enclosed in South Wales manors
and parishes were, in the main, the uncultivated common
and waste lands "upon which no severalty rights attached".
In 1795 it was estimated that the acreage of common
lands and waste lying unenclosed in South Wales was as
follows:

	Acres
Brecknock	256,000
Carmarthen	170,666
Monmouth	67,520
Radnor	200,000
Cardigan	206,720
Glamorgan	107,200
Pembroke	22,222

The total number of acres remaining unenclosed was
1,030,328, most of which was wild mountain land, unsuit-

[5] Badminton MSS. (N.L.W.), First Series 2737.

136

able for cultivation. But between 1795 and 1885, however, a further 204,540 acres were enclosed, which still left 825,788 acres open and unenclosed.

Reports by Officers of the Board of Agriculture show that before parliamentary enclosure really got under way, open or common fields were, however, rarely met with in South Wales, and existed only "where ecclesiastical property and private property are blended".[6] In south Cardiganshire most of the land in 1794 was either enclosed or enclosing, while in the north of the county, most of the low-lying lands were "pretty well enclosed" but hilly and exposed areas were mostly open. The only tract of common field was an extent of land reaching along the coast from Llannon to Aberaeron, which still remains open and divided into 'slangs' or *llainiau* (Fig. 15).

In Carmarthenshire about two-thirds of the country was enclosed, but the enclosures were found to be small in proportion to the farms, and frequently ill-shaped. Reporting to the Board of Agriculture in 1794, Charles Hassall stated that: "In no county were the inclosures so irregularly shaped. The deformity may have arisen from slow progress of inclosure in former times when the major part of the farms were open, and small portions of land were occasionally fenced in for the purposes of tillage, without much regard to the form of the plot." In time, these fences grew so thick "as to be found useful for sheltering the livestock, and on that account preserved". In consequence, it was not uncommon to see on the landscape "fifteen or twenty little crooked awkward fields upon a farm of fifty or sixty acres".

In Breconshire, hedges were formed of different curves— "scarce ten yards of a straight hedge can be seen together in the county". This added much to the beauty of the country, and to the inconvenience of the ploughman. It is

[6] Walter Davies, *General View* . . . (London, 1815).

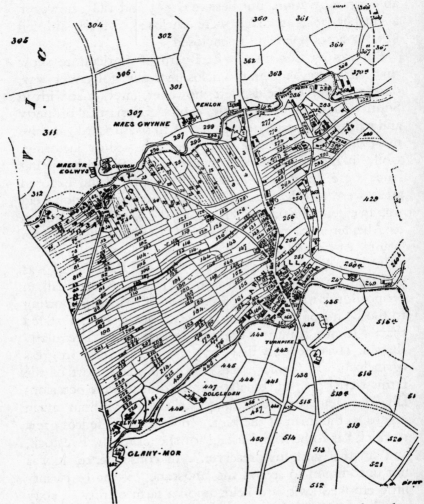

Fig. 15. Strips in open fields near Llannon, Cardiganshire, where they are still visible, and known locally as *llainiau* or 'slangs'.

interesting to note that farmers in Breconshire made their hedges crooked in the belief that "a crooked hedge affords more shelter to cattle than a straight one".

By the end of the eighteenth century the areas liable to enclosure were the upland moorlands, coastal waste, low-lying marsh and valley land, and what little remained of open arable fields. The Napoleonic Wars (1792–1815) certainly created an increased demand for home-grown food, and this was reflected on the landscape by a speeding-up of parliamentary enclosures. Between 1800 and 1895, there were 104 enclosure awards made applicable to the South Wales counties, as compared with four awards made previous to 1800, representing the enclosure of 154,715 acres and 5,784 acres, respectively. The acreage enclosed in each of the counties, together with the number of awards, was as follows:

	Acres	Percentage[7]	Awards
Breconshire	3,666	2	16
Cardiganshire	57,000	$27\frac{1}{2}$	12
Carmarthenshire	26,373	15	23
Glamorgan	7,421	6	9
Monmouthshire	11,222	16	16
Pembrokeshire	1,571	10	5
Radnorshire	47,463	$23\frac{1}{2}$	29

A mode of enclosure which is sometimes overlooked, but yet was registered on the landscape in many parts of South Wales, was brought about by encroachments made by landless squatters, and were the results of the *tŷ-unnos* tradition, whereby it was popularly believed that if a cottage could be erected on the common in one night, and with smoke rising from its roof by morning, the builder held a legal right to the dwelling, and to the land "within one axe-throw in every direction". An interesting example of this process of settlement may be found in the area known as Trefenter in

[7] Percentages refer to the proportion of the total of commons and wastes as given in 1795.

north Cardiganshire, in the parish of Llangwyryfon. According to the Tithe Map (1843), Trefenter was made up of forty individual homesteads occupying about 160 acres of land, or an area a quarter of a mile square, each with an average of four acres—an area wholly inadequate to maintain a family. Consequently it was necessary to graze their animals on the common—a cow, some sheep and geese—during summer time. Piecemeal enclosure and encroachment which followed, would probably have been the original nucleus of many of the present-day farm holdings.

Conspicuous changes occurred on the landscape of north Cardiganshire subsequent to the Llanfihangel Genau'r-glyn and Llangynfelin Enclosure Award of 1814, which involved about 10,000 acres including Cors Fochno. What were once commons and waste lands, became enclosed with public highways and private roads running through, over and along them for the convenience of the public. Sometimes it was necessary to broaden such tracks as already existed to the usual breadth of thirty feet, according to the 'lines and marks' laid down by the Commissioners. In the parish of Llangynfelin, what was once seventy-four acres of open land, became, in due course, five separate fields, which process involved one Richard Griffiths in the task of diverting the natural course of the river Lerry, near Ynys Las, and erecting new bridges.

The more revolutionary changes that were sometimes brought about on the landscape following parliamentary enclosures may be illustrated by a brief reference to one or two of the more outstanding enclosures in South Wales. For instance, in Pembrokeshire, the waste ground called Narberth Forest and Narberth mountain (which was well stocked with deer during the reign of James I, 1603–1625), containing 1,200 acres, plus waste land in the manor of Templeton, called Templeton Mountain containing 700 acres, Molleston Mountain 500 acres, and Robestone Grove

50 acres, making a total of 2,450 acres, were enclosed in consequence of an Act dated 1786. When Richard Fenton visited the area fifteen years or so later, he was so impressed that he remarked: "This immense tract of land so lately remembered a cheerless waste is now most pleasingly metamorphosed, having been for some years in a state of high cultivation and judiciously parcelled out into several large farms, interspersed with small portions of copse wood in a thriving state; a change in appearance contributing greatly to ornament as well as the wealth of the county . . .".

About twenty-five years earlier, in 1762, an act was initiated by the Duke of Beaufort for the dividing and enclosing two pieces, or parcels, of open and unenclosed land called the 'Town Hill' and the 'Burroughs' in the Borough and Manor of Swansea, Glamorgan, which together contained 750 acres. The Act deprived the burgesses of the privileges of depasturing and the cutting of furze and fern. An allotment of 150 acres of the best land of 'Town Hill' was made to the Duke of Beaufort, while the burgesses were granted the remaining 350 acres. Before long this landscape was completely transformed: new roads 'at least thirty feet wide' were laid out by surveyors, and along these several farms were built with characteristically square and rectangular fields separated by hedges (Plate 25). When, in the years following the First World War, the Corporation built a new 'garden city' on this site, the avenues of houses followed fairly closely the lines of the farms and fields marked out by the surveyors in the years immediately after 1762 (Plate 26).[8]

A similar transformation in the landscape occurred when the Great Heath and the Little Heath (or Mynydd Bychan and Waun Dyfal) in Cardiff were enclosed after the Act of 1801. This comprised an area of 1,200 acres, upon which the cattle of the townsmen had in former times been

[8] Frank Emery, *The World's Landscapes: Wales* (London, 1969), p. 90.

pastured. There had been earlier encroachments in the form of small plots on the fringes of the Heath, probably claimed by the practice of building *tai unnos*. An ejectment order was upheld against twelve persons who had thus encroached, and after a great deal of violence and public protest, the plots were vacated in October 1799. This was the prelude to the enclosure which followed in 1801–2. Various allotments were made, but most of the land enclosed eventually ended up in the private ownership of Lord Bute, upon which many building projects were subsequently initiated by him.

Of all the large-scale enclosures in South Wales, perhaps the most spectacular was that of the Great Forest in the county of Brecon between 1815 and 1818. We saw earlier how this tract of country, 50 square miles in extent, was once a great reserve for game, jealously protected partly for the diversion of the Norman lord Bernard de Newmarch, and partly to furnish a supply of fresh venison during the winter season. Dwellers within the Forest had, by long usage, established the right to 'housebote', 'hedgebote', to take turves for fuel, to dig limestone, and to graze their animals. Since the Middle Ages the area of the Forest had shrunk, through portions being disafforested from time to time through appropriation to adjacent holdings by assert or by secret enclosure, so that by the early nineteenth century, before the Enclosure Award, its area was calculated at about 39,390 acres. It is not necessary, here, to dilate on the long-drawn-out process of litigation that preceded the Enclosure Award, suffice it to say that the immediate effect of the enclosure on the landscape was to reduce the area available for future commonage to less than half of the original extent, 14,000 acres going to the Crown, and 8,000 acres having been sold to defray the expenses of the operation. In short, of the 39,390 acres formerly contained within the Forest, more than 21,484 acres were withdrawn from the common to pass into private hands.

It is important to note that the 14,000 acres awarded to the Crown constituted an extensive area in the middle of the Forest which, in effect, divided the 17,000 acres awarded to the commons into two broad tracts, namely the mountain ridges of the Fan Hir and Moel Feity on the west side, and the Fan Llia and the Fan Fawr as far as the river Taff on the east side. The heavy costs involved in parcelling and enclosing the land with stone walls led the Commoners to seek an option of holding their entire tract in common. Moreover, the considerable contraction and division of the commonage limited the number of sheep that could be grazed on the Commoners' Allotment. But in contrast, the Crown Allotment was admirably suited to sheep raising on more commercial lines. The area attracted many farmers from the Scottish Lowlands to settle on farms in the region during the 1860s who became prominent sheep ranchers. Foremost among the settlers was Robert McTurk, whose Cnewr Company leased the whole of the 13,000 acres of the Crown Allotment as a unit to allow of sheep farming on extensive lines. By the beginning of the twentieth century he had sheep runs carrying flocks of 14,000 sheep. The homesteads of these Scottish settlers eventually became recognisable on the landscape by belts of conifers planted by them as shelter. Thus the changes from being a deer reserve to being a vast sheep run was a long process brought about by a changing economy which also changed the landscape of the Forest, giving it its present guise.

The result of parliamentary enclosure movement in South Wales was that large parts of the agricultural area of the country were greatly modified and transformed. The movement in Wales, however, had a different emphasis from that in England. New hedges, fences and access roads were certainly created, as in England, but there were far fewer changes in farming practice. For example, the newly enclosed upland moors were divided by a network of earth balks or dry stone walls, but often stock was depastured on rough grass in precisely the same way as it had been before enclosure, except that instead of being able to range freely, the animals were contained within the large new fields. Little was done to improve the quality of the grass. Probably the most notable feature of examples studied is that post-enclosure holdings were often fragmented. In some areas plots of land were sold, or exchanged, in order to produce compact holdings, but in the upland areas many of the large blocks of land, detached from original properties became self-contained hill farms.

There are, perhaps, upwards of 300,000 acres[9] of common land remaining in South Wales which offer us some distinctive and unspoiled natural scenery, flora, fauna and wild life. In Radnorshire, for instance, there are some 47,650 acres of common land, nearly half of which is a simple continuous area in the gathering grounds of the reservoirs in the Elan and Claerwen valleys. In Brecon there are 135,570 acres of common land, of which the Brecon Beacons form one massive area, while in Cardiganshire there are still about 23,682 acres legally accessible to the public, much of which remains unexplored, while other parts are known only to the solitary shepherd or forester. The bulk of common land in Pembrokeshire is to be found in the Presely Mountains, and the neighbouring hills, inlcuding Mynydd Melyn, Mynydd Dinas, Freni Fawr and Freni Fach. Common land in Monmouthshire includes the famous Sugar Loaf, near Abergafenni, with 2,760 acres, the Black Mountain, 2,670 acres, and Hatheral Hill, 2,173 acres. In the heart of industrial Glamorgan it is still possible to climb the hillsides of

[9] Evidence concerning the extent of common land in Wales is fragmentary and unreliable, and the best guide is still: L. Dudley Stamp and W. G. Hoskins, *The Common Lands of England and Wales* (London, 1963), pp. 227–41.

the valleys and reach, in a matter of minutes, the mountain summits to enter another world—no house in sight, nor a single spoil heap on the skyline, only an unbroken expanse of moorland grazing tenanted by flocks of nomadic sheep. In winter these sheep descend from the hills, and are frequently found invading the gardens and scavenging the streets of the valleys below.

Agricultural Societies and the landscape

Enclosures certainly created the conditions that were conducive to the employment of more progressive and productive agricultural practice in South Wales, but even so, there were many improvements in methods which were still overdue at the beginning of the industrial era. The rotation of crops and the nature of farm implements were generally far behind those employed in England. To effect improvements in these areas became the chief concern of the Agricultural Societies, the first of which to be formed was the Breconshire Society founded in 1755, and followed in 1772 by the Glamorgan Society, with Cardiganshire in 1784, and Carmarthen and Monmouth both formed before 1794. The Pembrokeshire Society, founded in 1784, was of short duration.

Premiums were offered for various improvements on the land. In Cardiganshire, for instance, in 1786 a premium of five guineas was offered "to the person who shall plant the greatest number of forest trees in order to raise timber, not fewer than 20,000, and effectively fence the same in"; of four guineas for the next greatest number "not fewer than 15,000"; of three guineas for the third greatest number "not fewer than 10,000". It is interesting to record that in 1789 Thomas Johnes, of Hafod, was thanked for having planted, in the course of a season, 104,000 forest trees, and in 1792 for having planted 200,000 trees. From what the Forestry

Commission staff has recently estimated, it is possible that Thomas Johnes had planted almost 5,000,000 trees over approximately 1,500 acres of his estate at Hafod Uchtryd, a poverty stricken area, which he had converted into an idyllic valley, the history of which has inspired Elizabeth Inglis Jones to write her *Peacocks in Paradise* (Plate 29). The whole landscape was changed, for Johnes realised the importance of protection for his saplings, and consequently he saw to it that his plantations were well enclosed—most of them with a stone wall five feet high. But in spite of his care in maintaining his walls and fences, in 1812 he was embittered because "my former plantations have been shamefully destroyed by the wretched management of sheep in this county".[10]

Between 1786 and 1796, a million forest trees had been planted in response to the premiums offered by the Cardiganshire Agricultural Society. In addition, thirty miles of hedging had been completed, and forty-six acres of land reclaimed. Premiums were also offered for raising the greatest length of wall "faced on both sides with alternate layers of sod and stone well planted with white or black thorn . . .". Again, premiums were offered for "the best crop of corn or pulse on the greatest number of acres (not less than twelve) or barren or waste land—inclosed and improved in the best and most effectual manner . . .".

The same incentive was given for afforestation and land reclamation by the Breconshire Agricultural Society. Afforestation included the encouragement of tree and hedge growth. From about 1766, the importance to farms of well-grown hedges as a means of controlling livestock and conserving crops was generally advocated. One of the major concerns of the Agricultural Societies which affected the landscape, was the improvement of communication by repairing and making new roads.

[10] Linnard, *Ceredigion*, Vol. VI (1970).

New roads in the landscape

The Agricultural Societies were further instrumental in bringing about signal improvements in the condition of the roads. Along part of the South Wales coast in 1684, the state of the roads was such that when the first Duke of Beaufort came to Muddlecomb during his 'Progress' through Wales, we are told that "Here His Grace made no long stay because he would not loose the advantage of the tydes being out, and the pleasantness of travelling over the sands, which was for almost the first four miles". Later, on his journey from Swansea to Briton Ferry, "The troop and cavalcade of His Grace's attendants divided about half a mile off Swanzey lest the great number should incommode His Grace's ferrying over. Those of less use to His Grace took another way over hills about four miles about."

The first Act of Parliament for repairing of roads in 1555 did not touch Wales, and even two centuries afterwards the roads were such that a journey from Wales to London was such a hazardous enterprise that "few had the hardiness to undertake it without first settling their affairs". The pattern of roads on the South Wales landscape at this time would have been twofold—deep in the centre of the plain or valley "where they approximated to public ditches" and steep up the brows of hills where they were "akin to public step-ladders". Many of these roads were so bad that wheeled carts could not move along them "and horse biers slung between two horses had to be used instead of hearses".[11] Between Chepstow and Cardiff in 1768, Arthur Young found the roads to be "mere rocky lanes, full of hugeous stones as big as one's horse, abominable holes".[12]

[11] D. J. Davies, *The Economic History of South Wales Prior to 1800* (Cardiff, 1933), p. 91.
[12] Arthur Young, *A Six Week Tour Through England and Wales* (1768), p. 120.

Indeed, the deplorable state of roads in Wales (as in Scotland) was partly due to the lack of wheeled traffic. The early roads were traversed by pedestrian travellers, mules and pack-horses. Bridges also were only designed to meet such traffic. With the development of wheeled traffic, the need for road improvement became urgent. The only stretches of road attended to outside the parochial 'statute labour' of villagers were those which led to Ireland. It was the legal obligation of the parishes to keep their roads in good repair, but it was difficult to enforce this in practice. Eventually, after their own private efforts had proved wholly inadequate, the authority of Parliament was sought in order to set up a Turnpike Trust—turnpiking being a device by which local inhabitants shifted part of their legal responsibility for the upkeep of parish roads on to those who used them. Indeed, until now there had not been a proper system for the upkeep of the roads since the decline of Roman authority.

In 1755 and 1758, two Acts passed Parliament permitting the construction of turnpikes in Monmouthshire, and these were soon afterwards extended throughout South Wales. The old landscape of road communication was now to be partly modified at the hands of twelve Turnpike Trusts in Carmarthenshire, four in Pembrokeshire, two in Cardiganshire, two in Radnorshire, one in Breconshire, and twelve in Glamorganshire. Following the building of a road through Breconshire and Carmarthen to Fishguard and Milford Haven, a road was constructed from Cardiff to Cowbridge, Neath and Swansea, and these were linked by roads running north and south, thus presenting a new network of roads on the landscape (Fig. 16).

Superimposed on this network were the turnpike gates placed at strategic points along roads leading into the market towns, and it was at these points that the changing landscape was at variance with the Welsh peasant farmers' sense of

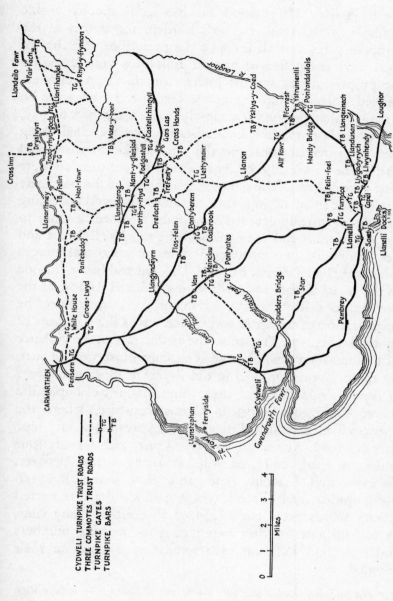

Fig. 16. The Cydweli and the Three Commotes Turnpike Trusts, showing the proliferation of toll gates and bars.

149

social justice. They stood on the landscape as visible symbols of the small farmer's burden, for it was at the turnpike gates that all users of the prescribed stretches of road were compelled to pay the tolls that were levied by the proprietors by way of interest on the large sums expended on road improvements. Gates and bars were so arranged that persons leaving the side roads had to pay, however short might be the distance they travelled along the Trust road. Consequently, towns like Swansea and Carmarthen were like besieged cities, so surrounded were they by toll gates. The genuine grievances of the peasantry against the growing injustices in the levying and collecting of tolls eventually erupted into open violence, leading to the destruction and removal of toll gates by 'Rebecca and her daughters' in a protracted series of nocturnal attacks which reached a climax in 1843. This sad and bitter episode in the social history of South Wales, referred to now as the the Rebecca Riots,[13] was a violent reaction against the proliferation of toll gates and chains across the junctions of by-roads (Fig. 17). The landscape against which the violence of the peasantry was directed is perhaps illustrated, in part, by the evidence supplied in the *Report of the Commissioners of Inquiry for South Wales*, 1844, respecting, for example, the Three Commotes Trust in Carmarthenshire, where the trustees had established twenty-one gates over fifty-nine miles of road. Again, the Cydweli Trust, with seventy-four miles of road, collected tolls at thirty gates. Between Swansea and Llanelli there were four gates along an eleven-mile stretch of road. Worst of all was the unrestricted liberty which proprietors enjoyed to erect as many additional toll gates as they required, if the existing numbers did not yield sufficient cash returns as interest on their money.

[13] For an authoritative account, see David Williams, *The Rebecca Riots* (Cardiff, 1955).

In 1789, the South Wales Association for the Improvement of Roads was formed. A survey of the road from Milford Haven to Swansea, carried out soon afterwards, showed that the greatest part of the Turnpike Road "being so extremely bad that it is not passable without considerable difficulty and danger, and some part of it (in the Cydweli area) even left in its original state so as never to have been amended or altered within the memory of man". In the four South Wales counties of Pembroke, Carmarthen, Glamorgan, and Monmouth, out of a total of 147 miles of road surveyed, 108 miles required immediate attention, and some modification. Numerous bridges along the road from Milford to Chepstow were found to be totally inadequate to meet the growing demands of a new industrial age, and the construction of new ones was strongly advocated. More specifically, seventeen new bridges were recommended, and fourteen existing structures required repair and extensive modifications.

The Enclosure Acts of the Georgian period led to further modification of the road system in South Wales. By authorising the enclosure of common land in certain localities, the Parliamentary Enclosure Acts made it necessary to make adequate provision for public highways, "private roads running through, over and along them", for the convenience and accommodation of the public. This sometimes involved the widening of such tracks as existed to the usual breadth of thirty feet.

Mills and lime-kilns

One part of the beauty of the Welsh scene is the natural landscape, while the other is found in the structures which man has sometimes planted upon it. Some of these have, in time, been taken for granted, just as much as a tree or a rivulet, yet some of them stand as monuments representing

THE WELSH RIOTERS.

Fig. 17 The Rebecca Riots, from an old print, 1843.

important developments in the history of man. In this category stand the water-mill, windmill, and lime-kiln, which were conceived and constructed to serve our earlier kinsfolk: like the farmhouse itself, they may be said to have constituted the tools and implements by which men and women sustained themselves and their families, and constituted, so to speak, their technical accessories. Mills are, indeed, ancient industrial monuments which served town and hamlet; they were used in agriculture and in industry, and their distribution may be seen by reference to the Ordnance Survey maps.

As stated earlier, rivers and streams were so numerous and convenient in most parts of South Wales that water-mills far outnumbered windmills. In Carmarthen alone, there were in all twenty-eight rivers and streams capable of turning mills. Many of the ancient water-mills were constructed in picturesque settings, and some are to be seen today in many parts of the countryside. For instance, the 'French mill' which stands on the shallow estuary of the river Carew, occupies a site upon which a mill has stood since before 1560—the present rectangular three-storeyed structure belongs to the late eighteenth century. It is, in fact a tide-mill, with water entering at high tide and dammed up by a barrage, and then let out in a controlled flow. The mills at Carew, called French mill and Mylton mill, were in great decay in 1565, and a sum of £30, it was said, would not suffice for their necessary repair. Recently, as a result of skilful craftsmanship, the French mill has been restored to working condition, and thus forms a realistic link with past centuries.

Despite their picturesque settings, many water-grist mills were placed inaccessibly for wheeled traffic, although this disadvantage mattered little for horses and pack-saddles (Fig. 18). But with the development of roads, many of the early mills, such as Buckland old mill, on the Usk, became little used, and fell into disrepair because new mills were erected on more accessible sites. The impact of the water-mill on the landscape may be gauged from the number of place names in South Wales containing the name *melin* (mill), e.g. Melin-Ifan-Ddu (Black Mill), Glamorgan; Felindre (mill villa), Cardigan and Glamorgan; Felinfach (little mill), Cardiganshire and Breconshire; Felinganol (middle mill), Pembrokeshire; Felinwen (white mill), Carmarthenshire. Many field names, too, bear testimony to the age-long importance of mills in rural society. Throughout the greater part of the nineteenth century, numerous grist and flour mills continued to flourish in the Vale of Glamorgan. Among these were the West Aberthaw mills above Booth House; Llandough mill near Cowbridge; and Gigman Mill, St Mary Church.

Windmills, in contrast to the water-mills, were to be found mainly on the dry southern limestone tract. Although they were not numerous in South Wales, they were visible on the landscape, probably as early as the thirteenth century.[14] They were in evidence mainly in Monmouthshire, St-y-Nyll, Llantrisant, Llantwit Major, Boverton, Wick (Plates 27 & 28), Merthyr Mawr, Newton, Llanrhidian, Kelvay Hall, in Glamorgan; and at Angle, Gelliwicke, Dalehill, St Bride's and St David's (Twr-y-felin) in Pembrokeshire.

It is surprising that the windmills of South Wales did not attract the attention of the tourists who travelled the Welsh countryside between 1780 and 1830, for, although few in number, they must certainly have stood out conspicuously on the landscape—"their halting alacrity of movement, their pleasant business making bread all day—their air, gigantically human, as a creature half-alive, put a spirit of romance into the tamest landscape".[15]

[14] White-Book Mabinogion (1907), p. 81.
[15] R. L. Stevenson quoted by Charles P. Skilton, *British Windmills and Watermills* (London, 1947), p. 8.

154

The distribution of windmills depended on relief, nature of farming, and alternative sources of power. Many farmers in the Vale of Glamorgan combined farming with milling, and erected windmills on their farms where water-mills would have been impracticable. Windmills were, sometimes, complementary to water-mills, and were located on elevated positions and at road junctions. One conspicuous windmill stood on the edge of an escarpment at an elevation of 307 feet in Newton Down, Glamorgan, the ruins of which are still visible today from nearby Mount Pleasant farm, where Neolithic man had established himself 2,500, or more years ago. About a mile lower down, between Newton Nottage and Porthcawl, stands Windmill House, whose construction shows unmistakable signs of its true origin.

Some idea of the size of the largest windmills of the Vale of Glamorgan is given in the specifications of a new structure to be built on the Boverton Place Farm in 1826: it was to have a tower fifty feet high, twenty feet diameter at base, and fourteen feet at the top; the wall was to be three feet thick at the bottom, and two feet at the top; it was to have three doors and three windows, and a gallery around the outside four feet broad and twenty feet from the bottom. The tower was to contain five lofts—three for the convenience of the tower, and two for the use of the mill—"the said mill to have five vanes each twenty-seven feet long and eight feet broad". The cost of the mill was estimated to be about £400—a substantial sum in 1826. About ten years or so previously, a windmill had been erected at Wick "at a very great expense".

The tremendous cost involved in keeping windmills in good repair, together with a change in farming practice and the use of steam, eventually rendered them obsolete, and by the end of the nineteenth century most of them in South Wales ceased to operate. The same fate attended the water-mills. With the development of modern machinery

Fig. 18 The old water-mill, St Florence, from a drawing c. 1841

and the opening of the railways after 1850, they gradually became obsolete, only to remain on the landscape as ruinous monuments to man's industry and ingenuity in an age which has long since died.

The scant attention paid by early observers to lime-kilns is particularly surprising, more especially because of their importance in the agricultural practice of the lowland regions of South Wales, and their proliferation across the countryside during the nineteenth century. Yet, the presence of lime-kilns provides us with a useful clue to the change of emphasis that occurred in the agriculture of South Wales from about the middle of the sixteenth century onwards into the latter decades of the nineteenth century. We shall never know when precisely the lime-kiln first appeared on the scene, but it is interesting to note that the Welsh name for lime-kiln—*odyn galch*—has been traced back to the old Cornish place-name 'Odencolc' which occurs in an Anglo Saxon Charter of Ethelwolf, King of Wessex, dated A.D. 826, "and concerns land in the South Hams district of South Devon".[16] Exactly what use was made of the lime burnt in the kiln at this early period may be the subject for a more detailed enquiry. It seems, however, from the evidence at present available, that lime-kilns did not appear on the South Wales landscape in any significant numbers until the seventeenth century, although lime-burning in kilns had been practised from remote times.[17]

Writing about 1600, George Owen records that limestone was dug from quarries "to the bignesse of a man's fist and lesse, to the end they might the sooner burne throwe, and beinge hewed smalle, the same is put to a kill [kiln]" which Owen describes as a wall:

[16] *B.B.C.S.*, Vol. XXIII, p. 116.
[17] Lime-kilns built on Merthyr Mawr warren and Ogmore Castle in Glamorgan, and at Kilgerran, Pembrokeshire, probably for building purposes, have been dated as belonging to the thirteenth and fourteenth centuries.

six foote high, four or five foote broad at the brimme, but growing narrower to the bottom, havinge two lope holes at the bottom which they call the kill eyes . . . In this kill first is made a fier of Coales or rather colme which is but the dust of the coales which is laid in the bottome of the kill, and some few stickes of wood to kindle the fier, then is the kill filled with these smale hewed pieces of lymestones, and then fier beinge geaven the same burneth . . . and maketh the lymestones to become meere red fierye coales which being don and the fier quenched the lyme so burned is suffered to coole in the kill and then is drawen where it is laied in heapes and the next showre of rayne maketh it to molter and fall into dust which they spreade on the land, and so sowe wheat or barlie therein as the tyme of the yeare requireth.

More significantly Owen further added:

This trade of lyminge hath been more used within these thirte or fortie yeares then in times paste and it destroyeth the ffurse, fearne, heath and other like shrobbes growing on the land and bringeth forth a fine and sweete grasse and quick changeth the hue and face of the grounde and hath greatlie enriched those that used it.

Such kilns as those described by George Owen contained from four to five tons of limestone, and were still to be seen in many places on the South Wales landscape during the early years of the nineteenth century.

Rice Merrick, writing of Glamorgan in 1578, noted that in the *Blaenau* there was in former times "allwayes great breeding of cattle, Horses and Sheepe", and "therein grew but small store of corne". But "of late yeares", he continued "since the knowledge and use of lyming was found, there groweth more plenty of grayne". At the time of the Conquest, Merrick states that the "mountaines in those dayes bore noe such corne as now groweth thereon, because lyming and marling of the ground was not used and, as I think, not known".

It would seem, therefore, that the sixteenth century marked a step forward in the use of liming (p. 96). When corn growing was profitable, and farming generally a paying pursuit, the cultivators of the soil never felt the necessity of applying anything other than lime and farmyard manure to the land. They had but very little scientific knowledge of its proportion, but they knew from experience that its application "pulverised strong soils, destroyed insects, checked the growth of moss and weeds, improved the quality of grain and grasses". The quantity applied was about three tons per acre, and in an area where limestone was to be obtained in great abundance, and coal and culm in ready supply for burning it, it was not surprising to find lime-kilns appearing in great numbers. During his 'tour' in 1772, Arthur Young observed that in the Llanvaches area in Monmouthshire, and Cowbridge in Glamorgan, "every farm has a lime-kiln".

In the Vale of Glamorgan there were but few public kilns for the sale of lime, and at the beginning of the nineteenth century, according to Walter Davies, "every farmer is a lime burner; raising the stone in the field to be manured", with the result that there was "scarcely an arable field to be found without having either at present, or formerly, a lime-kiln within it". It was reported in 1844 that "everyone builds a lime-kiln for 40s. or 50s. on his own farm".

The extension of the uses of lime as a manure on the farms of South Wales represented a minor revolution in agriculture, which for centuries was manifested on the landscape, not only in richer arable acres and lusher pastures, but also in the proliferation of lime-kilns along the coastline nearest to those areas in Pembrokeshire and Cardiganshire where lime had to be transported from other areas. By the end of the nineteenth century they were becoming generally disused because of the increasing application of artificial manures which were, in comparison, cheaper to obtain and to handle. There was also a general decrease in the growth of wheat in the 1880s. As the ruined Norman castle indicated the decline of manorialism and the feudal system, so did the ruined lime-kilns represent, in a less spectacular but in an equally significant way, the changes which agricultural methods were undergoing in South Wales at the close of the nineteenth century. By the end of the First World War, most of the smaller lime-kilns were in "glorious ruins, or becoming so", more especially along the sea coast.

SELECT BIBLIOGRAPHY

Bowen, Ivor, *The Great Enclosures of Common Lands in Wales* (London, 1914).

Clark, John, *General View of the Agriculture of the County of Brecknock* (London, 1794).

Davies, Margaret, 'Rhosili open field and related South Wales field patterns', *Agricultural History Review*, Vol. iv (1956), pp. 80–96.

Davies, Walter (*Gwallter Mechain*), *A General View of the Agriculture and Domestic Economy of South Wales*, 2 vols (London, 1814).

Edmunds, Henry, 'The History of the Brecknockshire Agricultural Society, 1755–1955', *Brycheiniog*, ii and iii (1956 and 1957).

Fenton, Richard, *A Historical Tour Through Pembrokeshire* (Brecknock, 1903).

Fox, John, *General View of the Agriculture of the County of Glamorgan* (London, 1796).

Hassall, Charles, *General View of Agriculture of the County of Monmouth* (London, 1812).

Hoskins, W. G. and Stamp, L. Dudley, *The Common Lands of England and Wales* (London, 1963).

Jones, T. I. Jeffreys, "The enclosure movement in South Wales during the Tudor and early Stuart periods' (University of Wales, unpublished M.A. thesis, 1936).

Lloyd, Thomas and Turnor, D., *General view of the agriculture of the County of Cardigan . . . Drawn up from the communications of Thomas Lloyd . . .* (London, 1794).

Pierce, Gwynedd O., *The place-names of Dinas Powys Hundred* (Cardiff, 1968).

Rees, William, *The Great Forest of Brecknock: a Facet of Breconshire History* (Brecon, 1966).

REPORT OF THE ROYAL COMMISSION ON LAND IN WALES AND MONMOUTHSHIRE, *Minutes of evidence*, 4 vols, *Appendices to the Report* (London, 1896).

Thomas, David, *Agriculture in Wales during the Napoleonic Wars . . .* (Cardiff, 1963).

Williams, David, *The Rebecca Riots* (Cardiff, 1955).

5. The landscape of religious and educational movements

Religion and the landscape. A unique socio-religious experiment. Education and the landscape. The National Eisteddfod

Religion and the landscape

OF ALL THE features connected with the human landscape of South Wales, perhaps none has received less attention in historical discussion than the local chapels, schools and other buildings of educational and cultural importance. Yet they form a unique part of the local landscape heritage, and are as significant as the medieval castles, monasteries, and abbeys in their time. No one who has passed through the industrial valleys and towns of South Wales will have failed to observe the marked frequency with which religious buildings and schools (to a lesser degree) dot the local landscape. Many of these buildings undoubtedly introduced a degree of architectural variety, if not elegance, into the numerous congeries of smoke-drenched 'works' and the squalid dust-strewn habitations of the labouring population. But they were not erected on account of their architectural qualities, and it would, indeed, be an empty exercise to study their presence in the landscape merely in terms of 'bricks and mortar' put together in accordance with a particular 'school' of architectural convention or design, be it Romanesque, Gothic or Classical: their real significance lies in their socio-economic background. It should be remembered in this context that within the plethora of industrial buildings and their accessories, together with the public and private buildings that made up the industrial scene, were the people—men, women and children—with their personal and corporate needs and aspirations which, in part, may be said to have found expression on the landscape in terms of chapel buildings, churches, schools, colleges, workmen's institutes, public libraries, theatres and cinemas. But these structures did not appear overnight. Their origins go back into history, and although this is not the place to dilate on historical events as such, it is nonetheless necessary to refer, briefly, to the more important events leading up to the filling-in of the landscape with sacerdotal buildings during the eighteenth and nineteenth centuries. The existence of so many chapels (i.e. Nonconformist church buildings) in the towns and villages of South Wales must be explained chiefly in conjunction with the religious revival sparked off *c.* 1735 by the preaching of its chief agent Howel Harris, a gentleman of Trefeca, in Breconshire, together with Daniel Rowland of Llangeitho, Cardiganshire, Gruffith Jones of Llanddowror, and William Williams of Pantycelyn, Carmarthenshire. These gentlemen deprecated the inefficacy of the Church of England in Wales—of which they were members—and strongly denounced the apathy and loose living of its clergy, and the languid state of religion in Wales generally. At the beginning of the eighteenth century "what spiritual earnestness there was . . . apart from exceptional clergymen of the Established church was due to the energy of Nonconformists".

Early nonconformity in Wales, as in England, may be said to have originated with the Act of Uniformity, 1662, although a number of ministers such as William Wroth, William Erbury and Walter Craddock, had been ejected from the Established Church some thirty years earlier because of their independent views. These men, along with others of the same convictions, became itinerant preachers whose work during the seventeenth century was, on the whole, "very largely confined to the English side of Welsh life . . . to the towns and the more Anglicised portions of the Principality".[1] The ocular evidence of the considerable impact which these early Dissenters—Baptists and Independents—had on Welsh affairs was minimal, and consequently we shall pass over the exciting events that were taking place in the religious life of Wales between 1662 and 1735 in order to examine, briefly, how the rise of Methodism, and its ultimate connection with Nonconformity uniquely influenced the human landscape of South Wales.

The Anglican Church had, long before the eighteenth century, lost touch with the peasantry (*y werin*) of the Welsh countryside. A pathetic picture of the state of the Church in the diocese of St David's in 1721 was drawn by Dr Erasmus Saunders. Church buildings, he said, were in a state of negligence, and only served for "the solitary habitations of owls and jackdaws"; one had even been let to the Dissenters; others were only half served, the service of the prayers being only partly read, and the means of preaching, catechising, and communion sorely neglected. In one church, we are told, the Sexton "to get a sorry maintenance was allowed the privilege of selling ale by the churchyard side". Sometimes this was also true of the clergy, and one is reputed to have stopped the service when there were customers. Other factors, such as the inability of the bishops to use the Welsh language, absenteeism, pluralism, and alienation of revenue, all contributed in varying degrees to undermine the influence of the Anglican church. A wide gap, therefore, existed between the Established Church in Wales and the peasantry of the countryside. The position

[1] Rhys and Jones, *The Welsh People*, p. 462; David Williams, *A History of Modern Wales* (London, 1950), p. 114.

was further exacerbated by the positive failure of the Church to respond effectively to the changes in population that were taking place in the industrial areas. Moreover, the old Dissenters—Baptists and Independents—had also failed to make any great impact on the populace. It is no wonder that during the fourth decade of the eighteenth century the people of Wales were captured by the spiritual and educational enlightenment represented in the teaching and preaching of the leaders of the Methodist revival of 1735. It was the beginning of a movement which was to revolutionise the educational as well as the religious life of Wales, and culminated in a significant filling-in of the landscape.

It is estimated that by 1851, the Nonconformists had *captured* nearly eighty per cent of the population (which itself had doubled during the same period) whereas, at the beginning of the century, the majority of the people belonged to the Established Church. The measure of this outstanding achievement in terms of chapel building is provided by the Religious Census of 1851. Here it is shown that out of a total of 1,863 places of worship which had hitherto appeared on the landscape, only 615 belonged to the Established Church, whilst the Independents had 367 buildings, the Welsh Calvinistic Methodists 302, and Baptists 264 buildings. A religious revival in 1859 led to an unprecedented surge forward in chapel building, so that by 1898 the Welsh Calvinistic Methodists alone had built 663 chapels and preaching houses, and by 1900 this total had reached 854. Another revival in 1904/5 did not, as is sometimes supposed, lead to a further period of intense chapel building.

By 1910 the strength of the Church of England[2] in South Wales was represented on the landscape by some 1,254

---

[2] After the Disestablishment Bill of 1914, which did not become law until 1919, Wales became a separate ecclesiastical 'province' outside the control of Canterbury, and henceforth was recognised as the 'Church in Wales'.

churches, with accommodation for 303,740 people. The Nonconformist denominations, however, were represented by 2,580 chapels and their adjoining schoolrooms, with 'sittings' (i.e. accommodation) for 1,228,448 persons. In Glamorgan alone there were, in 1905, about 1,074 Nonconformist chapels (valued at £1,383,577) with sittings for 568,119 persons out of a total population of 900,000, that is, for six out of every ten of the population. This was, indeed, in sharp contrast to the Established Church with its 247 churches, and accommodation for only 98,698 persons, that is, for about one in every ten of the population. The great period of chapel building in South Wales extended roughly from 1860 to about 1912, after which date there was little, if any, building of new churches, apart from re-building, extensions, and modifications of the older buildings.

The early chapels, both in the rural and industrial areas of South Wales, were drab single-storey buildings, having strong affinities with the Welsh farmhouse, especially in the rural areas of Cardiganshire and Carmarthenshire. Most of the chapels were of humble origin, their members meeting initially in stables, barns and farmhouses—the era of 'garrets and cellars'—where religious instruction was enthusiastically sought and given. In the industrial areas, where the problem of accommodation was more acute, the two-storey[3] and three-storey buildings, or the two-storey structure with adjoining vestry, predominated. In many instances these industrial chapels originated in private houses, colliery buildings, and even the long rooms of public houses. It is not surprising, therefore, that many of the early chapels in the coal mining areas of South Wales

---

[3] As used in relation to chapels the terms single-storey and two-storey denote the number of rows of windows on the main entrance elevation, whether or not there is a gallery inside. J. B. Hilling, *Cardiff and the Valleys,* p. 131n.

closely resembled the rectangular colliery winding-houses, fan-rooms and lamp-rooms which were, more often than not, built of the same stone, hacked out of the same local quarries. For example, in Gilfach Goch, Glamorgan, Noddfa and Libanus chapels originated in carpenters' shops on neighbouring colliery premises, and at Pontrhydyryn ("The bridge of the ford of the ash trees"), Monmouthshire, the Baptist Church there started in an assorting room of the local tinplate works. It is interesting to observe that Tabor chapel, the first to be built in Gilfach Goch, was easily converted into a colliery lamp-room when the expansion of the Britannic colliery compelled the worshippers to build another chapel elsewhere.

Although the early Wesleyan Methodists' preaching houses in England, up to about 1790, were octagonal in shape, there seems to have been no such pattern of building adopted by the Wesleyans in Wales. It would appear that the only octagonal chapel to be built in South Wales, if not in the whole of Wales, was Beulah chapel in the little village of Groes, near Margam, Glamorgan, belonging to the Presbyterian Church of Wales.[4] It was built in 1838 on a piece of land given by Mr Talbot, of Margam Castle, at a cost of £800, on condition that the building would be octagonal in shape (Plate 35). The only octagonal church that appeared on the South Wales landscape was that built at Georgetown, Merthyr Tudful, at the expense of the Crawshays, the local iron masters of Cyfarthfa. In 1803 Malkin described this building as "a spacious and elegant chapel-of-ease . . . an octagon building to be furnished also with its own organ".

Built at the expense of the members themselves, and often at great personal sacrifice, the Nonconformist chapels were

[4] The village has now been demolished to make way for the extension of the M4, but the chapel has been dismantled stone by stone and rebuilt at the Tollgate Park, Margam, half a mile away.

sited at points where they were most needed, but as their respective congregations swelled, and the wealth and social influence of their members increased, the small unpretentious buildings often gave way to more ornate and grandiose structures, with more sophisticated interior furnishings and decoration. Tuning forks, in time, gave way to harmoniums, or American organs, which were, in turn, in many of the larger chapels superseded by two- and three-manual pipe organs, with their ornamental casings, putting many a parish church organ to shame.

Perhaps the most striking architectural feature of the Welsh chapels has been the consistency in the way in which the barn-like form of building was adhered to for well over one hundred years from the early years of the nineteenth century until the twentieth century. As John Hilling has recently shown, "The gable-ended roof, traditional in Wales and easier to construct, became the dominant feature, culminating in massive pediments over single- or double-storey fronts. The design of the gable façade characterises the development of the chapel style more than any other single feature. Here is the focus of all the artistic and architectural expression of Nonconformism . . ." which was, with the exception of the English-language chapels, "nearly always a classical rather than a Gothic expression". The English-language chapels at first resembled the Welsh chapels in their rejection of the symbolism associated with the Church, but from about the middle of the nineteenth century, English chapels tended to become more and more like "poor men's versions of the Anglican Church",[5] Welsh Nonconformity, on the whole, remaining more conservative.

The multiplicity of 'denominational' chapels which grew up on the landscape was probably an outward expression of the differences that prevailed in the theological specula-

5 John B. Hilling, *Cardiff and the Valleys* (London, 1973), p. 130.

tion of the leaders of the various sects whose members were forever divided on two fundamental issues, namely, of religious dogma, and of forms of church government. There were also present in the atmosphere of chapel building schemes socio-religious factors, too complex to isolate, for "it was seldom possible in the nineteenth century to disentangle social and economic considerations from religious motives".[6] Moreover, the variety in the structural design of the chapels which obtruded on the landscape during the post-1870 period is most striking, with each architectural nuance possibly representing the subtler social, if not spiritual, feelings of 'otherness', not only between groups of differing religious persuasion, but also between groups within the same denomination, as if in their buildings they vied with each other in exciting feelings of awe, wonder, sublimity, and other high emotions (Plate 34). Speaking of mid-nineteenth-century chapels, John Betjeman states:

Not since medieval days had the people clubbed together to adorn a place of worship, and this time it was not a shrine but a preaching house ... They were anxious not to look like the Church which held them in contempt, nor like a house, for they were places of worship; nor like a theatre, for they were sacred piles. They succeeded in looking like what they are—chapels, so that the most unobservant traveller can tell a chapel from any other building in the street.[7]

Of more subtle significance than the Nonconformist chapels themselves were, perhaps, their names, deeply engraved, or heavily lettered, on their prominent plaques. A large number of these Welsh chapels were given Biblical

[6] David Williams, *A History of Modern Wales* (London, 1950), p. 246.
[7] John Betjeman, *First and Last Loves* (1952), pp. 102–8.

place-names which, in a sense, betrayed the 'mythical' element that was present in no small measure on the periphery of Welsh Nonconformist thinking, namely, of identifying Wales with the Holy Land. Such names as Bethabara, Nazareth, Rehoboth, Bethesda, Bryn Seion (Mount Zion), Calfaria (Calvary), Libanus, Moriah, Gosen, Piscah and Jerusalem, have been given many times over to different chapels in South Wales (and North Wales), and these stand out in sharp contrast to the names of the Saints to whom most of the neighbouring Episcopal Churches have been dedicated. Moreover, many official signposts in the landscape point to such places as Bethania, Nebo, Joppa, Horeb, Hebron, Salem, and even to Bethlehem (Carmarthenshire), where many people from a wide area are attracted at Christmastide in order to send their greetings cards through the village Post Office. Such names give a distinct Palestinian flavour to their respective localities. It is interesting to note, however, that many of these communities represent previous squatter settlements on the rugged fringes of the moorlands which originally had no centres or focus except, perhaps the Nonconformist chapels whose names they adopted[8] (Plate 33).

Although Nonconformity had made considerable headway by the mid-nineteenth century, the Established Church had not been altogether indifferent to the widening gap that separated it from the peasantry and, in particular, the labouring classes of industrial areas. Malkin, when revisiting Merthyr in 1806, found that the parish church he had described in 1803 as "not sufficiently large" had been taken down "and is rebuilding on a larger scale".[9]

Later, parish boundaries were adjusted to meet the

[8] E. G. Bowen, 'The dispersed habitat of Wales' in *Man and His Habitat* (ed. Emrys Jones) (London, 1971), pp. 191–2.

[9] Benjamin Heath Malkin, *The Scenery, Antiquities and Biography of South Wales* (London, 1807), Vol. I, p. 276.

requirements of a changing pattern in the distribution of population, and a programme of extensive re-building and restoration of old church buildings and parsonages followed, as well as the building of new churches in the industrial areas. For example, in 1869 the Parish of Ystradyfodwg was one incumbency, with four clergy, two churches, and two mission rooms, but by 1921, nine new parishes had been formed, and thirty-two new churches and schoolrooms erected. In the same area there were, however, over 150 Nonconformist chapels.

In the final analysis it may be said that the Nonconformist chapels, more than the churches, represent in the South Wales landscape, a complex of historical forces which have not yet been fully analysed. It was within these Nonconformist chapels, for example, that Welsh hymnody had flowered, and where countless numbers had been taught to read and encouraged to write; it was the dialectic method of the Welsh Sunday Schools (conducted mainly in the chapels) that encouraged and sustained interest in discussion, debate, and conversation of high quality on theological, Biblical, and political topics. The close association between the Calvinistic belief in universal theological education and its connection with a popular training in the Bible was, according to H. A. L. Fisher, "not manifested more clearly anywhere than in Wales".[10] In the Rhondda, by 1860, Dissenting chapels had become real centres of mental as well as spiritual activity for "they gave to the ordinary working man scope for exercising his initiative and administrative capacities" and before the coming of Friendly Societies and Trade Unions, "they were the only means whereby the Rhondda miner could learn the essential lessons of voluntary co-operation and self-government."[11]

Progressive changes in religious outlook and opinion,

[10] H. A. L. Fisher, *A History of Europe* (London, 1943), p. 545.
[11] E. D. Lewis, *The Rhondda Valleys* (London, 1959), p. 195.

together with recent redistributions of local population
have rendered superfluous many church and chapel buildings insofar as they have outlived their usefulness as
religious meeting houses. In consequence many have been
demolished in the cause of modern 'development' building,
or bull-dozed unceremoniously and irreligiously into piles
of rubble for modern road improvement schemes. Others
have survived as shells deprived of their former interior
furnishings and converted, for secular purposes, into
garages, furniture store-rooms, and social centres, etc.
Nevertheless, the Nonconformist chapels that still remain
on the South Wales landscape represent, more than any
other surviving buildings, the spirit of Nonconformity
which has directly or indirectly affected the whole course
of Welsh life, and exalted its national ideals.

A unique socio-religious experiment

If Howel Harris had been one of the prime movers in the
religious awakening that stirred Wales in the early eighteenth
century and which, ultimately, led to the building of upwards of 2,500 Nonconformist chapels in South Wales, he
was also a pioneer in a unique experiment at Trefeca,
Breconshire, which has left a conspicuous mark on the
landscape, and one which is, perhaps, more directly
associated with Harris's name than any other (Plate 32).

In 1751, strong differences of opinion on certain doctrinal
matters had led to a complete rupture between Howel Harris
and his fellow Methodist reformers and, in particular, Daniel
Rowland. Harris consequently withdrew to Trefeca where,
in addition to his own patrimonial estates, he acquired some
765 acres of land upon which to establish a Utopian community called 'The Family' based on the Moravian principles of Zinzendorf's *Brüdergemeine* at Herrnhut in Saxony,
and Fulmack in Yorkshire. A kind of 'religio-industrial'

community, it was, perhaps, the only experiment of its kind to have been undertaken in South Wales.[12] In one of his diaries, Harris relates how the building had proceeded between 1753 and 1759: ". . . I had, in addition to the dining hall and sleeping rooms put up a cold bath, balcony, cupola and clock; a printing press, a tucking mill, a kiln, wool spinning machines and looms, a workshop, bake-house and an infirmary. The chapel was opened in 1858."

When John Wesley visited Trefeca in 1763, he described what he saw on the landscape thus: "Howel Harris's house is one of the most elegant places which I have seen in Wales. The little chapel and all things round about it are furnished with an uncommon taste, and the gardens, orchards, fishponds, and the mount adjoining, make the place a little paradise." At that time about a hundred and twenty persons had joined the Family. A rather prejudiced Malkin described Trefeca in 1803 as: "Here a Gothic arch! there a Corinthian capital! Towers, battlements and bastions! Peacocks cut in box, and lions hacked in holly! Who has thus deluged his native country with bad taste . . .? It is a preacher of the gospel professedly of the strictest persuasion and most mortified habits." In 1772 the buildings extended in length for about a hundred and fifty feet; and were divided into three houses, with seventy rooms in the first, fifteen in the second, and thirty-four in the third, besides the stables, the hay-loft and other accessories.

Howel Harris's involvement in the day-to-day management of his estates at Trefeca led him to become keenly interested in agricultural improvements, if not reform, and

[12] It should be mentioned, however, that in 1847, 220 acres of land at Garnlwyd, Carmarthenshire, was taken over by an Owenite 'community' of fourteen members who supported themselves by producing dairy goods, boots and shoes for sale to the Leeds Redemption Society. Lack of capital for improving the marginal land on which they had settled, resulted in the abandonment of the experiments in 1855.

it is said that he was instrumental in founding the Brecknockshire Agricultural Society in 1755, becoming an Honorary Member of that Society on 5th May, 1756. His involvement in his estates had earned for him the title 'Squire Harris'.

After Harris's death in 1773, the fortunes of the Family turned, and gradually declined. In 1803, Malkin saw Trefeca "obviously falling" but it was not until 1847 that the last member of the Family died. However, in 1842, the buildings that had housed Harris's Family since 1751, became one of the two colleges.[13] of the Welsh Calvinistic Methodists where generations of young men were to be trained for the same Ministry which Harris had done so much to organise, despite his withdrawal to the monastic life of the Family.

An earlier college had been established at Trefeca in 1768, when Lady Huntingdon leased a farmhouse, Trefeca Isaf (Lower Trefeca), and converted it into a college,[14] with its chapel, in order to train young men in the Ministry. It was an all-denominational college, staffed initially by teachers who had been expelled by the University of Oxford for forming private Methodistical conventicles. Although Howel Harris himself did not return to the Methodist movement, he did become reconciled with the leaders of the Welsh Methodist cause, and Lady Huntingdon's college, in a sense, reflected that *rapprochement*. The building, however, still remains in the Breconshire landscape as a reminder of the religious 'enthusiasm' that will for ever be associated with Howel Harris, Lady Huntingdon, and others, who had laboured indefatigably in the cause of religious and educational enlightenment in the eighteenth century.

[13] The other was located at Bala, in Merionethshire.
[14] In 1792 this college was removed from Trefeca to Cheshunt, near London, and later to Cambridge.

Education and the landscape

The few grammar schools that had been built in South Wales in the sixteenth and early seventeenth century stood out as the main visual evidence of the provision made to meet contemporary educational needs of the population until the early decades of the nineteenth century. For the Charity Schools, developed in the eighteenth century, were conducted mostly in an upper room of a house, in a cottage, or sometimes in a room over a stable. Hardly any new school buildings appeared, despite the many bequests made by private individuals for their erection. Similarly, the eighteenth century 'Circulating Schools', associated with the immortal Griffith Jones of Llanddowror, were held in lowly places, and although they represented a powerful educational effort, no specifically visual evidence marked the progress of the education they provided. In short, it was not until the early nineteenth century that the landscape began to show definite signs of educational progress in South Wales. This was brought about mainly by the work of two societies which were formed in England with a view to providing education for the poorer children. One of them, the Royal Lancastrian Society, founded in 1808 (renamed the British and Foreign Society), was to be entirely undenominational in its teaching, and the other, the National Society for Promoting the Education of the Poor in the Principles of the Established Church in England and Wales, was founded in 1811. When these societies began their work in South Wales, the socio-religious differences that divided Nonconformists and the Established Church in 'matters spiritual' were clearly projected on to the educational scene. The Nonconformists were generally inclined to regard education as an essential part of religious training and as they objected to state control of religion, they objected to a state system of education. They were determined to prevent the Church from having control of education.

This determination became more tenacious after the publication of the findings of the three Commissioners appointed in 1846 to enquire into the state of education in Wales. Their Reports, published 1847, expressed the view that the illiterate and immoral condition of the Welsh people at that time was due, mainly, to the prevalence of the Welsh language (the 'mother tongue' of the over-whelming majority of the population in 1847), and Welsh Nonconformity. "The Welsh language", the Commissioners reported, "is a vast drawback to Wales, and a manifold barrier to the moral progress and commercial prosperity of the people. It is not easy to over estimate its evil effects." The Reports were, therefore, invested with the epithet *Brad y Llyfrau Gleision* (the treachery of the Blue Books), and are still referred to as such.

Meanwhile, in 1853, the Rev. William Roberts (the bard Nefydd) was appointed by the British Society to act as their agent in South Wales. On his appointment there were only fourteen British Schools throughout the whole of South Wales, but on Roberts' retirement ten years later, in 1863, the number had increased to 164.

The position which many of the British Schools occupied in the landscape very often reflected the difficulties with which agents were confronted in obtaining sites for them. According to the Committee of Council's regulations, grants could not be given for building a schoolroom unless the sites were freehold. Consequently, partisanship often compelled schools to be sited in unhealthy and inconvenient places. Where the land was the property of gentlemen belonging to the Church of England and those generally of the Tories and High Church party, sites were not available at all in some areas for the building of British Schools. For instance, at Bryn-mawr, Breconshire, a British School had been built there in 1844 "in a healthy place", but by 1854

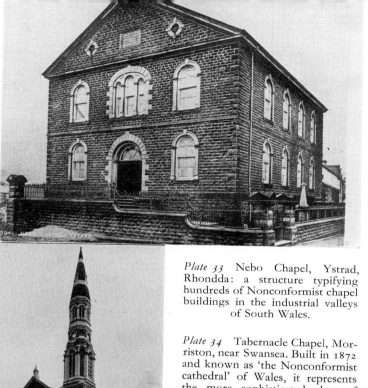

Plate 33 Nebo Chapel, Ystrad, Rhondda: a structure typifying hundreds of Nonconformist chapel buildings in the industrial valleys of South Wales.

Plate 34 Tabernacle Chapel, Morriston, near Swansea. Built in 1872 and known as 'the Nonconformist cathedral' of Wales, it represents the more sophisticated class of Nonconformist church buildings that appeared in the larger industrial towns.

Plate 35 Beulah, in the village of Groes, Margam; the only octagonal chapel in Wales, as it stood before it was recently dismantled. See p. 167 n.

Plate 36 Cowbridge Grammar School, founded in 1609, was the oldest endowed school in Glamorgan.

Plate 37 Ewenni Nati School presenting marked ecclesias appearance—a fea which characte most National Schoo

Plate 38 Bryndu British School, Glamorgan, displaying the architectural austerity that marked the British Schools in the nineteenth century.

Plate 39 St David's College, Lampeter, established in 1836 as a Church of England in Wales college. Today it is one of the constituent colleges of the University of Wales.

Plate 40 University College of Wales, Aberystwyth—'the College by the Sea'. Aberystwyth Castle is seen in the background on the right.

Plate 41 The Six Bells Colliery, Abertyleri, Monmouthshire, showing, in the background, row upon row of terraced houses lining the hillside.

Plate 42 Park Dare Workmen's Institute. Similar Institutes were established throughout the South Wales coalfield, providing reading rooms and other educational and recreational facilities.

Plate 43   The National Library of Wales from the south.

Plate 44   The Eisteddfod Gorsedd circle, Haverfordwest, viewed from the south. (Cf. Plate 2.)

Plate 45 *Pont-y-tŷ-pridd* ('the earthen house bridge') in 1795, now known as Ponty-pridd Bridge. Built in 1757, after three previous attempts by the local architect, William Edwards, to link the Hundreds of Miskin and Senghennydd; it was one of the most remarkable bridges in Europe, and its single-span arch of 140 feet remained the largest arch in Britain until 1831.

Plate 46 Crumlin Viaduct in 1890. It was demolished early in 1966.

Plate 47   Tramroads or waggon-ways, with horse-drawn waggons loaded with coal,
near Neath Abbey, as seen by Edward Donovan, *c.* 1804.

Plate 48   The Waterston and Gulf Refinery, Pembrokeshire, showing the rural
community engulfed by industry.

Plate 49 Milford Dock, Pembrokeshire: aerial view from the south. The rectangular plan of the old town above the herring market is Greville's original of 1780. The dock gates are from 1874–1908, the ice-factory (far right) from 1901; the mackerel market is in the foreground. Its future is now uncertain as high prices threaten to kill the fishing fleet.

Plate 50   Aerial view of Barry Docks.

had been surrounded by other buildings such as a slaughter-house, stables, gas works, etc., "rendering the neighbourhood very unhealthy". It was, therefore, desirable to have a new school erected more in accordance with the approved plans, but the Duke of Beaufort, being the owner of the whole neighbourhood, would not grant a site in Fee Simple which had to be the case in order to receive Government aid.[15]

The fundamental differences that characterised the educational thinking of the National Society and the British and Foreign Society were subtly displayed in the distinctive architectural style of their respective school buildings. The majority of the National Schools, with their stone walls, dormer-pointed windows (sometimes embellished with stained-glass), doors designed to resemble those of the Anglican churches, and belfries, presented an unmistakable ecclesiastical appearance that was intended to emphasise on the landscape the intimate relation between education and the Episcopal church which the National Society wished to establish (Plate 37). In sharp contrast, however, the British Schools were built of brick, following rather austere or puritanical lines, resembling barns, and the early Non-conformist chapels, with square and oblong windows (Plate 38). These buildings, in turn, represented the British and Foreign Society's separatist attitude, and its complete detachment from the 'National' movement in its schools. There were, however, local variations in the design of school buildings, such as could be found in Dowlais, where the school was built like an Oxonian quadrangle, with large Gothic windows. But here, we had an 'industrial' school, built by Lady Charlotte Guest, wherein was exhibited a greater degree of 'individualism' in design and divorced from obvious sectarian motivation.

The year 1868–9 saw the opening of thirty-four new

[15] E. D. Jones, 'The Journal of William Roberts (Nefydd)', *National Library of Wales Journal*, Vols VII–X.

British schools, including two new schools at Merthyr Tudful and Morriston, each costing £4,500. They were described as "an ornament to those towns" providing for the education of 1,000 scholars. Between 1853 and 1871, the British and Foreign Society alone had built 205 schools in South Wales.[16]

Although the National and British Societies had, together, succeeded in erecting hundreds of school buildings, there were still many parishes in South Wales without school buildings. The School Boards which were set up in consequence of the Education Act of 1870 were instrumental in providing hundreds of new school buildings, more especially after 1891 when elementary education was made free. In 1889 another important step forward had been made in the struggle for educational provision in Wales, when the Welsh Intermediate and Technical Education Acts were passed. The result was that Intermediate Schools, or County Schools, were built in most of the market towns of Wales, where they stood out conspicuously.

By about 1910 the overall achievement in the field of primary and secondary education was visually represented in terms of about 1,300 school buildings, with their playgrounds and school-yards. Thus a new, and highly significant element appeared in the South Wales landscape, both in the rural and industrial scene.

There was not a single building in South Wales at the beginning of the nineteenth century that could be associated with real University education. But in 1827, St David's College, Lampeter, was opened for the education of young men intended for Holy Orders (Plate 39). The college was founded by George IV, at the suggestion of Dr Thomas Burgess who was then Bishop of St David's, incorporated by royal charter and endowed by Act of Parliament. The

[16] Of this total, 68 were located in Glamorgan, 23 in Monmouthshire, 28 in Cardiganshire, 35 in Carmarthenshire, 8 in Breconshire, 18 in Pembrokeshire.

impact the college had on the local landscape at that time must have been spectacular. Even before the foundation stone was laid in 1822 several quarries were opened in Lampeter from which stones were to be procured for the college building.[17] After its completion in 1827, the college was appropriately described as Lampeter's "principal architectural ornament" which, incidentally, had been the means of promoting the prosperity of this "small and straggling" town "consisting for the most part of low houses indifferently built . . .".[18]

Nonconformist sects, too, made provision for the higher education of ministerial candidates. The Independents founded a college in Brecon, while the Calvinistic Methodists established a college at Trefeca in 1842. The Baptists, in turn, built a college at Pontypŵl in 1836, and later at Haverfordwest. The Presbyterian Academy was founded in Carmarthen in 1704 on a non-denominational basis, but it was not until 1840, when it acquired its own buildings, that it could be identified in the landscape.

Nothing significantly visible was then done in the sphere of higher education in South Wales until the opening of the University College of Wales at Aberystwyth in 1872, which was followed in 1883 by the University College of South Wales and Monmouthshire at Cardiff. It was not until 1920 that the University College of Swansea was built to take its place as one of the constituent colleges of the University of Wales which was formed by Royal Charter in 1893.

The architectural quality of these educational buildings cannot be discussed at length here, but it must be said of them that their noble structures, conceived by men steeped in the Classical and Gothic tradition of symmetry and balance, considerably enriched their contiguous landscapes.

[17] John S. Harford, *The Life of Thomas Burgess* (London, 1840), p. 319.
[18] S. Lewis, *Topographical Dictionary of Wales,* Vol. II (London, 1833), p. 319.

For example, the structure of the "College by the sea" at Aberystwyth was, in fact, begun in 1864 to serve originally as an hotel.[19] This project, however, fell through, but despite the repair and rebuilding that were later necessary, particularly after two fires had left what has been described as "a complex pile of most disparate character", it has been claimed by one authority that "the bowed section on the sea front"—originally the hotel bar, later the college chapel!—and the "entrance and stair tower on the rear" are in fact "among the grandest and most boldly plastic fragments produced in this period" and that "neither Oxford nor Cambridge has anything of comparable quality".[20]

The University College of South Wales and Monmouthshire, the largest of the constituent colleges of the University of Wales, found its first home at the Old Infirmary Building in Newport Road, Cardiff. It was not until 1909 that it became identified in the landscape with its permanent home in Cathays Park, where it is flanked by the National Museum of Wales. The expansion that has taken place in the University of Wales since 1945 has resulted in considerable new extensions and new buildings which, in turn, have introduced a still greater variety of architectural taste and design in the respective landscapes at Cardiff, Swansea and Aberystwyth, where familiar and mellowed settings have been transformed almost beyond recognition.

By the end of the nineteenth century, therefore, there stood in the South Wales landscape a kind of network of special buildings representing a national system of education ranging from the primary-school level to the University, and perhaps it would not be an exaggeration to say that they were a tangible expression of "the chief event

[19] This formed part of an ambitious scheme by which Thomas Savin hoped to make Aberystwyth the 'Brighton of Wales'. Savin had provided Wales with much of its railway accommodation.

[20] Henry Russell Hitchcock, *Architecture: Nineteenth and Twentieth Centuries* (Penguin Books, 1958), p. 187.

in the special history of Wales" during the nineteenth century.

In this context reference should be made to two other national institutions located in South Wales, namely the National Library of Wales and the National Museum of Wales, the former occupying a dominant position over-looking the town of Aberystwyth, and the latter in the Civic Centre in Cardiff. Both these institutions received their Charters in 1907. The National Library was constituted with the object of "preserving and maintaining manuscripts, books, pictures and works of all kinds in Welsh or any other Celtic language . . . as well as literary works in any language on any subject which might help to attain the purposes for which the educational institutions of Wales were created, especially the furtherance of higher education, and of literary and scientific research". The National Museum was founded with a view to preserving the material remains of Wales, thus complementing the work of its sister institution, the National Library, by promoting advanced studies in the field of natural history, archaeology, art, and the folk culture of Wales (Plate 43).

We should also mention here the Public Libraries and Mechanics Institutes which appeared throughout the industrial South, and which may be regarded as a part of the main national educational movement. Neither should we forget the Workmen's Halls which, in turn, became centres of cultural and recreational activities. Some of these are still to be seen in the valleys but, like the chapels, many of them have been abandoned or converted for alien uses (Plate 42).

The National Eisteddfod

Visitors to Wales will find, somewhere on the landscape in or near most of the major towns, a fairly imposing circle of standing stones presenting such an appearance of great antiquity as might lead the unsuspecting to associate them with the 'mausoleums' of prehistoric times! They are, in fact, known as the Gorsedd Circles representing, perhaps rather crudely, a ritual which was introduced into the National Eisteddfod of Wales in the early nineteenth century by Iolo Morganwg (Edward Williams, 1747–1826) and purported by him to be connected with the ancient druids. But it was not until about the middle of the nineteenth century that this ritual developed into an indispensable part of the general administration of the National Eisteddfod, as no National Eisteddfod of Wales may be held without a ceremonial Proclamation by the Gorsedd at least a year and a day in advance, and a formal presentation of the first copy of the list of competitions to the Archdruid. This presentation takes place, if the weather permits, in the open air within the Circle of Stones (Plate 44). It is not necessary to expatiate here on the 'mystical' significance of the Gorsedd Circles, and suffice it to say that they are significant features in the Welsh landscape, reminding the observer of another important aspect of the 'national' movements that characterised the history of the Welsh people in the nineteenth century. A uniquely Welsh institution, and not to be confused with the annual International Eisteddfod held at Llangollen, the National Eisteddfod is peripatetic, whereas the other national institutions occupy permanent sites. It is an annual festival invited to different towns in North and South Wales in alternate years, and takes place throughout the first week of August, when competitions are held in vocal and instrumental music, in reciting or composing poetry, and in arts and crafts of every kind, the winners in each contest being awarded the coveted prizes. These events, which are conducted in Welsh, are, at present, held in a transportable pavilion erected on open ground on the outskirts of the host town which is regarded as the 'cultural capital' of Wales during the Eisteddfod week.

SELECT BIBLIOGRAPHY

Archdall, H. K., *St. David's College Lampeter: Its Past, Present, and Future* (Lampeter, 1952).

Board of Education, *Education in Wales, 1827–1947* (Bi-lingual) (London, 1948).

Ellis, E. L., *The University College of Wales Aberystwyth, 1872–1972.* (Cardiff, 1972).

Evans, Leslie Wynne, *Education in Industrial Wales, 1700–1900* (London, 1971).

—— *Studies in Welsh Education . . . 1880–1925* (Cardiff, 1974).

Hilling, J. B., *Cardiff and the Valleys: Architecture in Townscape* (London, 1973).

Jones, Anthony, *Chapel Architecture in Merthyr Tydfil, Glamorgan* (Merthyr Tudful, 1962).

Parry, Thomas and 'Cynan', *The story of the Eisteddfod and the National Eisteddfod and Gorsedd of today* (Bilingual) (Liverpool, n.d.).

Rees, Thomas, *History of Protestant non-Conformity in Wales* (London, 1883).

Religious Census (1851, H.M.S.O.).

Reports of the Commissioners of Enquiry into the State of Education in Wales, 3 vols (London, 1847).

Richards, Thomas, *Religious developments in Wales, 1654–1662* (London, 1923).

Rhŷs, John and Jones, D. Brynmor *The Welsh People . . .* 4th ed. (London, 1906).

Roberts, Gomer M. (ed.), *Hanes Methodistiaeth Calfinaidd Cymru. Cyf. 1. Y Deffroad Mawr* (Caernarfon, 1973).

Williams, David, *A History of Modern Wales* (London, 1950).

6. The landscape of the industrial revolution

Woodlands and their deprivation. Canals, tramroads and railways. Bridges and viaducts. Quarries

Woodlands and their deprivation

THE TERM 'INDUSTRIAL' was not current in the seventeenth century. Even in the early decades of the nineteenth century the terms generally used, in published and manuscript sources relating to Wales, to describe the organisation employed in the processes of converting raw material into more sophisticated articles of consumption were 'works' and 'manufactories'. 'Industrialism', as distinct from the rural industries, came only to certain areas in the uplands and littoral regions of South Wales. It is customary to consider its development almost exclusively from *c.* 1760 onwards, but throughout the greater part of the preceding two hundred years, coal mining and iron, lead and copper smelting had been carried on in various centres on a limited commercial scale.

The Act of Union, 1536, by establishing a single constitution, gave English prospectors a greater sense of security to venture their capital in mining enterprises in Wales, and between the years 1564 and 1568, ironworks multiplied, particularly in Glamorgan, when Sir Henry Sidney, with other Sussex ironmasters, came to the county to exploit its natural resources. Another enterprising ironmaster who came to South Wales during the mid-sixteenth century was Capel Hanbury who established furnaces at Pontypŵl for smelting local ore. Iron smelting soon spread along the northern rim of the coalfield to Blaenavon, Llanelli (Breconshire), and Hirwaun.

The early industrial undertakings in South Wales depended almost entirely on the abundant supplies of timber that were available over extensive areas of the region to obtain the charcoal required for smelting. It has been estimated that the wood from an acre of forest was required to produce three tons of iron. It is no wonder, therefore, that Rice Merrick, the renowned Glamorgan historian from Cottrell, near St Nicholas, who, in 1578, listed about forty-one woods and forests in Glamorgan, observed "many in our dayes, about Iron Milles, were spoyled and consumed".

It should be remembered that in the sixteenth and seventeenth centuries, long before the so-called 'industrial revolution' had gathered momentum, there were approximately forty-five furnaces and forges in the South Wales region producing iron, lead and copper, of varying quality and quantity all of which were dependent on the supply of local timber for fuel, and local water for power to drive the water-mills. They were concentrated, mainly, in the upper- and lower-Taff valley, reaching from Aberdâr and the Cynon Valley to Cardiff. The Melin Griffith works in the lower-Taff valley drew its supplies of fuel from the charcoal produced from the cordwood obtained from the woods of Pentyrch, Llanishen, Cefn Mably, Castleton and Fonmon, and other woods in the Vale of Glamorgan. In the Cynon Valley the consumption of wood from the adjoining countryside had been so ruthless and complete by the end of the eighteenth century that the ultimate effect on the landscape is reflected in the words of Walter Davies who, *c.* 1814, wrote: "Within any convenient distance of the great ironworks, the valleys have been stripped of their grown timber." The extent of the denudation was earlier lamented by a bard who grieved that

> No more the badger's earth we'll sack
> Nor start a buck from the glade;
> No more deer stalking in my day,
> Now they've cut Glyn Cynon's shade.

The neighbourhood of Coety, near Bridgend, Glamorgan, was a centre of early industrial activity where, in 1589, Sir Robert Sidney (later Viscount Lisle and Earl of Leicester) and his wife, Barbara (heiress of the Gamages of Coety), sold to John Thornton and John Savage all the iron 'myne' on their manor in Coety Anglia, together with the timber for the making of 'coles' for ironworks, with liberty "to build a work for smelting, making and casting iron sows, to make iron by forge or furnace or other means". In 1611, Viscount Lisle's forest of Coed-y-mwstwr, of about 500 acres, which stood almost adjacent to the parish of Coety, was let at 4s. per acre. A local bard later lamented the fact that there was neither shelter nor firewood available in Coed-y-mwstwr because of the devastating effect of these ironworks on the landscape—"ni chair klydwr ynghoed mwstwr / na phrenn ar dan, gan waith haearn". A few miles to the north of Coed-y-mwstwr, three forests known as Garth Maelog, Allt Griffith and Talyfan had become, by 1596, "a fair and large sheep leaze",[1] their wood having been sold to the ironworks started by Henry VIII in the Park, near Llantrisant.

The same account follows the early efforts at winning non-ferrous metals. The centres of activity were to be found at Llaneilfyw, in Pembrokeshire, Rhandirmwyn, near Llandovery, Carmarthenshire, where there had been

[1] Rice Lewis, 'A Breviat of Glamorgan'.

workings since medieval times, but by the time of Henry VIII, other workings had been started at Cydweli, Abergwili and Llanelli. Lead mining had been actively developed on the monastic grange of Briwnant in Cwmystwyth, Cardiganshire, from an early date, and so much had the landscape here been modified in consequence, that when Leland visited the area he saw: ". . . on the right hand on a hillside Cl(awdd)-mwyn where hath bene great digging for leade, the melting whereof hath destroid the wooddes that sumtime grew plentifulli thereabout" and that ". . . summe menne suppose that it sesid (ceased) bycause the wood is sore wastith".

In 1583 the tenants of Usk, Caerleon, and Trelech, in Monmouthshire, complained that Sir William Herbert, Henry Morgan and Richard Hanbury, had enclosed 2,000 acres of their commons in the woods Wyeswood, Glascoed and Gweheleg, and were going to fell 60,000 great timber trees. The social consequences of this onslaught on the landscape were likely to "decaie seaven or eight thousand households by taking awaie theire herbage in the said commune and pannage and estovers".[2] By 1596 the woods in Ogmore were "reserved to the ironworks", and much litigation took place concerning the felling of trees for charcoal.

Around the year 1632, the tenants on the manor of Narberth complained that one Barlow "had engrossed the greater part of the woods of Pembrokeshire, that he intended to set up iron works within the woods of the lordship of Narberth, and they had thus lost, not only their rights of common of pasture and estovers, but the whole country was likely to be cleared of timber".

Perhaps the extent of the denudation of woods in South Wales was indicated by George Owen who, in the early

[2] T. I. Jeffreys Jones, *op. cit.*, p. 48. Quoted from *C.S.P.* 140/40 (May 24 Eliz.).

seventeenth century declared of Pembrokeshire that "this Countrie groneth with the generalle complainte of other countries of the decreasinge of wood". Doubtless, the almost limitless demand for charcoal in industrial under-takings was the principal cause for this, and George Owen reminds us of another result, namely the increasing preva-lence of stone buildings, "for that," he says, "I finde in old tyme there was in manye places of the countrye sufficient store of timber to have framed fayer buildings".

It is impossible to contemplate the rapidity with which the South Wales landscape changed under the impact of early industrial enterprises. The felling of thousands of acres of trees in order to maintain industrial processes soon resulted in a growing concern about their dwindling sup-plies. Such was the position in the Aberafan district where, in 1759, it was required that horses carrying charcoal from the woods at Margam should "be muzzled in such manner as they shall not graze or browse the lands or young growth in the woods . . ."

It should be remembered in this context that the grazing of domesticated animals and the processes of cultivation often prevented, in many areas, the regeneration of trees on cleared land, and checked the invasion of open areas by shrubs and trees. In Pembrokeshire, George Owen found "by matter of Recorde that diverse great Corne fieldes were, in tymes past, great fforestes and woodes". About 1620, William Morgan, lord of the manor of Wentsland and Bryngwyn, in Monmouthshire, had sold to Richard Hanbury all the timber on the lands which were not enclosed and used in severalty at the Dissolution. Since the land had been cleared of its timber, "tillage had in-creased and methods improved" by liming the ground for corn. Similarly, at Trelech Grange, in Monmouthshire, tenants said that since they had been selling the timber from their lands to the ironworks, "their lands had been made more profitable and more acres had been devoted to both arable and pasture".

By the end of the eighteenth century it was observed that in Glamorgan generally, where estates had formerly been sold at an inferior price, "in consequence of their being crowded with timber" the situation was such "that a few straggling trees and even coppices of sapplings are to be taken at an exclusive valuation by the purchaser of an estate by auction".

Apart from the demands made upon local arboriculture for the smelting of lead and iron, shipbuilding, along the South Wales coast and in the naval yards at Portsmouth, Plymouth and in Cornwall, caused further inroads into the woodlands of South Wales. For example, in 1729 a number of contracts were drawn up between Bussy Mansell of Margam and the Commissioner for H.M. Navy, to deliver substantial quantities of timber to the Naval stores at Plymouth and Portsmouth. The wider economic significance of such undertakings was reflected on the landscape by the need for "finding, providing and procuring a good and sufficient way or passage through Y Faerdre, in Llangyfelach to the highway near Melinyfran in Llansamlet".

Besides the increasing demands for timber in industry and commerce, it is worth pointing out that in the agrarian economy that predominated in South Wales previous to 1760, the domestic requirements of an increasing population had an indirect effect on the landscape. Furniture and domestic utensils were still made mainly of wood, and contemporary probate wills serve to emphasise the high premium placed on timber as a source of wealth and a medium for settling debts. Testators frequently instructed their executors to fell their timber in order to discharge their debts. William Phillips, for example, a Swansea mercer who died in 1716, had commanded his executors to "fell, fall, all timber growing on [his] demesne lands called Llanerch . . . for and towards the payment of my debts".

The denuding of the countryside of its trees—a process which gained momentum until the exploitation of the South Wales coalfield began—must have transformed the landscape within a fairly wide area along the coastal regions and in certain areas in the uplands. But besides stripping the countryside of its trees, industrial operations were beginning to foul the countryside by leaving in their wake heaps of industrial waste which, in later years, were to disfigure almost beyond recognition the green valleys and mountain slopes of South Wales.

Besides denuding the countryside of its woodlands, iron and lead mines involved digging and quarrying. Hundreds of tons of spoil appeared in the virgin areas where iron mines were sunk. These often appeared like pockmarks on the landscape. At the royal park, near Llantrisant, in 1531, three mines had been sunk, viz. at St Peter's mine with a shaft seven feet wide and forty-two feet deep; St John's mine with a similar dimension and St Thomas's mine just three feet deep. In time hundreds of tons of waste would lie adjacent to these shafts, despoiling the agricultural countryside. Similarly, there had been a considerable prospecting for coal in the parishes of Neath and Baglan in Glamorgan since the seventeenth century. In the parish of Baglan alone there were, in 1696, "severall veines of coale to the number of forty at least in which, from time to time, there hath beene a world of coale dig'd".[3] The search for coal during the first half of the eighteenth century was continued with growing vigour. Between 1700 and 1740 there were seven collieries operating at Briton Ferry and sixteen more at Swansea. That the natural landscape was now being sacrificed, almost indiscriminately, in the search for coal is

[3] Edward Lluyd, *Parochialia* (1697), *Arch. Camb.*, Supplement (July, 1911), p. 33.

seen on lands in Henllan, near Cadoxton-juxta-Neath, where, in 1724, several workmen had been employed for many months "to search for coale in a great many places and in a great many fields closed, and meadows . . .", and in so doing "thirty holes were bored" and "four or five pitts were sunk". With the multiplication of such undertakings and trial borings, the problem of disposing of industrial waste was already present. In the 1730s we find John Popkins, a prominent Swansea coal proprietor was paying 10s. per annum to the Duke of Beaufort "for liberty to lay rubbish near his coal works".

During the second half of the eighteenth century, there was a further growth and expansion of pockets of industrialism in many parts of Glamorgan, especially in the hinterland around Swansea and along the coastal areas between Baglan, Neath and Landore. But the supplies of local timber for fuel began to diminish, and consequently became more expensive. The iron trade declined until it was found that coal was even better for smelting purposes than wood, thanks to the great discovery at Coalbrookdale in England. Therefore, from about 1756 to 1810, most of the South Wales iron works were established, and eventually extended from Blaenavon, in Monmouthshire, to Hirwaun in the northern reaches of the Glamorgan hills.

Within this complex stood Merthyr, which became world famous as a centre of 'industrialism' in all its harsh realities, both in terms of human exploitation, and the desecration of the natural landscape. In 1696, Merthyr was merely "a village with about forty houses". In 1760, the landscape still bore clear evidence that its inhabitants were mainly "hedgers, ditchers, farm labourers, few craftsmen, a shopkeeper, several publicans, the parson and the Squire". There were, then, about ninety-three farms in the entire parish of Merthyr, but almost immediately after the first furnace was built at Cyfarthfa in 1765, twenty of these farms were engulfed by the Cyfarthfa works. The same ruthlessness was meted out at Dowlais, where several farms were converted into agents' houses and warehouses, while many others were 'tipped over' and so undermined were the foundations of others by coal and iron works, that they eventually tumbled down.

It would seem now that the natural state of the countryside was being sacrificed to the requirements of industrial processes. For example, the pre-industrial magnificence of the country surrounding the Gnoll, in Neath, was by the middle of the eighteenth century being cruelly tarnished by the works that lay adjacent to it. When Sir Harbottle Grimston visited Sir Humphrey Mackworth's residence at the Gnoll in 1769, he observed that:

> If I were to consider the beauty of a place abstracted from its trade and manufactory, I should condemn the copper works, the coal mines, and the different engines to get rid of superfluous water, as being too much within view of the house, but as from hence the riches of the place are collected, the man who owes his support to it should look with satisfaction on the source, and rather consider them as appendages on the beauty of his place than blemishes.

Such an attitude reflected a new ethos. Mineral or industrial wealth was at a premium, and was to be vigorously sought at the expense of the natural landscape or of any social cost. The stage was rapidly being set for the indiscriminate raping of the countryside.[4]

In 1804 it was observed that the 'prodigious manufacture' of copper, brass and spelter, erected on the banks of the

---

[4] Moelwyn Williams, 'The economic and social history of Glamorgan, 1660–1760' in *Glamorgan County History* (ed. Glanmor Williams), Vol. IV (Cardiff, 1974), p. 366.

river Tawe yielded such great volumes of smoke that it quite changed the face of the country: "vegetation forsakes the surrounding hills . . . and the scene of barrenness for miles in the exposed direction, evidently declares how deleterious the effects are to vegetable life". And the same smoke from the different manufactories, which at night appear in so many distinct scenes of smoke and flame, "give you an idea of the Solfaterns in the vicinity of Vesuvius".

Canals, tramroads and railways

The South Wales canal system was, in the main, the creation of the last decade of the eighteenth century. Canals were constructed in order to provide a more expeditious means of conveying iron and coal from the upland areas to the sea-ports which had previously been reached by pack horses and horse-drawn vehicles, moving along roads that were still difficult, and often dangerous and perilous to traverse. The canals ushered in a new civilisation in South Wales (Fig. 19).

The impact made on the South Wales landscape by the construction of canals must have been tremendous by bringing, as they did to some areas, stretches of water courses where none had previously existed, and to others additional stretches of water running parallel with unnavigable rivers. One observer, commenting on the South Wales canal system in 1804, thought "that time will come when our posterity will smile at the plan of making an artificial river by the side of a natural one", rather than "rendering those which nature has made fit for all the purposes". In fact, efforts had been made to make navigable the estuaries of the Tawe, Neath and Taff, but the results were inadequate. Small canals leading from local collieries and limeworks had been built in South Wales long before 1790. Indeed, between 1695 and 1700, Sir Humphrey Mackworth had been

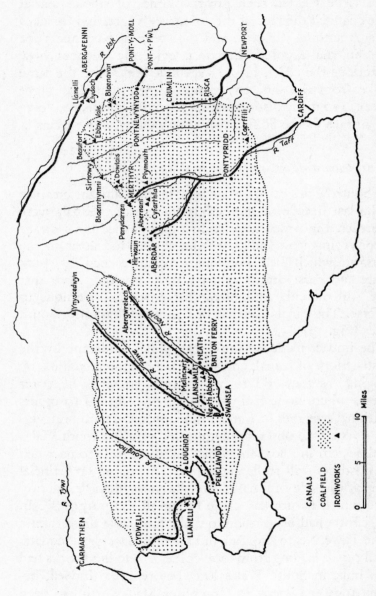

Fig. 19. The canals that served the South Wales iron and coal industries from 1789 until the coming of the railways.

194

forced to build a tidal cut 18 to 20 feet wide and 300 yards long, from a pill in the river Neath in order to enable small craft to navigate to within 400 feet of the Melyn lead and copper works. The first authentic canal in South Wales may have been built by Thomas Kymer from Little Gwendraeth River, near Cydweli, to the Great Forest at Pwll Llygod in Carmarthenshire, following an Act of 1766 authorising its construction. But the great age of canals in South Wales did not dawn until 1790.

Our canals have not been sufficiently considered in relation to the landscape changes that followed in the wake of their construction. The building of a major canal involved considerable modifications to its immediate surroundings in the landscape. In 1790, an Act was passed authorising the building of a navigable canal from Merthyr to Cardiff (later known as the Glamorganshire Canal), a distance of twenty-six miles. It was to run through the parishes of Llanfabon, Eglwysilan, Whitchurch, Llandaff, St John and St Mary in Cardiff, to Penarth Point. In its construction the proprietors were empowered to make such reservoirs, feeders, aqueducts, and set up such engines and machines as were necessary for supplying the canal and reservoirs with water. They were also empowered "to bore, dig, cut, trench, sought, get, remove, and lay earth, stone, soil, clay, rubbish, trees, beds of gravel or sand, or any other matters or things . . .". It was necessary, too, to "make, build, erect and set up, in or upon the said canal or adjoining lands, and to repair, support, vary or alter such and so many bridges, piers, arches, tunnels, aqueducts, sluices, locks, wharfs and quays, etc." as would be necessary. The extent of land to be taken or used for the canal and towing paths, and the ditches, drains and fences to separate them from adjoining lands was not to exceed twenty-six yards in breadth. Such an undertaking represented an unprecedented interference with the natural landscape. This canal took four years to complete, and was crossed by more than forty bridges; it had forty locks throughout its twenty-six miles, eighteen of which were within a one mile stretch, and eleven others within a short distance of a quarter of a mile. At Cardiff it entered the river Taff near Penarth Point where it communicated with a large lock admitting ships of 200 tons to the town's quays that had been built on its bank.

Similar modifications of the landscape were authorised in the construction of all the South Wales canals, though in varying degrees. The Monmouthshire Canal, completed in 1792, ran from Newport to Pontypŵl, following the course of the Afon Lwyd across the Usk Valley at Abergafenni. It was later extended from this point to Brecon. The Brecon–Abergafenni Canal extended for thirty-three miles, and was completed in December 1811 at a cost of £170,000. Its construction involved the building of a tunnel 220 yards long at its junction with the Monmouthshire Canal: it was crossed by 62 stone and 14 wooden bridges, and had 11 aqueducts, 31 culverts, and 185 locks of 180 tons of water each. Travelling on horseback along a considerable stretch of this canal in 1797, one visitor has recorded, "we were frequently obstructed by the bridges which are placed at different distances, and under whose arches we were forced to ride".

In 1791 the Neath Canal was begun, and was projected up the Vale of Neath from the Brickfield near Melincrythan Pill to Pont-Neath-Vaughan in the upper extremity of the Vale. It was later extended south to Briton Ferry, to connect with a "convenient shipping place" built for loading vessels with coal. This canal was thirteen miles long, with sixteen locks. Soon afterwards another canal was built along the Tawe, from Swansea to Ystradgynlais in the Breconshire hills—a distance of sixteen miles.

The construction of canals and the sea-port terminals

they served constituted the first major adjustments to the landscape that man deemed necessary to lubricate the process of industrial development in South Wales. The masters of industry were consistent in their policy of deliberately moulding the landscape to serve their works in the essential process of distribution. With the opening of the Glamorgan Canal in 1794, many people saw the dawn of a new era, and hoped that "with the iron treasures of our hills, to grow daily more truly rich than the Spaniards are with their mines in Mexico and Peru", while others genuinely lamented the building of the canals. On visiting the Briton Ferry region in 1804, one observer remarked, "But the admirer of nature will lament that the privacy and silence which tend to produce and enhance the pleasurable effects of rural scenery, are now invaded and destroyed by the continuation of the Neath Canal, but for an easy delivery of coals for exportation." Yet, man's interference with the natural landscape was justified according to the same observer, because "it must be acknowledged that beauty should be subordinate to utility".

Transport by land and water continued to complement each other until the railway age dawned. Production, however, tended to outpace the capacity of the means of transportation as provided by the canals.

The work of the canals was generally supplemented by tramroads and railroads. In many places, however, tramroads had appeared on the landscape long before the canals. One of the earliest records we have of surface tramroads or waggon ways refers to the wooden railway constructed *c.* 1697 by Sir Humphrey Mackworth leading from his coal works in Neath (Plate 47) on what was formerly "a pool of dirt and water . . . made [into] a good and firm way . . . for all sorts of carriages . . .". Along this track Mackworth experimented with the novel idea of attaching sails to the wagons, which a contemporary described as "the wonder of the world" with "one horse doing the work of ten and, if the wind was good, even twenty". Thomas Yalden (1670–1736) was so impressed with this 'wonder' that he sang the praises of Mackworth thus:

> Thy fam'd inventions, Mackworth, must adorn
> The miner's art, and make the best return.
> Thy speedy sails, and useful engines, show
> A genius richer than the mines below . . .
> The winds, thy slaves, their useful succour join,
> Convey thy ore, and labour at thy mine.

Chauncy Townsend was granted authority by the Duke of Beaufort in 1750 to construct waggon ways over the highways and wastes within the Manor of Kilvey. In 1755 another waggon way was constructed over Mynydd Bach Common in the parish of Llanrhidian in Gower for carrying coal. Most of the early tramways were wooden.

In the year 1791 there was not a single yard of iron railroad on the South Wales landscape. By September 1811, the completed railroad connected with canals, collieries, iron and copper works in Monmouthshire, Glamorgan and Carmarthenshire amounted to nearly 200 miles. A railway from Swansea to Mumbles (claimed to have been the first passenger railroad in the country) was opened in 1804. It ran a distance of about five miles along the sea-shore, on which coals and limestone were brought down, and provisions were taken back. A car upon tram wheels, carrying about sixteen or eighteen persons, ran twice a day during the summer, each passenger paying a shilling fare.

The canal system in South Wales had spurred the ironmasters and coal owners to build an extensive network of tramroads leading to and from the more inaccessible places to link with canals at convenient points. They were also constructed over wide areas within the confines of the collieries and ironworks, and meandered from these works to adjacent quarries. A French traveller passing through Swansea on his way to Tenby in 1810 "crossed several iron railways leading from foundries and coal-mines in the country to the sea". These railways were at first iron grooves, along which ran the cast-iron wheels of the trams. Later, the grooves were placed on the circumference of the wheels, and the rails became a mere ledge of iron upon which stones and other impedimenta could not lodge. It has been estimated that by about 1830 there was a network of 350 miles of tramroads in South Wales. The South Wales industries were entirely dependent on the canals and their subsidiary rail-roads for transportation to the sea-ports.

One important and historically significant stretch of rail-road we must note in passing is that constructed by William Crawshay from his Penydarren works to link with the Glamorgan canal at Quakers Yard, a distance of nine miles lower down the valley. It was along this line that Richard Trevithick, on 21st February, 1804, successfully ran his steam locomotive whilst drawing a load of ten tons of iron, and seventy persons. This, it is claimed, was the first steam locomotive in the world to run on rails. It was also the beginning of developments that were eventually to render the canals obsolete. Indeed, the traffic along the canals reached its peak between 1840 and 1850.

The first major railway in South Wales was the Taff Vale Railway, opened in 1841, running from Cardiff to Merthyr. This line was followed, in 1846, by a railway connecting the Llynfi valley and Porthcawl, and another stretch linking Swansea with the Amman Valley. In 1850 the South Wales Railway was opened and ploughed through the landscape from Gloucester to Swansea. The line was further extended to Carmarthen, and had reached Haverfordwest by the end of December 1852. There were, by now, about 300 miles of railway visible in the South Wales landscape, all of which connected, directly or indirectly, the iron and coal producing areas with the ports. A new pattern of communication lines was also emerging. For whereas the old lines of communication tended to run from west to east, the new routes ran from north to south. This trend was further emphasised from 1860 onwards when there was a further filling in of the landscape by additional railway tracks. During this period, one of the more far-reaching projects was that undertaken by the Barry Railway Company in 1888 in constructing a complete system of docks and railways to serve them (Fig. 20). The main railway extended from Barry to Trehafod, in the Rhondda Valley, where it connected with the Taff Vale Railway. Several branch lines fanned out from the main trunk line, the most important being the Vale of Glamorgan Railway which ran a distance of twenty miles through the picturesque vale to the junction at Bridgend, where it linked up with the main line to London, Swansea and Milford, and with the branch lines serving the Llynfi, Ogmore and Garw valleys. The impact made on the landscape by the Barry Railway Company's undertakings may be judged from the fact that it eventually owned 86 miles of main and branch railways, besides over 140 miles of sidings connected therewith, of which nearly 100 miles were around the docks at Barry itself, and occupied an area of over half a million square yards, or about 104 acres. Such dramatic changes in the landscape around Barry were matched only by the spectacular changes in the social scene. In the year 1881, for example, the population of Barry was barely 100 persons, occupying a few scattered cottages, whereas in 1891, it had risen to 13,000, and by 1921 it had reached a total of 38,900. The number of houses and other buildings necessary to sustain such a phenomenal increase of population transformed what had been a completely agricultural landscape, into one predominantly urban and commercial. But these events were only an epitome of the changes which had

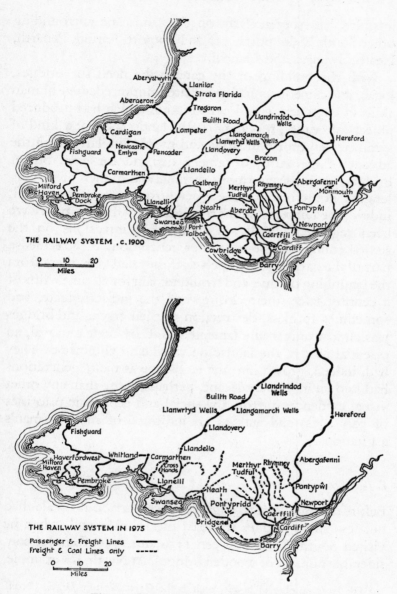

THE RAILWAY SYSTEM , c. 1900

0   10   20
Miles

THE RAILWAY SYSTEM IN 1975

Passenger & Freight Lines ———
Freight & Coal Lines only - - - - -

0   10   20
Miles

Fig. 20. The railways of South Wales.

intruded less spectacularly on the landscape surrounding other South Wales ports such as Newport, Cardiff, Penarth, Neath, Swansea and Llanelli.

With the building of the canals, the need for bridges, locks, and aqueducts had stimulated unprecedented human skills in engineering and construction which had produced objects of beauty, revealing on the landscape a new kind of symmetry and form in stone and metal. Similarly, with the advent of the railways came a demand for even bigger bridges, viaducts, enormous cuttings and tunnels of varying lengths, not to mention the signal boxes, crossing gates and, indeed, the railway stations themselves.[5] All these must have been regarded initially as abominable intrusions on the settled countryside, but to later generations they seemed a part of the natural landscape—as if they had been there from the beginning of time, and would remain for all time. Almost a century later, their closure and the indiscriminate, and sometimes ruthless, destruction of their tracks and bridges was almost universally lamented as if, by their removal, an essential part of the landscape was being eliminated. They had, indeed, grown into the landscape as many generations had known it. The landscape, perhaps, more than any other visual evidence, mirrors the social and economic priorities of past ages, and acts as an indicator of modern man's aspirations.

Bridges and viaducts

Before the middle of the eighteenth century South Wales had but few stone bridges to boast of. John Leland, when he visited South Wales between 1536 and 1539, found a considerable number of wooden bridges. At Neath, for example,

[5] The large number of hotels, such as the Great Western Hotel, Cardiff, built by the railway companies provide further evidence of the impact that the Railway Age had on the appearance of South Wales towns.

the bridge across the river was of timber—"Ponte Castelle Nethe of tymbre"—while the river Taff was crossed in four places by wooden bridges. Of the forty Glamorgan bridges referred to by him, twenty-three were wooden structures, and seventeen were of stone. The importance of roads and bridges was reflected in contemporary wills. Roger Seys, of Boverton, was one of many in the sixteenth century who left "ffower pounds towards the reparacion of the bridge and the church way from the hamlet of Boverton to Llantwit".

With the development of trade and commerce which occurred during the Tudor period, and the increased traffic that followed the advent of industry the old bridges were found wholly inadequate, and sporadic efforts were made to improve them. The bridges of South Wales began to display real elegance about the middle of the eighteenth century, when a self-taught genius named William Edwards brought the art of bridge-building to a high degree of perfection. Born in 1719 at Eglwysilan, Glamorgan, Edwards acquired an unusual expertise in building, which earned the admiration of his fellow craftsmen. By 1755, after three previous unsuccessful attempts, this local genius had succeeded in building over the river Taff what was regarded as the world's largest single-arch bridge (Plate 45). This bridge, called Pont-y-tŷ-pridd (now Pontypridd), had a span or chord of 140 feet, and stood 35 feet above the river and gracing a landscape described by Francis Grose in 1775 as "nothing . . . more picturesque . . . environed on all sides by woody hills, cornfields, most luxuriant trees, and some neat cottages . . .". Edwards's fame spread rapidly, and he was soon engaged in building a large and handsome bridge over the river Usk, at the town of Usk, which was followed by other bridges such as a three-arched bridge at Swansea, a single-arched bridge at Pontardawe with a span of eighty feet; Betws bridge, Carmarthenshire; Pont-dolau-hirion, across the Tywi, about two miles outside Llanymddyfri on the road to Lampeter; Morriston bridge across the Tawe, Aberafan bridge, Pontycymmer bridge, and the bridge over the Wye at Glasbury, near Gelli, Breconshire.

With the intensification of coal mining in the valleys, and the consequent need to improve the lines of communication between the pit-heads and the ports, a new network of railways developed on the South Wales landscape, more especially after 1850. Many railways had to extend into seemingly impenetrable regions and in order to overcome the many natural obstacles, the construction of formidable bridges and viaducts was of paramount importance. New demands were thus made on engineering skills, and in this respect, perhaps the finest accomplishment of its day was the Crumlin viaduct (Plate 46).

A noble piece of engineering, the Crumlin viaduct was constructed entirely of iron to carry a branch line of the Newport–Abergafenni and Hereford Railway over the Crumlin valley in order to complete the connection with the Taff Vale, and other railways of the district. The main valley was over 1,000 feet wide, and 200 feet from the bottom of the level at which the railway ran. Adjoining this, was another valley 500 feet wide and about 100 feet high, and separated from the former only by a projection in the rock. When the viaduct was eventually constructed, and opened on 1st June, 1857, its total height from the level of the rails to the water beneath was 198 feet. A noteworthy fact indicating the magnitude of the structure is that eleven tons of paint were used in providing two coats on the ironwork. The Crumlin viaduct is no more, but with its savage demolition early in 1966 a construction of rare magnificence disappeared from the landscape.

Other viaducts of different dimensions were built where gorges had to be crossed by rail. Built of stone, from local quarries, they invariably introduced an element of architectural elegance to many rugged and unattractive parts such as at Pontrhydyfen near Port Talbot and Cefn-coed-y-cymer near Merthyr; sometimes they added to the natural scenery. An outstanding example of this is the picturesque viaduct which spans Porthkerry Park in the Vale of Glamorgan, where it forms a vital link in the once important Vale of Glamorgan Railway which served the collieries in the West and the agricultural districts between Bridgend and Barry. It still remains as a monument to the great engineering skills of its builders who took from 1894 to 1897 to complete it. It stands 110 feet at its highest point and comprises 18 piers spanning 1,125 feet across the valley.

Quarries

Although the industrial development of South Wales after about 1760 led to a transfiguration of many areas by the building of canals, bridges, railroads, and the proliferation of industrial buildings and human habitations, large sections of the natural landscape were being hacked and blasted away in order to provide the raw materials required for their construction. Thus numerous quarries in the Pennant Grit rock in the upper divisions of the coal measures were exploited as fiercely as were the coal seams beneath them and they still stand out on the landscape as evidence of man's savage and indiscriminate exploitation of his physical environment (Plate 54). The same applied to the agricultural landscape, more particularly after the sixteenth century,[6] when stone was being used increasingly in the construction of farm buildings. Thus on many farmlands may be seen old disused quarry pits, now grown into grassy or wooded hollows, that once provided the stones to build the local farmhouses, cottages, and other agricultural buildings.

The industrial quarries may be seen more especially in

[6] George Owen, *Description of Penbrokeshire, 1603 (Cymmr. Rec. Soc.*, 1892), p. 40.

such places as Pontypridd, Craig-yr-hesg, Cilfynydd, Treforest, Llanbradach, Nelson, and Quaker's Yard. Again in the Vale of Neath, Cwar Mawr Ynys Arwed (The Great Quarry of Ynys Arwed) and the Clwydau Quarry are prominent features of the local landscape, the latter being particularly noted for its echoes "even to the yapping of the dogs in the Vale below". Another quarry known as Cwar-y-capel provided the stones from which were built the majority of the pre-1939 houses at Resolven.[7]

The Trias rocks are quarried in the neighbourhood of Bridgend, the best known being the 'Quarella Stone'—a fine, even-grained calcareous sandstone, varying from a white to a pale green colour. Lias beds are quarried at Penarth, Cogan, Barry, Leckwith, Cowbridge, in Glamorgan, and at Liswerry, near Newport, Monmouthshire. The variety known as 'Sutton Stone' is one of the best stones in the Cardiff region. The quarries in the Lias at Lower Penarth, Bridgend, Stormy Down, are chiefly for lime and cement. Limestone for steel and cement are still quarried in vast quantities at South Cornelly, near Porthcawl, and on the coast at the famous Aberthaw limestone quarries. Quarrying for road metal chippings is carried on very extensively near Conwil Elfed, in the Gwili Valley, Carmarthenshire, with savage effects on the local landscape.

We must not, however, look upon our quarries merely as scars on the landscape but also as the sources of a variety of building stones the quality and colour of which have been important factors in determining the appearance and character of our towns and villages. In the Rhondda valley ninety per cent of the houses built in the last century were constructed of local Pennant sandstone.[8] Indeed, the dominating feature in most of the coalfield valleys is the mono-

[7] D. Rhys Phillips, *The History of the Vale of Neath* (Swansea, 1925), pp. 312–14.

[8] E. D. Lewis, *The Rhondda Valleys* (London, 1963), pp. 143–4.

tonously dull greyish colour of the Pennant stone in the houses which climb the hillsides, row upon row, in disorder and congestion, presenting a 'specialised landscape' universally associated with the South Wales coalfield.

SELECT BIBLIOGRAPHY

Davies, D. J., *Economic History of South Wales Prior to 1800* (Cardiff 1933).

Davies, Margaret, *Wales in Maps* (Cardiff, 1958).

Hadfield, E. C R., *The Canals of South Wales and the Border*, 2nd ed. (Cardiff, 1967).

Hilton, K. J. (ed.), *The Lower Swansea Valley Project* (London, 1967).

Humphrys, Graham, *Industrial Britain: South Wales* (Newton Abbot, 1972).

Jones, Arthur Grey, *A History of Ebbw Vale.* [Risca] (1970).

Lewis, W. J., *Lead-mining in Wales* (Cardiff, 1967).

Lloyd, John, *The Early History of the Old South Wales Iron Works, 1760–1840* (London, 1906).

Rees, D. Morgan, *Mines, Mills and Furnaces* (London, 1969).

Rees, William, *Industry Before the Industrial Revolution*, 2 vols (Cardiff, 1968).

7. The landscape of towns

The early towns. Planned towns. Industrial towns. Port towns. Lighthouses. Resort towns. Promenade piers

The early towns

NO PRE-INDUSTRIAL town in South Wales is of Welsh origin. The Romans, although they developed a formidable system of military forts and camps linked together by roads, it was at one point only, at Caerwent (Venta Silurum), that they seem to have established a town. With the final withdrawal of the Roman legions sometime in the fifth century, the town of Caerwent declined and finally decayed.

The making of boroughs in South Wales certainly originated with the Norman Conquest, and, as far as we know, the nature of the native economy up to that time hardly required the existence of towns. There were, however, three elements in the early settlement pattern of Wales which acted as pre-urban nuclei, namely, the fortified Roman camps, the monastic settlements of Celtic missionaries, and the native *maesdrefi*—the primary settlements of the Welsh princes. Of these elements, it would appear that the Roman forts were in fact the most important in providing a base for some degree of continuity, but only to a limited degree. Roman and Norman strategic centres have only in few instances continued to have an urban association. Brecon and Carmarthen, for example, have for special reasons continued to this day to be urban centres. We know that the Normans built their castles at the same strategic points as many of the pre-existing Roman camps, and it was around the Norman castles that urban activity in South Wales eventually developed. But one would look in vain for continuity on actual urban sites on the landscape. Perhaps Cardiff is the best example of direct continuity of site, and Caerleon, perhaps, the only example where the Roman fort had any influence on the later development of the town. The Roman fort at Y Gaer, in Brecon, is sited nearly three miles away from the present town, whereas modern Neath grew around the Norman Castle, sited a mile away from the Roman Fort (Nidum) and actually on the opposite side of the river.

Towns can only prosper if their economic functions can be sustained permanently, and when the causes which originally brought them into existence languish and disappear, so do the towns themselves decay and wither. In the same way we saw whole villages deserted, and in some areas completely vanished. No matter whether the original cause for founding a town was religious, military, political, or economic, it can only continue to fulfil an urban function if it is set within a living countryside. It was mainly for economic reasons that Llandaff had to give way to Cardiff as a centre of urban life, and Llanbadarn Fawr (Cardiganshire) to Aberystwyth.

Again, in the sixteenth century, Leland found that the old town of Cydweli was nearly "al desolited" whilst the new town of Cydweli which was "three times as [bigge] as the old" in turn declined: for "Sins the haven [of] Vedraith Ve[han] decaied," says Leland, "the new toune is sore de[caied]". Meanwhile we find that "Cairmardine [ha]the incresid sins Kidweli Havin decaied". It was not until a new economic base was provided during the industrial era that

Cydweli again revived and developed into an important industrial centre fulfilling an urban function.

Llanstephan castle, which stands on the opposite side of the estuary to Cydweli, was ideally placed for guarding the "estuarine highway" to Carmarthen. But although it commanded a rich agricultural area, and was in medieval times, a centre of maritime activity, it failed to develop into a town. Its position was awkward and the tides difficult, and Carmarthen, some eight miles up river, was already bridged and able to facilitate river and road traffic. Instead, Llanstephan developed into a small resort, a retreat for nineteenth-century middle-class families. The castle lost its significance, and the Plas, an eighteenth-century porticoed mansion, succeeded it. The landscape, too, took on a new appearance, for the new landlords, who settled there, planted their oaks, beeches, and rows of Scotch pine to add to the outward splendour of their residences.

The process of early town building in South Wales was directly related to the policy of castle building within its several Norman lordships—i.e. the bastide town. George Owen, the renowned Pembrokeshire historian described the process thus:

> And the saied lordes, att their first coming to those lordships by conquest, espyenge out the firtile partes in ech countrye, builded their castles for themselves and townes for their owne soldiors and countreymen wch came wth them to remayne neere about them as their guarde and to be allwayes ready to keep under such of the countrye inhabitants as wold offere to rebell . . . and by this meanes all the townes and castles in most part of Wales . . . were first built.

Throughout the medieval period, Welsh towns survived mainly upon the trade and commerce sustained by an agricultural society, despite the small non-agricultural undertakings that were carried on in many parts, more particularly in the Swansea and Neath areas. In short, the medieval towns were principally small market towns set, as one would expect, at convenient and strategic points along the South Wales lowland and coastal regions from Chepstow in the east to Aberystwyth in the west.

Some of these market towns, such as Newport, Cardiff, Aberafan, Neath and Llanelli, later developed into large industrial and port towns. Others, such as Bridgend and Cowbridge in Glamorgan, Llandeilo, Llandovery, in Carmarthenshire, and Tregaron and Lampeter in Cardigan, have survived mainly as market towns supported by agricultural and ancillary industries.

Planned towns

There are but few so-called planned towns in South Wales, that is, towns that originated as deliberate settlements. There are, perhaps, three such towns that may be noted here, namely Milford, in Pembrokeshire, Aberaeron in Cardiganshire, and Morriston, near Swansea, in Glamorgan. Milford and Aberaeron were 'planned', with a view to exploiting their geographical positions as sea-ports, by private individuals who had capital to invest in such ventures, while Morriston was planned to provide enlightened accommodation for industrial workers.

In 1800, Aberaeron was merely a low-lying tract with a creek or inlet near the sea. In 1807 the Aberaeron Harbour Act was passed, and the town of Aberaeron was born. It came into existence because the Rev. Alban Thomas Jones (who later adopted the surname Gwynne) saw the commercial potentialities of a harbour, and envisaged a centre of trade serving an area extending to Tregaron, Lampeter, Pumsaint, Llanwrda, Llandovery, etc.

The harbour was completed by 1811, and building sites were granted by landowners on ninety-nine year leases. All building operations had to follow a prescribed plan and design, which account for the grid-iron plan of the early Aberaeron streets, and the conspicuous larger corner and centre houses in the street. For some years before the advent of the railway, the town of Aberaeron developed according to plan into a busy commercial centre, and the landscape filled in as more and more entrepreneurs were attracted to the area. Rows of houses were speedily built, and business houses were soon established, manufactories producing edge tools were set up, and three shipbuilding yards were established. In the course of forty years, it was said that from fifty to seventy ships were built in the Aberaeron yards in which "almost every family had a share, as they had in herring nets".

The coming of the steamships and the railways eventually sounded the death knell of Aberaeron as a flourishing port. With the decline, and ultimate cessation, of its maritime trade, Aberaeron stagnated, and the town has remained relatively static ever since. Here, then, at Aberaeron, we have an example of a nineteenth-century 'planned' town which failed to develop, and declined rapidly after the economic base upon which its survival depended was removed by the force of events.[1]

Milford, in Pembrokeshire, came into existence through the individual endeavours of Charles Francis Greville (1749–1809) who had inherited the estate around Hubberston and Pill from his uncle Sir William Hamilton (1730–1803) who had succeeded in 1790 to have a Private Act passed through Parliament to develop the areas around Hubberston and Pill by building quays, docks, piers and roads. The implementation of these plans were, however, entrusted to Greville (Plate 49). The site earmarked for development was

[1] *Ceredigion,* Vol. IV (7–13).

carefully chosen on the finest point in the haven, and Greville proceeded to the ground plan of the streets designed by Louis Barallier of Toulon, who had been engaged as designer and architect. Their layout followed a pattern of parallel lines, running due east and west, in the direction of the shore, having short streets of communication intersecting them at right angles. The lower street was to be formed of one row of houses fronting the water. The new town was called Milford.

Malkin, who visited Milford about 1806, made the following observation: "The new town is making rapid progress; and the style of building in general is far superior to what this part of the country has hitherto been accustomed to adopt. Whether the commercial visions, which magnify the future Milford into a rivalship with our first trading towns, are likely to be realised, I pretend not to conjecture. . . ."

By 1815 the new town of Milford consisted of about 160 houses, some of them elegant structures, including a chapel built and endowed by Greville, occupying a distinctively planned grid-iron core, around which more recent buildings have been erected. Greville invited a group of American Quakers to settle there and develop South Sea whaling, and also induced the Navy Board to commission the building of frigates on the site. Its original function, however, was not wholly realised. Fishing smacks began to use the docks originally intended for use for South Sea whaling and later as a Naval dockyard, and step by step Milford became a fishing port, the foremost in South Wales. The chequered story of the changing fortunes of the port has been fully related by Sir J. F. Rees, who brought the story up to the 1950s. In more recent years, however, Milford has become a vast oil port where four oil company terminals and three refineries have been established on the shores of the haven, as well as a gigantic oil-fired power station. The impact on the landscape of current developments may be gauged from the fact that along its shores there are facilities for handling, annually, some 19 million net register tons of shipping carrying upwards of 40 million tons of oil. Moreover, some £200,000,000, has been spent on the development of industry directly dependent on the port. The natural advantages of Milford Haven have been known for centuries, and even Shakespeare asked (in *Cymbeline*, Act III, Scene 2) "how Wales was made so happy t'inherit such a Haven"? The town, however, was planted there as a speculative venture which, in a sense, failed; and had it not been for the alternative economic uses to which the haven could be put within the framework of modern economic requirements, Milford, like Aberaeron, would have stagnated.

Another example of a deliberately planned settlement was that which grew up at Morriston, near Swansea (Fig. 21), and was so named after Sir John Morris, a progressive and enlightened proprietor of extensive copper works and collieries in the Swansea area. He realised the importance of human labour and of providing 'civilised' accommodation for his own employees. The first step was taken about 1750 when he built a "Tennement House or Flats for workers" sometimes referred to as Morris Castle—a "lofty castellated mansion" accommodating about forty families. mostly colliers. This edifice was, perhaps, the first workers' flats in Wales, if not in the country, and its remains are still visible on the landscape above Landore and Plasmarl.

In 1790, however, Morris began building a new town according to a plan furnished by William Edwards, the renowned bridge-builder who had for twenty years or more superintended the construction of Sir John Morris's copper works. The land upon which the town was to be built was in the Fee of Trewyddfa near Nant Felin, upon which stood a farm, but from 1790 to 1796, this rural landscape was transformed.

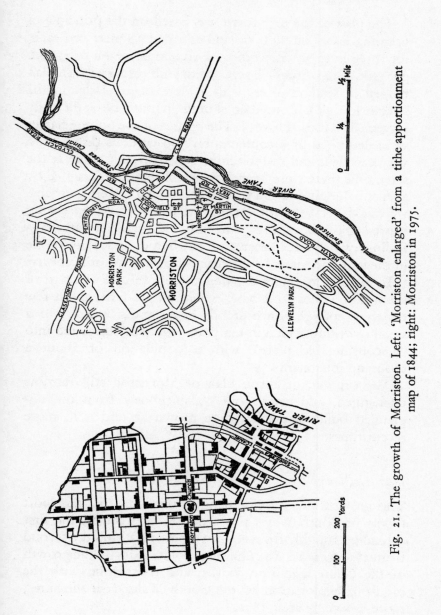

Fig. 21. The growth of Morriston. Left: 'Morriston enlarged' from a tithe apportionment map of 1844; right: Morriston in 1975.

The plan of the new town was based on the principle of granting leases on plots of land of about a square rod each, for three lives, or fifty years, at an annual rental of 7s. 6d. per plot. The workers' houses were built on a grid-iron plan ranged in straight lines, with a view to regularity in the streets lest "their number should in time be sufficiently increased to form a town". The houses of the poorer classes were described by a contemporary observer as being "of a very excellent and commodious construction" while at the same time there were "very respectable edifices occupied by agents belonging to the works, and others". Here, perhaps, we find in embryo the feelings of class distinctions being expressed on the landscape in early industrial settlements— feelings which later became much sharper and more subtle in the larger industrial complexes of the nineteenth century.

In Morriston, therefore, we have an example of a part of the South Wales landscape, where only a farm and a few thatched cottages once stood, being transformed into a small township which in ten years had been converted into "a considerable place" with a population of about a thousand inhabitants.

The original grid-iron plan of Morriston still remains unchanged, and stands out conspicuously from the un-planned buildings which have grown around it in more recent times.

Industrial towns

The growth and development of the industrial and port towns of South Wales proceeded in two stages, the first extending roughly from about 1760 to 1850, and the second from 1850 to 1921. The first stage coincided with the growth of the Glamorgan iron works, and the second with the vigorous exploitation of the South Wales coal measures, more especially after 1870.

The initial impact of early industrialism on the unspoiled landscape of the South Wales valleys must have been violent and cataclysmic. Farms and farmhouses were quickly despoiled, and the industrial scene which rapidly emerged displayed on the landscape the most striking evidence in the whole country of the squalor and depredation that accompanied the haphazard urban growth following the almost maniacal appropriation of the bountiful supplies of ironstone and coal that lay beneath the green pastures of the Welsh hills and valleys. The most representative towns of the first phase of the industrialisation of South Wales are Merthyr Tudful, Dowlais, Ebbw Vale, Rhymney and Tredegar. During this early period the production and distribution of iron dominated the social and economic scene in the upland regions of Glamorgan and Monmouthshire, when, "A dozen conspicuous families ruled the valleys with rods of iron, disembowelled their depths of their vital energies, piled into the sky pyramidical heaps overtopping the ridges of hills, black monuments of the benificent rules of the modern Pharaohs".[2] It was in such a setting that the 'iron' towns developed.

The landscape of the industrial towns presented, on a wider and more intricately knit canvas, the same kind of visual evidence of social distinctions as were to be seen on the rural landscape. In the countryside the numerous farm labourers' cottages and farmhouses lay in the shadow of the baronial castles and stately houses which stood out in marked contrast, both in dimension and design. The parish church, too, which was invariably associated with the patronage of the castle and the mansion, further emphasised, visually, the presence and power of the 'establishment'. The small Nonconformist chapels that intruded on the rural scene were normally associated with the small farmers and the yeoman class. The social dichotomy that characterised

[2] Thomas Jones, *Leeks and Daffodils* (Newtown, 1942).

Welsh society was still more conspicuous in the industrial towns where large houses, built by the ironmasters for themselves and their managers and agents, were almost invariably sited away from the main concentration of the workers' houses. Cyfarthfa Castle, and Dowlais House in Merthyr, Nant-y-glo House, Ebbw Vale House, to mention only a few, were as conspicuous, if not as formidable, in the industrial settlements as the castles had been in the Normanised coastal regions and, in a sense, represented on the landscape the same kind of feudal relationship.

The pattern of settlement was first dictated by the immediate requirements of the ironmasters, namely, an adequate and constant supply of human labour, planted within easy distance to operate the works. Consequently the nucleus, or core, of the settlement would be around the furnace or mine, with the workers' houses located in close proximity to these centres of production. Writing about his impression of Merthyr during the second decade of the nineteenth century, one observer stated that:

> nothing can be more irregular, or more offensive to the eye . . . than the arrangement of the streets and houses. Indeed, it is scarcely correct to say that there is in the place what can properly merit the name of a street. The houses were originally erected in the situation which best suited the convenience of the proprietor of the ground, without any regard to plan, or to the situations of other similar buildings. As the increasing population called for new erections, the same method was successively followed, until the present collection of houses arose, spreading over an immense extent of ground in every possible direction, communicating with each other for the greater part by narrow lanes and avenues, which are generally choked with filth.

It is interesting to note also that the houses of the proprietors whose "first consideration would be convenience" were built near the works. Penydarren house, for instance, occupied in 1818 by Mr Crawshay, was "the only one that aspires to elegance of structure and pleasantness of situation", and was placed "in the midst of the works, and close to the principal forge, the hammers of which are continually in action". Other proprietors and managers had, likewise, "placed their residence in the situations best adapted for the supervision of their concerns".[3]

As the population increased, additional houses to accommodate an expanding labour force could eventually be built only along hill slopes of the elongated valleys overlooking the railways, tramways and roads, that intertwined like serpents to fill the valley floors. That is to say, the technical and commercial requirements of the ironworks determined the original pattern of human settlement in the industrial towns of South Wales, and largely dictated the direction of all future development. But physical conditions affecting the building of houses were common to the whole of the industrial valleys of South Wales. The narrowness of the valleys provided "length with little breadth", and the industrial towns straggled lengthwise instead of fanning out from a centre. A leading characteristic common to almost all the towns and villages of the South Wales coalfield and ironworks is the absence of any kind of plan, and "scarcely a trace of any consciousness that a town should be something other than a fortuitous aggregation of houses". The result of the absence of an original plan may be seen in the haphazard location of schools, places of public worship, recreational centres and other buildings for public purposes. There were, in short, no town centres as such.

The magnitude of the impact which the ironworks made on the landscape of South Wales in terms of human settlement

---

[3] T. Rees, *South Wales: or, original delineations . . . of that part of the Principality* (London, 1818), pp. 646–8.

is shown by the population figures. In 1801, the population of Glamorgan was given as 70,879, of whom 7,700 persons, or nearly one person in every ten in the county, resided in the Merthyr area, while 6,821 resided in Swansea, and only 1,870 in Cardiff. By 1850, the most populous area in the whole of South Wales was at Dowlais and Merthyr, where the Guests, the Crawshays, the Hills and the Homfrays had established a 'mineral kingdom' extending from Hirwaun to Blaenavon. Within this vast industrial complex Merthyr Tudful, Dowlais, Rhymney, Ebbw Vale and Tredegar, were probably the largest urban settlements that originated with the large-scale production of iron.

Bare landscape evidence of the pattern of early urban growth—that is, the filling in of the landscape with human habitations, industrial and public buildings etc.—only partly reflects the actual living conditions inflicted upon the early settlers, in both the iron and coal-mining towns of South Wales, by landlords, iron masters and coal-owners. Without a deeper insight into these conditions, the true implications of the industrial townscapes of the region in terms of human experience cannot be fully felt. That is to say, unless the man-made landscape can be related to man's experiences and aspirations, the landscape itself becomes meaningless. The apalling conditions in which working-class families were compelled to live became the subject of numerous reports to the General Board of Health during the middle years of the nineteenth century. The first Public Health Act was not passed until 1848, but this was, in fact, only a voluntary act, insofar as it was optional for a district to adopt the provisions of the act or not. The greater part of the industrial complex of Merthyr was built before the passing of the act, at a time when the population was already about 46,692. Reporting on the state of Merthyr for the *Health of Towns Commission* in 1845, Sir Henry de la Beche stated that Merthyr contained "networks of filth emitting noxious exhalations", and in the district called the Cellars, near Pont Storehouse, de la Beche was appalled by what he saw. "The space between the houses [was] generally very limited, and an open, stinking and nearly stagnant gutter, into which the house-refuse is, as usual, flung, moves slowly before the doors. It is," continued de la Beche, "a labyrinth of miserable tenements and filth." Despite these horrific conditions, it may seem incredible to us today that when an application was made in 1849 for the adoption of the 1848 act to Merthyr, the opposition was tremendous. Indeed, "there was no room large enough in the town to hold the persons who wished to be heard against the adoption". The enquiry, which lasted nine days, was eventually held in the open air at the market place. The Inspector who held the enquiry "seemed doubtful whether the application for adoption should be granted or not", and adjourned the enquiry until the autumn for further consideration. It appears that workmen were predisposed to oppose the act "on the grounds that the sanitary condition of the town was less a cause of illhealth than conditions of work and lack of food". Meanwhile, however, cholera broke out, and within three months had claimed 1,500 lives in Merthyr. This was enough, and in 1850 the Public Health Act of 1848 was adopted, and the Local Board of Health was set up. At last, when the population of Merthyr was nearly 50,000, a start was made to end a state of affairs in which builders were allowed unrestricted freedom to build houses according to their whim and fancy, with the result that courts were numerous, houses were built back to back, over and under, and against the earth. It was such houses as these that, in later years, presented local councils with problems of slum areas, of closing insanitary houses, and of erecting new ones.

Within the town of Merthyr in 1840, the average expectation of life was said to be 18 years 2 months, and 47 years 10 months for those who survived the first twenty years of life. The cause of this monstrous mortality was probably to be found in the wretched local government of these new towns. Other new towns had added to their population numbers, but the institutions of the old town had usually been capable of some sort of imperfect extension into suburbs. Merthyr, Ebbw Vale and the other new iron towns were appendages to no former nucleus or rather to one, the institutions of which were wholly inadequate to regulate a large population. A Report of the General Board of Health in 1853 stated that "Merthyr Tudful presents one of the most strongly marked cases of the evil of . . . allowing a village to grow into a town without providing the means of civic organisation". (We have considered in Chapter 5 the significance of some of the religious, educational and other public buildings which formed part of these industrial townscapes.)

An examination of the physical layout of most of the industrial towns of South Wales would provide a study in contrast between the earliest settlement cores and those parts which grew up during the late nineteenth century, more especially after 1875, when a number of Reports of Select Committees on health and sanitation in large towns culminated in the passing of two acts of parliament, namely the Public Health Act of 1875 (which empowered local authorities to introduce by-laws for the design and layout), and the Housing of the Working Classes Act of 1890, which introduced municipal house-building. The landscapes of the industrial valleys of South Wales reveal gradations of improvement in building which occurred from about 1870 onwards, during the second period of the industrial revolution, when the houses of workers were of a decidedly superior quality to the earlier stone cottages. Many of these still stand out in a number of areas in the valleys in sharp contrast to the later houses which generally consisted of a parlour, a middle room, kitchen, and two or three bedrooms.

In Ebbw Vale, where, in 1790, a blast furnace and a cast-ing shop were built on the lands of Penycae farm, the same pattern of settlement is exhibited. The first cottages were built by the Company as an integral part of the works and so formed a nucleus of what was to become a major industrial town which, like Merthyr Tudful, developed without any initial planning, but rather in a haphazard fashion following the vicissitudes of the ironworks. The early cottages were built of stone with tiled roofs and stone floors, large fire-places and small square windows. There were no sanitary arrangements, and no water supply, and many of these early houses were erected on sloping ground. They had three storeys on the lower side and two on the upper, with spiral stairways, usually of stone. These three-storey houses were greatly favoured in the early days of the ironworks and were to be found also in the coal-mining areas of the Rhondda and Ogmore Valleys.

The second phase of the industrialisation of South Wales from about 1850 onwards brought a greater blight on the landscape than ever before. The industrial economy of South Wales was now based principally on coal-mining, and the industrial towns and villages of the Aberdâr, Ogmore, Garw and Llynfi valleys grew up because of the national and international demand for coal, and particularly steam coal. From 1870, coal production in South Wales increased con-sistently until 1913, when 56,800,000 tons of coal was produced by a labour force of some 235,000 persons. This amount represented about twenty per cent of the total output of Great Britain as a whole. During this period, too, the population of Glamorgan increased from 317,752 in 1861, to 1,120,910 in 1911, whereas during the first industrial phase, the increase was from 70,879 in 1801 to 231,849 in 1851.

The same haphazard development we found in the iron towns of Merthyr, Dowlais and Ebbw Vale, also charac-terised the newer towns in the South Wales coalfield in providing dwelling places for their teeming populations. An official report revealed that in 1853, there were four iron-works, and more than a dozen collieries operating in Aberdâr, there were hundreds of newly built houses which had no drainage at all, and the inhabitants "got rid of their refuse by throwing it into the street". There were also "whole rows of houses without any privy at all; the inmates having no place to go excepting the fields. Sometimes they make use of utensils which are kept on the premises; but, generally, they resort to the fields or bye-ways, or even the streets, and they are not too particular to go far out of the way." Houses were "built in lines", but "no street has been paved excepting Bute Street".

In the "worse quarters" of the town, however, conditions were described as follows: In *Green Bach* (Little Green) there "are a large number of houses crowded together upon a very limited space without any street paving, drainage of any kind or ventilation". *Cobbler's Row* was described as "a cluster of houses without back doors, back windows or back openings of any kind". A row of houses called Arch Row, and another called Big Row, were described as "double houses", that is, "houses below and houses above being built in the side of a steep hill; the upper houses being entered from what would be the back of the lower ones if they came up so high". None of these houses had back doors, and the lower ones no back-lets of any kind. In a small outlying district called *Roberts Town* there was "a collection of sixty or eighty houses built upon a plot of low-lying ground near the river Cynon, being but a few feet above the bed of it. It has been completely severed by tram-roads and railways from the rest of the parish, and has no road communication with it, so that no cart can pass from or to it." Such bestial conditions prevailed because there was no statutory guidance or control on house-building.

Perhaps the most striking and dramatic urban development occurred in the Rhondda valleys. At a time when Merthyr Tudful had become a "metropolis of ironmasters" and the Aberdâr and Cynon valleys were producing large quantities of steam coal, the Rhondda Valley remained almost entirely rural in character. In the first decade of the nineteenth century, Malkin, the oft-quoted antiquary, referred to Ystradyfodwg in 1807 as exhibiting "such scenes of untouched nature, as the imagination would find it difficult to surpass; and yet the existence of the place is scarcely known to the English traveller". The banks of the Rhondda rivers were clothed with "woods and groves as are rarely to be found". Malkin described the upper reaches of Ystradyfodwg "as untameably wild as any thing that can be conceived; and the few who have taken the pains to explore the scattered magnificence of South Wales, agree in recommending this untried route to the English traveller, as one of the most curious and striking in the Principality not excepting the more known and frequented tour of the northern counties". The district was thinly peopled, and appeared to be deserted of human habitations.[4]

The parish of Ystradyfodwg was still unspoiled in 1836, and its wild natural beauty continued to attract the attention of discerning tourists. Even in 1861 the population of the area did not exceed 4,000 souls, but by 1871 it had increased by over 400 per cent to 16,925, and by 1921 it had soared to the incredible total of 162,717—a figure representing a population density of 23,680 per square mile of the built-up area of the Rhondda Valley.

Urban development in the coal-mining valleys followed the same pattern as characterised the iron towns. Although the configuration varies usually, the valleys have a common pattern, with the floor of the valley dominated by the river, the collieries, the railways, and the main road, each side of

---

[4] B. H. Malkin, *The Scenery, Antiquities and Biography of South Wales* ... (London, 1807), Vol. I, pp. 83, 84, 285, 295.

which is lined with shops and dwellings, etc. Above this level, houses and public buildings have been pushed up the lower hillside, sometimes at tremendous gradients. Any conventional layout that was applied elsewhere to level sites, if followed in the valleys, resulted inevitably in ill-planned streets and housing congestion. The Welsh Garden Cities Ltd., Cardiff, however, was one agency which aimed at providing an improved layout of workers' houses in the industrial areas, and the 'Garden Village' at Gilfach Goch, whose foundation stone was laid on 17th March, 1910, was probably the first of such villages in South Wales. Even so, in the Rhondda, Garw, Ogmore and Llynfi Valleys, open country and vast stretches of moorland are within a few minutes' walk of the main streets—a fact which lends some relief to the drabness of urban conditions which is in sharp contrast to the 'unrelieved blight' found in many of the industrial towns of Britain.

Port towns

The major port towns of South Wales owe their development to the existence of rich coalfields—probably the finest in the world. They extended approximately thirty miles from east to west, and averaged about fifteen miles from north to south, producing every variety of coal that was needed for different commercial purposes. The Monmouthshire, or eastern, part of the coalfield contained the bituminous coal, excellent for locomotives and other purposes when quick steam raising was necessary (Plate 41). The port of Newport served this vast hinterland, which was also rich in iron stone. In the Rhondda, Aberdâr, Merthyr, Rhymney, Llynfi, Ogmore and Garw Valleys, was to be found the world-renowned semi-bituminous coal, known as Best Admiralty,[5] and gave high calorific value, as well as a low

---

[5] So called because it was highly favoured by the Admiralty and, having "the necessary elements in the exact proportion for marine engines" was used exclusively by the Royal Navy after 1872.

percentage of ash, economy in consumption, and an almost complete smokelessness. It was in order to cope with the increasing overseas demand for this coal during the late nineteenth century that Cardiff, Penarth, Barry (Plate 50) and, to a lesser degree, Porthcawl, came into prominence as port towns. In the western region of the coalfield were vast deposits of anthracite coal, the exportation of which gave a further impetus to the older metallurgical ports of Swansea, Port Talbot, Neath, Briton Ferry, Aberafan, and Llanelli.

Some of the earliest industrial developments in South Wales were located in the Neath area, where coal outcropped to the surface on both sides of its long winding estuary. Here coal had been worked from time immemorial for domestic purposes in levels, and shallow pits. From about 1586 copper ores from Cornwall were brought across to Neath for purposes of smelting by the use of pit coal. This practice was encouraged because of the magnificent seaboard of Swansea Bay. By 1705 it was acknowledged that "the convenience and cheapness of coal both occasioned the building of great work houses or manufactories in Neath for the smelting of lead and copper ore, for extracting silver out of lead, and for making lytharge and red-lead for the use of the Mine Adventurers". This may, indeed, be regarded as the beginning of the geographic concentration of metallurgical industries in the Swansea district which were facilitated by the inward curve of Swansea Bay, and its extension further inland into the coalfield along the tidal waters of the Neath, and along the Tawe. Thus Neath and, subsequently, Swansea possessed a valuable geographical advantage in the days of small sailing vessels. Such advantages were further enhanced by the ample supply of water in the streams that flowed rapidly down from the Breconshire mountains and which, in turn, facilitated the establishment first of ironworks and tinplate works, then the manufacture of steel, of tubes of galvanised sheeting in the areas. These were the beginnings of the metallurgical development of the Swansea Valley district, and the port towns of Neath and Swansea.

The ample deposits of cheap semi-anthracite steam coal "suitable for use in reverberatory smelting furnaces" brought the smelting industry to Swansea Valley. Between 1717 and 1856, at least thirteen copper smelting works were established in the Lower Swansea Valley, and about ninety per cent of Britain's copper smelting capacity was concentrated between the more extended littoral lying between Neath and Llanelli. With copper smelting came spelter or zinc smelting, tinplate and steel. These, and subsidiary industries, increased the population of Swansea from 21,533 in 1851, to 114,326 in 1891, and 157,554 in 1921, and consequently the number of structurally separate dwellings that appeared on the local landscape increased from 4,027 in 1851 to 20,866 in 1891, reaching a figure of 28,920 in 1921. The houses built around the copper smelting and tinplate works in the Swansea region were small terraced cottages of stone, or stone and slag blocks, with slate roofs. The commercial and business premises of Swansea presented more sophisticated architecture and design, as will be found in almost all the port towns.

An aspect of the landscape effects of the copper smelting processes is one which is sometimes overlooked. The poverty of the local vegetation in the Swansea Valley is now a landscape feature which is taken for granted. But as far back as 1804, the Rev. John Evans observed that "The volume of smoke from the different manufactories contribute to make Swansea, if not unwholesome, a very disagreeable place of residence." This was due to the same factors as existed in 1848 when "about 92,000 tons of sulphurous acid a year, or 65,900 cubic metres a day, were released into the atmosphere by the copper works". Consequently the concentration of fumes in the valley for nearly a hundred years resulted in almost a complete destruction of its vegetation. The indigenous sessile oak and birch wood-land of Kilvey Hill, and all grass and heather in the area disappeared. The topsoil, no longer held by plant roots, was washed off the valley sides, leaving the subsoil to be eroded into gullies. The area became a virtual desert, and the effects are still visible today (Plates 51 and 52).

During two hundred years of industrial activity, the Lower Swansea Valley, once a beautiful river valley, was wholly transformed into a barren wilderness three and a half miles long and a mile wide and the river, in turn, becoming "an industrial sewer". Early in 1960 this "stark monument of the reckless exploitation of the past" became the subject of a major pioneer investigation by a group of experts (drawn from the University Colleges of Swansea and Cardiff, Swansea Corporation, and industry) "to establish the factors which inhibit the social and economic use of land in the Lower Swansea Valley, and to suggest ways in which the area should be used in the future". As a result of this Project,[6] which produced twelve study reports of high quality, a number of sites have by now been cleared and relandscaped, and a fresh greenness is gradually replacing some of the desolation.

Cardiff, in the eastern sector of the South Wales coalfield, developed dramatically during the latter decades of the nineteenth century. It mushroomed into the premier town of Wales, and the foremost coal exporting centre in the world, mainly as a result of the frenzied exploitation of the rich coal basin of the Rhondda Valley. It was during this period that the landscape outside the town walls rapidly filled up, and the acceleration of the over-spilling explains, in part, why Cardiff, like other South Wales industrial towns,

[6] K. J. Hilton (ed.), *The Swansea Valley Project* (London, 1967).

has an appearance of haphazard building: there was, in fact, no previously consistent architectural tradition to follow.

Before 1829, the most important single factor contributing to the development of Cardiff was the Glamorganshire Canal which stretched from Merthyr to a tidal lock at Cardiff. But a new boost was given to it when John Crichton Stuart, the second Marquis of Bute (1793–1848) termed 'The Creator of Modern Cardiff', ventured £350,000 of his own money on converting the marshlands along the east bank of the Taff estuary into the first dock at Cardiff, the West Bute Dock, which was opened in 1839. Its opening gave a great impetus to the coastal and foreign shipments from Cardiff itself, and greatly stimulated the economic activities of the interior of the coalfield. Then, in 1859, the Bute East Dock was opened to be followed in 1887 by the Roath Dock, and in 1907 by Queen Alexandra Dock. The completion of these docks marked the culmination of schemes initially conceived by the second Marquis of Bute, whose lamented death in 1848 had deprived the town of its "most powerful and munificent friend whose purse was always open to every call for the improvement of the town and for the promotion of every charity". Indeed, it would not be an exaggeration to say that in the history of Cardiff, no less than in the history of the South Wales coalfield, "the Butes played a very real part in determining the pace and pattern" of its development. "By creating the Bute Docks they placed themselves in the front rank of British landlord entrepreneurs",[7] for these docks became the greatest centre of coal export in the world. In a sense it is distressing to realise that in recent years we have witnessed the undoing of so great an enterprise undertaken four generations ago at so great a cost in human effort.[8] Yet, it is a salutary thought that on

[7] John Davies, 'The Second Marquis of Bute' in *Glamorgan Historian*, Vol. XVIII, pp. 15–16.
[8] William Rees, *Cardiff, A History of the City* (Cardiff, 1969), pp. 265–6.

this site, which had once been a gateway to the world, will stand the National Industrial and Maritime Museum of Wales.

With the building of the Cardiff docks, Butetown developed into an important shopping centre where the residential part was laid out on a grid-iron plan, and included a variety of dwellings ranging from "rude cottage terraces" and elegant looking three-storey blocks of dwellings, to the "genteel rustic terrace of Windsor Esplanade". Moreover, the river Taff, which at one time frequently flooded the Cardiff High Street during spring tides, was diverted, and today the famous international rugby stadium, the Cardiff Arms Park, stands where once the Taff carried shipping to a point near the present Quay Street—famous as one of the entrances to the rugby stadium.

With the development of the railways, beginning in 1840 with the opening of the Taff Vale Railway, and followed by the South Wales Railway from Gloucester to Swansea in 1850, Cardiff grew apace. The population increased from 10,077 in 1841 to 164,333 in 1901, thus outstripping the older port of Swansea whose population had increased from 19,115 to 94,537 during the same period.

Cardiff, therefore, is mainly Victorian, and despite its phenomenal townscape changes during the last twenty years, it retains a strong Victorian atmosphere within which the social divisions of the pre-war urban society are still discernible in the architecture and planning of the houses. The chapels and churches, too, provide an interesting land-scape study, reflecting the traditional dichotomy in Wales between 'Church' and 'Chapel' which characterised the industrial towns. The Church Building Act of 1818 was followed by a spate of church-building, mainly in the style of the revived Gothic movement. But side by side with the churches of the Establishment, Nonconformist chapels multiplied at a much faster rate, and even the chapels were now set in Gothic architecture, with pointed arches as if to emphasise the feeling of equality with the Established Church.

The story of Cardiff has been admirably presented elsewhere by Professor William Rees and others,[9] and it is not necessary to dilate on the subject here. However, it should be noted that from the point of view of the landscape, the present city centre, together with the docks area and Cathays "coincide with the area included within the borough of Cardiff from Norman times up to 1875" and the addition of Roath and Canton represents the limits of Cardiff up to 1922.[10] But although Cardiff has sprawled during the last century, the core of the town around St John's Church and the Castle has remained substantially the same in layout to the present day (Plate 57).

But without a doubt one of the most outstanding features in the Cardiff landscape today is the famous civic centre in Cathays Park which stands adjacent to the Castle and just north of the city centre. This 60-acre site which was once "an expanse of semi-waste ground studded with occasional clearings and small enclosures"[11] became dominated by the most impressive and grandiose collection of buildings in the Principality, forming one of the finest civic centres in the country, if not in Europe. Conceived on spacious lines, it consists of avenues running down the two long sides of a central rectangular park, with the major public buildings arranged along the front and at the sides of the avenues. The City Hall, faced in Portland stone occupies a dominating position, and its clock tower brilliantly conceived and most subtly designed represents one of the most successful of all nineteenth-century classical towers in Britain. The white

[9] William Rees, *op. cit.*; J. B. Hilling, 'The buildings of Cardiff: an historical survey' in *Glamorgan Historian*, Vol. VI.
[10] J. B. Hilling, *op. cit.*
[11] William Rees, *op. cit.*

Portland-stone buildings in parkland surroundings are always extremely attractive, and with the full blossoming cherry trees in spring they present a truly idyllic setting. As an architectural collection Cathays Park has been described as "an extraordinarily fine assembly of twentieth century Neo-Classical buildings—in fact a monumental and permanent exhibition".[12] It is indeed fitting that such a gem should be set in landscape of the capital of Wales.

The decline of 'King Coal' in the South Wales valleys after 1921 saw a contraction in the activities of those port towns whose growth and survival depended largely on the export of coal. During the last quarter of the nineteenth century, however, another movement which contributed substantially to the survival of the sea-port towns was the removal of a number of steel works to the seaboard, and the abandonment of several inland tinplate works for sites near the coast, where raw materials could be more conveniently and economically assembled, and the product placed more readily on the overseas market. Newport, Port Talbot, Cardiff, Swansea and Llanelli all benefited in varying degrees by this process of relocation of industry, and their townscapes were modified accordingly. The contemporary scene in the industrial ports of South Wales will be discussed in a later chapter.

Lighthouses

The expansion of maritime trade around the South Wales coast from the seventeenth century, besides necessitating the building of new harbours and docks and ancillary installations, made it increasingly vital to promote measures to ensure a high degree of safety for the mariners and their ships along this notoriously treacherous coastline. Numerous wrecks had occurred along the coast from St David's Head

[12] J. B. Hilling, *op. cit.*, pp. 145–60.

in Pembrokeshire to the Bristol Channel, because of faulty navigation and bad weather, while far too many had been deliberately perpetrated by the callousness of the wreckers who, by kindling fires on various eminences along the coast, lured vessels to the fatal shores.

In 1600, it appears that only one lighthouse stood on the whole coast of Britain, whereas by 1700 there were fourteen, and by 1819 there were thirty-seven.[13] This increase reflected the rapid expansion of sea trade and the growing recognition of the lighthouse as a means of preventing wrecks. One of the first lighthouses to appear on the Welsh sea-scape was at St Anne's Head, near Milford Haven about 1662.

It was not until 1737, under great pressure from Bristol sea traders, that Trinity House agreed to establish a lighthouse on Flat Holm island near the mainland of Cardiff. The stone tower was erected, and is said to have first shown its light on 25th March, 1738. The present lighthouse is essentially the same as that of 1737, with its walls almost seven feet thick at its base, and three feet thick at the top at a height of sixty-eight feet. Until 1820 the light was provided by a coal fire which was replaced by an oil lantern until, in 1839 a dioptric apparatus was installed. A decision in 1866 to fit a new lantern with helical glazing and new powerful optic necessitated an iron gallery to accommodate it, and this increased the height of the tower to ninety-nine feet, and the light to about 164 feet above sea level.

In Swansea Bay the first lighthouse was erected on the outer of the two islets near Mumbles, under the powers of the Harbour Trustees Act of 1791, but it was not completed for some years, and was first lit, after the manner of the times, by a coal fire on 30th April 1794. In 1796 a further Act of Parliament gave the Trustees power to improve the light, and accordingly the newly introduced Argand lamps were substituted, the date being recorded in an inscription

[13] D. Alan Stevenson, *World Lighthouses Before 1820* (London, 1959).

on the base of the iron lantern which stated that it was 'executed' by Charles Collins Esq., Portreeve, at Neath Abbey, 1798. The battery was erected in 1860.

At Nash Point, near Marcross, Glamorgan, two light-houses dominate the landscape (Plate 59). The higher of the two lights stands 113 feet high, having a diameter of 27 feet 10 inches, and walls 4 feet 2 inches thick. The lower house was originally 67 feet high and 22 feet 6 inches in diameter. Completed in 1862, only the higher of the two houses is now in operation.

Other lighthouses were constructed at Emsger (or South Bishop), Great Castle Head, and Chapel Points on Caldey Island in Pembrokeshire, Burry Port in Carmarthenshire, Whitford Point on the north Gower coast, at the entrance to the docks at Swansea, Barry and Cardiff, and each side of the mouth of the Usk estuary. The 'pepper box' type of light-house once stood at the end of the stone pier in New Quay, Cardiganshire, and a similar one still stands at the harbour entrance at Porthcawl, Glamorgan.

By today many of the South Wales lighthouses that once protected ships, and the lives of those who sailed in them, have been rendered obsolete by more sophisticated naviga-tional aids. Most of these lighthouses are handsome and commanding structures. Their towers are invariably white in colour, and consequently are made as available for day marks as their lights are for the night.

Resort towns

Few towns in South Wales have developed solely as resort centres without depending on some form of subsidiary func-tion, or service, to under-pin the local economy. Llandegley Wells enjoyed considerable fame as a spa from the eighteenth century to the middle of the nineteenth century. The chaly-beate and sulphur waters are still there, yet they were not sufficient in themselves to sustain a permanent spa town. Only a small derelict building in the middle of a field now remains to remind us of former glories.

Llanwrtyd Wells and Llangamarch Wells, too, were noted for the medicinal quality of their waters (*Y Ffynhonnau*). As early as 1804, the Rev. John Evans described Llanwrtyd as a "celebrated spa for the South Walian gentry; and though the access is difficult and the accommodation bad, it is surprising how well they are frequented during the summer months, and the gaiety displayed in this obscure part of the kingdom". After the coming of the railways in 1864, tens of thousands of visitors frequented these places annually from about May to October, but their appeal was short-lived, and as towns they, too, stagnated.

Builth, like Brecon, was a charter town and grew up originally as a market town under the shadow of its Norman castle. After the castle fell, Builth, however, continued to be a thriving market town, and in the nineteenth century the local wells provided a further amenity which made it into one of the mid-Wales spa towns. The attraction of the wells was again short-lived but Builth, like Llandrindod, continued to keep its urban status because the spa was not indispensable to its basic economic structure.

Llandrindod Wells, once referred to as the Welsh Montpellier, did not develop into a resort town until the late nineteenth century, although the salubrity of its air, and the curative properties of its local springs had been well known for almost two centuries previously. The *Gentleman's Magazine* for October 1748 carried the following lines under the heading 'Nature's Pharmacopoeium':

> Let England boast Bath's crowded springs,
> Llandrindod happier Cambria sings,
> A greater, though a modern name
> By merit rising into fame . . .

For here at Llandrindod were:

> Three streams a different aid bestow,
> As sulphur, salts, and minerals flow,
> Uniting all that medicine claims
> And answering Nature's various aims.

The extent of the first accommodation for visitors to Llandrindod was limited to a few farmhouses. Then in 1749, a Mr Grosvenor converted an old mansion (located near the old church), known as Llandrindod Hall, into an hotel capable of accommodating several hundred visitors. After nearly forty years, the Hall was closed down on account of the disreputable excesses of some of the guests who frequented the place annually, and was later converted into a small woollen factory.

The first Pump House was built in the early nineteenth century, and Llandrindod Wells eventually developed principally around this nucleus. In 1801 the population of Llandrindod was only 192, and described as a parish of 2,884 acres, of which 1,500 were enclosed, and the remaining 1,384 unenclosed. The 1870 Swydd Neithon Manor Enclosure Act made it possible to release 3,220 acres of land for building, and before 1870 houses began to spring up, streets were laid out, and shops were erected on the virgin landscape, but it was not until 1891 that the first real impact was made upon it. By Local Government Board Order (No. 26,809) which came into operation on 14th April 1891, part of the Civil Parish of Cefnllys was constituted the Urban District of Trefonen, which was afterwards re-named Llandrindod Wells. In 1891, the new town had a population of 920 accommodated in 172 houses. By 1961 there were 1,104 houses accommodating a population of 3,251, compared with the peak figure of 4,596 in 1921 when the spa was at the zenith of its popularity. Here, then, is an example of a spa town having outlived the attraction of the therapeutic value of its natural springs as a viable economic concern, because a new economic base had been established.

South Wales coastal resorts are again of recent origin. Aberystwyth, now a resort and university town in north Cardiganshire, came into existence with the building of its castle *c.* 1277 (Plate 40). It occupied a magnificent strategic point at the mouth of the Rheidol, where it was surrounded on three sides by marshland, and on the fourth by the open sea. The first castle, however, was sited some distance inland along the river Ystwyth, and was properly called Aberystwyth[14]—a name subsequently, but inappropriately, applied to the stone castle built in 1277, near the mouth of the Rheidol. The shell of the second castle still stands upon an eminence commanding a view, in faint outline, of the immediate environs of the old castle town. It appears that the old medieval town had two main streets, one leading from the castle to the great darkgate (Great Darkgate Street), while a second led from the gate near the bridge (Bridge Street) to the shore north of the castle (Weeg Street/Pier Street). At the carfax, that is, where the streets crossed at right angles, the market cross was probably located. A subsidiary street ran from Weeg Street, almost parallel with Great Darkgate Street, to a third gate, the east gate, now perpetuated in the name Eastgate or Little Darkgate Street. The stages in the development of the town may be illustrated by the diagrams in Fig. 22.[15]

There had been no real significant changes in the development of the town of Aberystwyth from the thirteenth to the eighteenth century. The activities of its port were insignificant, and although lead mining was developing in the

[14] The element 'Aber' in Welsh place-names denotes the mouth of a river, or the point of conflux of two or more rivers or streams.

[15] Harold Carter, *The Towns of Wales: a study in urban geography* (Cardiff, 1965) is still the only extended study available on the development of Welsh towns.

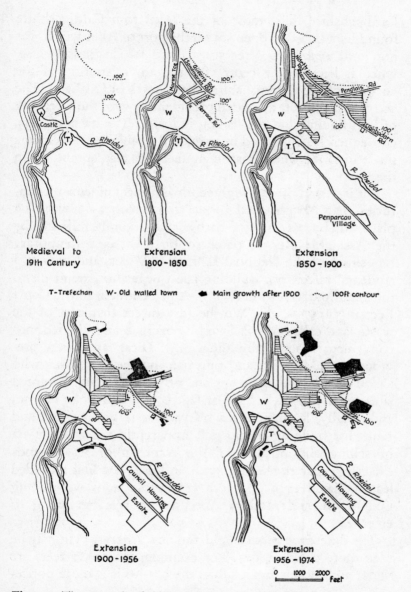

Medieval to
19th Century

Extension
1800-1850

Extension
1850-1900

T-Trefechan   W-Old walled town   ◀ Main growth after 1900   ·····100ft contour

Extension
1900-1956

Extension
1956-1974

0   1000   2000
feet

Fig. 22. The growth of Aberystwyth. (After Harold Carter to 1956.)

239

Cardiganshire hills, most of the lead from Cardiganshire found its way to the open sea *via* the port of Aberdyfi. It was not until 1770 that Aberystwyth had its Customs House, when it became the centre for the administration of the customs of the Cardiganshire creeks north of Cardigan. The activity of the port increased considerably with the extension of lead mining and the fishing industry. The harbour was, consequently, improved in 1780, and further improvements made in 1836, when small manufactories also sprang up in the town.

But it was in the late eighteenth and early nineteenth centuries that Aberystwyth began to develop as a watering place, and by 1810 Marine Baths had been built, followed by the Assembly Rooms (later to be used as a temporary repository of the National Library of Wales, and now as a students' refectory). Building soon began to extend on to the Sand Marsh (Morfa Swnd). A presentment in the Court Leet in 1813 stated, "We the jury direct that part of the waste land called Morfa Swnd be mapped and divided into convenient spots for building. . . ." These lands were previously used for grazing purposes by the burgesses who jealously guarded their ancient privileges. They "granted sites for a Chapel, House of Correction and Poor House; and, finally, let their lands on various terms of years and rents, for building purposes". Apparently not a single act of selling any portion of the common or waste lands exists—"every transaction was 'on lease', the first recorded lease is dated 1759".[16] From 1813 these lands were being built upon, and modern Aberystwyth was beginning to emerge.

The difference between old and new Aberystwyth may be seen quite clearly today. For example, the new streets are wider and more spacious than the old—this is more notice-

---

[16] George Eyre Evans, *Aberystwyth and its Court Leet* (Aberystwyth, 1902), pp. 163–4.

Plate 51   An industrial scene in the lower Swansea Valley: The Hafod and Middle Bank Works, *c.* 1840 (from Hachette's *La Tour du Monde*, 1865).

Plate 52   The view from the same position in 1975.

Plate 53   Rheola open-cast site—aerial view of Maesgwyn Cap and Rheola Forest. The foreground shows land shaped for planting in contrast to the savaged country in the centre and background.

Plate 54   A stone quarry on the coastal plain between Newton and Margam, Glamorgan.

Plates 55 and 56   Two photographs of Quay Parade, Swansea, viewed from the same position. Above, *c*. 1920; below, 1975.

Plate 57 Cardiff Civic Centre, 1974.

Plate 58 Cwmbran New Town showing modern high-rise blocks in the foreground.

Plate 59 The lighthouses at Nash Point, near St Donat's, *c.* 1850, by J. Outhwaite after Gastineau.

Plate 60 Trecco Bay caravan site, Newton, Porthcawl. In the seventeenth and eighteenth centuries sailing vessels plied regularly from Newton Bay (left background) to Minehead and Bristol, carrying thither agricultural goods and commodities, and returning with more exotic items to be sold in the local shops.

Plate 61 Llysfran Valley, Pembrokeshire, looking east, before construction of the reservoir commenced.

Plate 62 The same view, after construction of the reservoir.

Plate 63 Fragmentation of human settlements in aid of modern transport in the neighbourhood of Gabalfa and Heath, Cardiff.

Plate 64 Coed Morgannwg, Glamorgan: the Ogmore Valley in the South Wales coalfields. Afforestation in this old industrial landscape has covered many scars, including some old colliery spoils.

Plates 65, 66 and 67 Gilfach Goch, Glamorgan: three views of its main industrial complex from approximately the same position:

c. 1900

1959

1975

able along North Parade and Terrace Road, leading to Marine Terrace along the sea-front.

Before the coming of the railways in 1864, Aberystwyth had had a strong Regency flavour, and counted among its annual visitors such people as Sir Robert Peel, Lord and Lady Grey, Lord and Lady Grosvenor, Lord and Lady Bolingbroke, the Duke and Duchess of Dorset, etc. Neighbouring gentry, too, made great use of Aberystwyth as a resort town. The railway made the town more accessible from north and south, and it soon became a popular attraction for middle and working-class family holidays,[17] particularly from South Wales.

This is not the place to dilate on the details of the architecture and style of houses that were built in Aberystwyth at different periods in its development, but the discerning visitor will still observe the four-storeyed Georgian houses in the Bridge Street–Pier Street area (once the residential quarters of the élite society) and the Victorian structures in North Parade moving away from the commercial core of the town. There are also an admixture of lesser houses exhibiting in clear outline the social and functional distinctions between the houses and their inhabitants. Perhaps the most interesting features left in the townscape are to be found in several large buildings in Regency style standing in Laura Place and Pier Street, within a bow shot of the Castle grounds, and those at the Western end of North Parade. As Professor Carter puts it, "These three localities epitomise respectively the reconstruction of the core, the infilling of spaces within the walls, and the first extension on to Morfa Swnd."

Further south, along the west Wales coast, Aberaeron and New Quay enjoyed a brief period of coastal trade, but with the extension of railroads, their sea-going trade declined, and they have survived to this day mainly as resort and

[17] W. J. Lewis, 'Some aspects of the history of Aberystwyth', *Ceredigion*, Vol. III (4), IV (1) (1959, 1960).

pleasure towns, attracting many of the *nouveaux riches* of the post-Second-World-War era.

In Pembrokeshire, Tenby developed as a resort town by virtue of its natural attractions. Leland has left us the following description of Tenby *c.* 1539: "Tinbigh town," he says "stondith on a main rocke, but not veri hy, and the Severn Sea so gulfeth in about hit, that at ful se almost the thirde part of the toune is inclosed with water. The toune is strongeli waullid, and welle gatid, everi gate having his portcolis *ex solido ferro.*" There was a "sinus and a peere made for shyppes" and the town for "very welthe by marchandyce". In 1566, however, its population was barely 800, and at the end of the eighteenth century it appears to have been "almost entirely deserted, excepting by the poorer classes and a few respectable tradesmen". But by 1800, it had become a favourite resort in summer for the "fashionable and luxurious".

In its development, the outline of the town of Tenby has been largely determined by the fact that it was strongly walled and well gated, as Leland put it. Its townscape is, on the whole, dominated by two parallel streets—High Street and Frog Street—between which run connecting streets. Although architecturally, Tenby is predominantly Regency in style, it does nevertheless preserve much of its distinction as a medieval walled town whose plan is dominated by the Castle wall, and its 'Five Arches'. A characteristic feature of the town is the system of alley-ways which intersect the buildings standing between the quay and the market square, reminding the observer of the former traffic in goods and commodities that existed between the harbour and the tradesmen of the town.

Very little need be said here about Swansea, Barry and Penarth. Although they still enjoy a wide reputation as resort towns, their main economic base continues to rest on the maritime and commercial activities of their respective hinterlands, and their urban outlines have been largely dictated by the requirements of these activities.

A word must be said, however, about the resort town of Porthcawl, for the growth and development of this urban settlement originally revolved around its small port, but since the turn of the century it has survived as one of the premier resort towns of South Wales. The area had become popular as a bathing retreat as early as the late seventeenth century when it was more commonly referred to as Newton, and where there was a summer annexe to Pile Inn. The *Torrington Diaries* tell us that here was a "Bathing Company: and a tavern and machines kept by the man of this Inn [i.e. Pyle Inn] . . .", and that Lord Porchester with his "fine family of children" had travelled "to a house he [had] hired on the coast for the benefit of bathing".[18] But it was not until the early twenties of the nineteenth century that Porthcawl's urban growth really began, when a horse-tramroad was constructed from the mining town of Maesteg in the Llynfi Valley to the newly-dug harbour of Porthcawl for exporting coal. In 1865 this tramroad was replaced by a railway, and the old inner dock, which was also constructed at that time, became the terminus of the locomotive railroads from the Llynfi and Ogmore Valleys. Trade increased rapidly from exporting 17,306 tons of coal in 1864 to 165,000 tons in 1873. But by 1878 the total coal shipments had fallen to 68,000 tons. In 1898 two new docks were opened, one at nearby Port Talbot, and the other at Barry, a little farther afield to the east. The advantages enjoyed by Port Talbot over Porthcawl soon became evident, and coal waggons from the valleys were gradually diverted from Porthcawl, and soon it was to lose almost all its trade. In 1903 only 2,767 tons of coal was exported from Porthcawl, and in 1907 the dock was finally closed. After the First World War, the inner harbour was used as a scrapyard

[18] *Torrington Diaries*, Vol. I, p. 293.

for obsolete naval vessels, but later it was filled in. By today, only the small tidal basin, the breakwater and the lighthouse, remain as landscape evidence of Porthcawl's former maritime history.

Although the features which characterise the Porthcawl townscape of today were initially controlled by the nucleus created by the dock and the railway, and later by the building along the Esplanade, the Inclosure Award of 1860 was to determine in great measure the subsequent development of Porthcawl. The Award released about 800 acres of land on Newton Down and Backs Common. The Commissioners laid out the lines of a number of public highways, occupation roads and public footways. Some of these were designed to give access to newly enclosed fields on Newton Down, but the Commission's No. 1 road gave access to enclosed parcels of agriculturally valueless land which became available for ribbon development. This road ran in the direction along which John Street, the main street of the town, was to develop. One of the most prominent families responsible for promoting the development of the resort town of Porthcawl was the Brogden family. John Street, already mentioned, perpetuates the memory of John Brogden (1798–1869), head of the family, and Mary Street and Caroline Street commemorate Mrs Brogden (Mary Caroline, daughter of Major John Bute), the wife of James Brogden, John Brogden's son. Many promoters were involved in the building of the resort town of Porthcawl, and the enclosure of Backs Common had resulted in the application of some degree of town planning in the late nineteenth century. By Local Government Order, Porthcawl was constituted an Urban District in 1893, and thereafter it developed into a foremost resort town in industrial South Wales. The growth and development of Porthcawl as a resort and residential town are reflected in the size of its population which, in 1851, was 958, in 1871 it was 1,455, and by 1921 it stood at 6,642. By 1971, however, there were 14,104 persons in Porthcawl occupying 4,565 houses.

Much of the characteristic features of the Porthcawl that grew up in the last century have undergone drastic transformations, and a new pattern of development is emerging which is designed to cater for a new breed of 'visitors' far removed from those whose demands John Brogden hoped to satisfy (Plate 60).

Promenade piers

A feature in the development of resort towns which added an element of novelty and charm to their coastlines, in Wales and in England, was the promenade pier,[19] as distinct from the more numerous stone piers that were extended into the sea (or tidal rivers) in order to protect a harbour, and form a landing place for vessels. The promenade pier was usually structured of iron or wood, supported by columns or pillars, and was intended for the purpose of pleasure and sometimes of providing a landing place for boating parties, etc.

In South Wales, however, despite a proliferation of stone structured piers in the vicinity of the natural harbours and tidal rivers along its coastline, only four promenade piers were erected, namely, at Aberystwyth, Tenby, Mumbles and Penarth. At Aberystwyth, the first pier projected for a distance of 690 feet into the sea. It was built at a cost of £13,600, and was opened on Good Friday, 1865.[20] The strength of its structure, however, did not match the height of the tempestuous winter tides of Cardigan Bay and, consequently, in January 1866 a hundred feet of its length succumbed to the rolling seas when "The iron supports

[19] The first of these was the Brighton Chain Pier, 1823.

[20] It appears that as early as 1740 there was a project on foot to build a pier at Aberystwyth for the "advancement of the fishery and other branches of the trade". See *Bye-gones* (1886–7), pp. 26–7.

snapped like so many columns of brittle glass and the timber was torn like rags." It was not until 1872 that the pier was replaced by a new one with a handsome refreshment pavilion surmounted by a balcony. Today its decayed state is a veritable "blot on the escutcheon".

The pier at Mumbles, near Swansea, and the one at Penarth, both provided added facilities for local pleasure seekers who, in former days, could be counted in their thousands during the holiday season. The Mumbles Pier was opened in 1898 in conjunction with the project undertaken by the Mumbles Railway and Pier Company to construct a railway line from Mumbles Head to Oystermouth, thus extending the first passenger railway in the world from Swansea to Oystermouth. These structures, though few in number, appeared in the sea-scape to supplement the natural seaside attraction for man's enjoyment in an age when the annual family holiday was beginning to establish itself in the life of the working classes.

If promenade piers in the landscape represented a purposeful achievement for public pleasure, domestic opulence, which became particularly conspicuous in the Victorian and Georgian landscape, was sometimes marked by eccentricities or follies—useless buildings erected for purely personal and fantastic reasons. South Wales was not devoid of such buildings. For instance, on an eminence near Llanarthne, overlooking the Towy Valley, stands 'Paxton's Tower', a Gothic structure, triangular in plan, with turrets at each corner. On the tower, which was restored recently to a reasonably good state of preservation, the following inscription may be seen in English, Welsh and Latin on each of its three doors: "To the invincible Commander, Viscount Nelson, in commemoration of deeds before the walls of Copenhagen, and on the shores of Spain; of the Empire everywhere maintained by him over the seas; and of the death which in the fullness of his own glory, though ultimately for his own country and for Europe, conquering, he died. This tower was erected by William Paxton."[21]

Again, on the site of an Iron Age hill fort on Pendinas, Aberystwyth; is an unfinished tower to commemorate the Battle of Waterloo. It was conceived by Captain Richards of Bryneithin, whose original intention to erect a statue of the Duke of Wellington on horseback on top of the tower was thwarted by financial difficulties. Another conspicuous columnar tower in the landscape around Derry Ormond, near Lampeter, was built to mark the defeat of Napoleon.

It was for an entirely different reason that the sham Castle of Clytha, Monmouthshire, was built. A tablet on its wall indicates that "This building was erected in 1790 by William Jones of Clytha House, fourth son of John Jones of Lanarth Court, the last surviving child of Sir William Morgan of Tredegar. It was undertaken to relieve a mind sincerely afflicted by the loss of a most excellent wife . . . and to the memory of whose virtues this tablet is dedicated" (Plate 22).

At Craig-yr-helfa Road, Glyntâf, near Pontypridd, stand the Round Houses which comprise a pair of three-storey towers with steep octagonal slate roofs. These are the most unusual structures in the area, being the follies of the eccentric Dr William Price (1800–1893). A qualified surgeon of no mean reputation, Price became fanatically involved in druidism, and practised druidic rites on the Pontypridd Rocking Stone. He habitually wore a white tunic over a scarlet waistcoat, trousers made of green cloth, and on his head he wore a large fox skin. He believed strongly in cremation, and on 13th January, 1884, on the death of his infant son, whom he had blasphemously christened Iesu Grist Price (Jesus Christ Price), he proceeded to burn the body in a barrel on the hillside at Caerlan, near Llantrisant Town. An angry crowd of onlookers, including a local

[21] i.e. Sir William Paxton.

constable, interrupted the operation. Price was arrested, and on 7th February, 1884 was indicted at the Cardiff Assizes with having attempted to cremate the body of his son. A verdict of 'Not Guilty' was passed, and on 14th March, 1884, Price made history by completing the task of burning the body of his infant son, using half a ton of coal, a gallon of paraffin oil, and sixpenny worth of wood. The legality of cremation had been established.

The Round Houses, however, were intended to be part of a scheme for a druidic museum and palace to be erected at the pseudo-druidical site of Y Maen Chwyf (The Rocking Stone).[22] Needless to say, the scheme fell through, but the two Round Houses still stand in the local landscape to remind us of the eccentric Dr William Price.

About the year 1858, Francis Crawshay, the son of William Crawshay the 'Iron King' (1788–1867), built a 'Tower' near Hirwaun, from which the local Tower Colliery got its name. The tower, originally thirty feet high, stands in ruin on the mountain slope. It was a three-storey building, having six-arched windows, with six roundholes in the tower wall, grouped in three pairs facing north, east and west. Two brass cannons were introduced into the tower,[23] which was lived in during the summer months. It was abandoned in 1858 after the closing of the Hirwaun Works, and remained in the landscape as a rare example of a 'folly' in a Welsh industrial setting.

SELECT BIBLIOGRAPHY

Carter, Harold, *The Towns of Wales: a Study in Urban Geography* (Cardiff, 1965).
Carter, H. and Davies, W. K. D., *Urban Essays: Studies in the Geography of Wales* (London, 1970).
Dyos, H. J. (ed.), *The Study of Urban History* (London, 1968).

[22] J. B. Hilling, *Cardiff and the Valleys* (London, 1973), pp. 106–7.
[23] *Glamorgan Historian*, Vol. X, pp. 77–8.

Evans, George Eyre, *Aberystwyth and its Court Leet* (Aberystwyth, 1902).

Higgins, Leonard S., *Newton Nottage and Porthcawl* (Gomerian Press, 1968).

Hilling, J. B., 'The buildings of Cardiff: an historical survey' in *Glamorgan Historian* (ed. Stewart Williams), Vol. VI (Cowbridge, 1969).

Howell, J. M., 'The birth and growth of Aberayron', *Cardig. Antiq. Soc. Trans.*, IV, 7–13.

Howse, W. A., *Radnorshire* (Hereford, 1949).

Jones, Emrys, 'Tregaron: a Welsh Market town' *Geography*, Vol. 35 (1950).

Jones, P. N., *Colliery settlement in the South Wales Coalfield 1850–1926* (University of Hull. Occasional papers in Geography, No. 14).

Leland, John, *The Itinerary in Wales In or About the Years 1536–9*, (ed. Lucy Toulmin Smith) (London, 1906).

Lewis, E. A., *Medieval Boroughs of Snowdonia* (London, 1912).

Lewis, E. D., *The Rhondda valleys: A Study in Industrial Development, 1800 to the Present Day* (London, 1963).

Lewis, S., *A Topographical Dictionary of Wales* (London, 1833).

Lloyd, T. Alwyn and Jackson, Herbert, *South Wales Outline Plan* (H.M.S.O., 1949).

Malkin, B. H., *The Scenery, Antiquities and Biography of South Wales . . .* 2 vols (London, 1807).

Randall, H. J., *Bridgend: The Study of a Market-town* (Newport, 1955).

Rees, James Frederick, *The Story of Milford* (Cardiff, 1954).

Rees, William, *Cardiff: A History of the City*, 2nd ed. rev. (Cardiff, 1969).

Williams, Glanmor (ed.), *Merthyr Politics: The Making of a Working-Class Tradition* (Cardiff, 1966).

8. The landscape of today and tomorrow

New lakes. New forests. New roads and runways. New industrial landscapes. New towns

IN THE FOREGOING chapters we have been discussing some of the features of the landscape which bear testimony to the variety of ways in which man has, throughout the years, utilised his physical environment in his continuous struggle to exploit the resources of nature—air, water, land and minerals—for his own preservation and enjoyment. The process goes on inexorably in our own day on a more sophisticated and grandiose scale, presenting on the landscape new expressions of the changing requirements of a 'new society'.

New lakes

Perhaps some of the more visually pleasing results of man's interference with the landscape today are expressed in terms of large reservoirs—man-made lakes—for the storage of water. With few exceptions, everyone today has a water-tap from which flows the everyday domestic water requirements. This was not always so, and perhaps it was the village pump that first represented on the landscape the necessity of providing a fairly reliable source of water for human consumption. But the increase of population that came in the wake of industrialism, particularly after 1870, and subsequent improvements in sanitary conditions, made it necessary to construct large artificial lakes in the upland regions of South Wales, where there is a plenteous supply of water.

One of the first extensive reservoirs to be formed in South Wales was in the Elan Valley, where the Elan Dam was built in 1904. Ironically, the water from this reservoir was never intended for Welsh consumption, but rather for supplying the City of Birmingham, seventy miles away from its Welsh source, as indeed did the Claerwen reservoir opened in 1952. The gathering ground of the Elan, and its tributary the Claerwen, contains a total area of 45,562 acres, that is, over twenty square miles—an extreme length of about fifteen miles, and an extreme breadth of eight miles. The formation of these reservoirs involved a considerable modification of the existing landscape, occasioning the destruction of at least two houses of some pretensions and literary interest, namely Cwm Elan and Nant Gwyllt. Both houses, now some fifty feet below the level of the Caban Coch reservoir, were associated with the poet Shelley.[1] In addition, an old church, Capel Nant Gwyllt—a small ivy-covered church—a Baptist chapel, a school house, as well as eighteen cottages[2] were submerged by the Caban Coch, Graig Goch and Pen-y-garreg complex of reservoirs.

If a new scheme, now under discussion, is finally approved, the Graig Goch reservoir in the Elan Valley will eventually be converted into the biggest in Europe, by

[1] Shelley visited his uncle, Thomas Grove, at Cwm Elan in July, 1811. In 1812 he returned to the Elan Valley having in the meantime married Harriet Westbrook, and entered into occupation of Nant Gwyllt, only to have to leave again in the same year.

[2] The submergence of these buildings was partly compensated for by the construction of a 'model' village at the lower end of the valley, undertaken by the Birmingham Corporation, and planned by the architect who designed the Cadbury village.

increasing its present capacity of 2,000 million gallons to
140,000 million gallons, raising its dam from 120 feet
to 400 feet high, and submerging another 1,530 acres of
land.

Of more direct benefit to the people of South Wales has
been the Llyn Brianne Dam, high up in the Towy Valley,
Carmarthenshire, opened in 1972. The dam stands 88·5
metres (approx. 288 feet) high—the highest yet built in
Britain—and has brought into existence on the landscape
a lake of 88 ha. (or 210 acres) holding 61,000,000 cubic
metres of water. The degree to which the surrounding area
was manipulated for the procurement of the raw materials
required in the construction of the dam is indicated by the
fact that it is formed of 515,000 cubic yards of clay, and
2,200,000 cubic yards of rock fill. One singular advantage
in the choice of the Brianne site was that there were no
occupied dwellings to be drowned, and the actual area
eventually submerged was, in the main, coniferous forest
and some moorland sheep-grazing. The valley itself was
previously served by an old country road and numerous
mountain tracks which had to be diverted around the
reservoir. Such an operation involved the construction of
approximately eighteen miles of new country roads and
a similar length of private roadways for the Forestry
Commission.

Another man-made lake which deserves mention is the
Llysfran reservoir on the Cleddau, Pembrokeshire, opened
in 1972, with a total capacity of 4,674 million gallons of
water, with the top water level 350 feet above sea level
(Plates 61 and 62). This lake will supply the domestic and
commercial requirements of an extensive area of Pembrokeshire. It will also be put to good recreational use, offering
facilities for fishing, rowing and sailing. The grounds at
Llysfran have been developed as a county park, providing
car-parks, roadways, viewing points, and picnic sites, which,

together, combine to present a completely new landscape, possessing a special beauty and attraction of its own.

In Glamorgan, too, man-made lakes are being converted into public amenities. The Llandegfedd reservoir, near Cardiff, has been developed into a most attractive and pleasing retreat of some 435 acres, with facilities for fishing, sailing and walking. Such man-made beauty spots offer an added attraction to tourists, and provide a fillip to the tourist industry.

New forests

Since 1920 the Forestry Commission has been actively engaged in South Wales restoring the forests to their former productivity, as well as increasing the over-all woodland area of the region (Fig. 23). About ten per cent of the total land area of Wales, or about 522,000 acres, is now productive forest. By far the greatest number of trees planted are conifers, and of the 23 million trees planted annually, about 10 million are made up of the Sitka spruce (from British Columbia), and another 5½ million are made up of Lodgepole pine and Japanese larch. The Sitka spruce and Lodgepole pine are used for planting exposed moorlands, sometimes at considerable heights. The remaining trees, such as Douglas Fir and Norway spruce occupy more sheltered places, often on steep hillsides which had been previously wooded.

Apart from the economic advantages which accrue from afforestation, the landscape is often scenically enriched, despite the fact that many unviable hill farms (the majority are about twenty acres) which become amalgamated into more viable units, lose much of their land and sheep walks in the plantations. Many derelict areas, too, are beautified, such as the forests in the Ogmore Valley, where the former greenness of the valleys is being restored, obliterating,

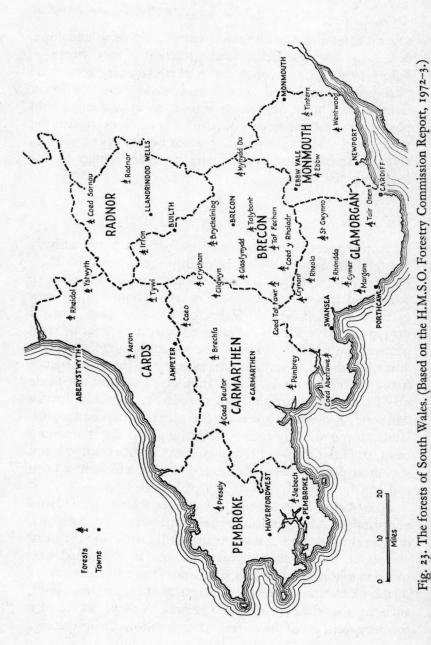

Fig. 23. The forests of South Wales. (Based on the H.M.S.O. Forestry Commission Report, 1972–3.)

254

for all time some of the ravages of a previous age of mineral extraction (Plate 64). In other areas the planting of new forests has completely changed the settlement pattern of dispersed farmsteads, and has given rise to entirely new settlements with a social identity of their own. An excellent example of such landscape changes is to be found in the new settlement known as Llandulas, which has emerged in recent years following the Forestry Commission's planting of the Crychan Forest some nine miles north-west of Llandovery.[3]

Like the 'new lakes', the 'new forests' have now settled on the landscape, and with the amenities they offer, they will in time be accepted as an essential ingredient in the modern man-made environment.

New roads and runways

In 1919 'motoring for the million' became an imaginative slogan at a time when, in fact, there were only 100,000 cars on the roads of Britain. Twenty years later there were two million cars, and by today it is estimated that well over one-half of households are car-owners—a situation which, coupled with the requirements of industry, has led to extensive road improvement schemes in South Wales. Further, it is officially recognised that the key to the economic development of South Wales is 'better access', and this spells bigger and better roads.[4] Programmes approved, or completed during the last decade or so, have increased the dual carriageway roads in Wales to 120 miles, the greater proportion of which has been constructed in South Wales where three-quarters of the population are concentrated (Plate 63).

The most striking road improvements already carried out

[3] E. G. Bowen, *Man and his Habitat*, pp. 196–7.
[4] *Wales; the Way Ahead* . . . (Cardiff, H.M.S.O., 1967).

in South Wales include the dual carriageways on the Neath by-pass, and the Port Talbot by-pass, which represent the the first urban motorway to be constructed in Britain. Again, the Heads of the Valleys road has improved communication between Swansea and the Midlands. Although some of these road 'improvement' schemes have sometimes produced a pleasing modification of existing roadways, others have certainly inflicted severe casualties on our landscape heritage by demolishing, sacrilegiously, many a structure of rare architectural beauty, and some hundreds of habitable dwellings that had, over the decades, settled neatly into the landscape. The completion of the Eastern Avenue, Cardiff, removed much that was pleasantly familiar on the landscape, while the trunk road between Cardiff and Merthyr Tudful completely transformed much that was once an essential part of the social and economic life of an earlier period.

The extension of air transport facilities has necessitated the acquisition of hundreds of acres of some of the most fertile agricultural lands in the area. At Rhoose Airport, Glamorgan, for example, there are two tarmac runways of 1,244 yards and 1,115 yards long, with a grass strip of 744 yards, occupying agriculturally valuable land which had been cultivated from early times, and producing some of the finest crops in the Vale. At Fairwood Common, Swansea, there are, in all, three tarmac runways of 869, 870 and 1,345 yards, respectively.

With the improvement of access roads into South Wales, far-reaching developments have taken place in the facilities afforded for the enjoyment of Wales' natural beauty. The proliferation of the motor car has been followed by self-catering holidays which have increased in popularity, bringing in their train new permanent features on the landscape in the form of extensive sites occupied by chalets, caravans, tents and holiday camps. The extent of the impact this has had on many virgin landscapes is indicated by the fact that of the 210,000 licensed caravan pitches in Britain, about one-fifth are in Wales. It is a sobering thought that by 1981 (if the Welsh Tourist Board's estimates are reliable) over 5½ million visitors will visit Wales, more especially as "The greater part of the increase is expected to result from the growing demand for self-catering holidays," that is, for more caravan sites, "although a large number . . . are likely to be converted into holiday camps . . .".

Subsidiary landscape changes to road improvement schemes have resulted in many old and secluded hostelries being refurbished beyond recognition, while new road-houses, with their annexed garages, filling stations and expansive forecourts, punctuate the roadways at fairly frequent intervals, where once continuous stretches of hedgerow trees and hedges added colour, variation and charm to our passage along the highways.

New industrial landscapes

A policy of rationalisation in the coal industry of South Wales has, in recent years, led to the complete abandonment of 'high-cost' collieries, concentrating production, mainly, at those more favourably situated, and which carry relatively heavier capital investment. Scores of old, yet relatively productive, pits have consequently been closed and, like the railroads that once served them, they have been elimated from the landscape, leaving wide expanses of lifeless dereliction in many localities where virile communities were once sustained. In other areas, however, old colliery sites have been cleared for the establishment of light industries to provide alternative employment for the local population. Other industrial buildings, and their surrounding spoil, have been systematically removed and re-landscaped, with a view to re-introducing the greenness that originally characterised the industrial valleys of South Wales (Plates 65, 66 and 67).

Since about 1943, however, a new form of mining—the open-cast system—has been undertaken at about sixteen different sites in South Wales where total production rose from 0.7 million tons in 1946 to 2.4 million tons in 1966. In distinct contrast with underground mining, open-cast involves the removal of 'super-incumbent strata', or overburden, which are discharged and dumped clear of the coal exposed by this method (Plate 53). One of the main criticisms that may be levelled against this form of mining is the inevitable scarifying effect it has on the landscape, and the consequent destruction of land values. It is claimed, however, that no appreciable decrease in the agricultural value of the land need occur if the soil is properly restored after coal has been extracted.

Although coal-mining is still an important industry in South Wales, it has been considerably run down, partly because of a growing demand for the use of oil. For instance, in 1948 the total production from the South Wales coalfield was 23 million tons, whereas in 1972 it was only 12 million tons. But, in marked contrast, the total crude oil distillation capacity at the various South Wales refineries increased from 2,600,000 tons in 1950, to 26,610,000 tons in 1972. This relative change in the demand for fuel is clearly emphasised in the region of Llandarcy, Pembroke and, more especially, of Milford Haven, where the technical installations represent about a quarter of the refining capacity of the United Kingdom, and the natural deep-water harbour now accommodating tankers of over 100,000 tons, could, with further improvements, provide for tankers of up to 200,000 tons, and more (Plate 48).

Side by side with the increasing demand for oil, there has been, since 1948, a trebling of electricity consumption in Wales as a result of its increased application to industrial and for domestic use. This extra demand has led to major construction programmes being undertaken by the Central Electrical Generating Board, resulting in tremendous modifications of the landscape. The mammoth coal-fired power-stations constructed at Uskmouth, Carmarthen Bay, Rogerstone and Aberthaw, stand out grimly against their skylines, reminding the observer of an additional source of energy employed by man for the pursuit of his economic and social ends.

A more pleasing enterprise has been the Rheidol Hydro-Electric Scheme, some ten miles north of Aberystwyth. This scheme was skilfully brought to fruition in 1962. Its surface accessories, although transforming a vast area of the surrounding hills and valleys, have settled easily into the natural landscape, bringing, in their train, a new dimension of beauty as an added amenity to the neighbourhood. The upper works are located in remote hill country rising over 1,000 feet above sea level, while the intermediate works are near Ponterwyd, at a level of about 800 feet above sea level, with the lower works sited at Cwm Rheidol, nearly 150 feet above sea level. The upper reservoir at Nant-y-moch is impounded by a massive buttress dam 172 feet high, with an overall length of 1,150 feet. It has a maximum capacity of about 5,700 million gallons, while the lower stage reservoir at Dinas, has a capacity of 185 million gallons. The whole hydro-electric scheme has probably necessitated the modification of sixty square miles, besides changing the original flow of the River Rheidol for several miles along its course. The power generated by the three power-stations in the Rheidol Scheme is received by the grid system for transmission to consumers in mid-Wales, but the transmission lines have been discreetly undergrounded, leaving a pylon-less landscape in this vast hydro-electric complex.

In other areas of South Wales, power is transmitted by

overhead cables, supported by massive transmission towers (pylons), bringing on the landscape an alien element perhaps too unmistakably organised for a mechanical world ever to be absorbed in small scale organic landscapes. In the Vale of Glamorgan, and in the Vale Towy, they may be seen on the intimate countryside like files of linked giants.

New landscapes have again appeared since 1945 in the vicinity of the gigantic steel producton plants at the Ebbw Vale Works, the Spencer Works at Llanwern, the Margam Abbey Steel Works with their associated tinplate works at Swansea and Llanelli, which are located along the South Wales littoral. They have brought into existence, for example, new deep water harbours such as may be seen at Port Talbot.

Inland, there is still a growing need for new industrial development sites, but it is highly significant that apart from the steel industry, over 80 per cent of the potentially suitable land for new industrial undertaking lies in the coastal plain stretching from Cydweli to Chepstow. These, and other developments have led to a population movement of some magnitude down from the valleys towards the coast, a movement which has been partly stemmed in Monmouthshire by the building of a 'new town'.

New towns

It has been estimated that some 5,000 to 5,500 acres will be required in South Wales during the next fifteen years for urban development. Much of this will, undoubtedly, be absorbed in the expansion of existing towns such as Swansea, but some land will be taken up by the development of new towns such as Cwmbran, in Monmouthshire —the first new town to be built in Wales—in consequence of the New Towns Act 1946, and the 1947 Act, now superseded by the New Towns Act 1965. The area designated for development is 3,147 acres. By the end of March 1972, the Corporation had built 7,800 dwellings to house the town's increasing population.

Cwmbran is a modern 'planned' town, developed under the planning control of the Cwmbran Development Corporation (Plate 58). It has been planned "on the basis of five main residential neighbourhoods grouped around the new town centre area". Moreover, each neighbourhood has its own "social, educational and shopping facilities providing for day-to-day needs, leaving more ambitious shopping to be done in the town centre". Great attention has been paid to landscape at Cwmbran, the Corporation having planted "more than one tree" to every house built, besides "many thousands of shrubs and hedges, and many acres of grass".

Another area which has been extensively urbanised is centred around the old market town of Llantrisant and its environs. A short distance outside the town's boundaries, the Royal Mint has been set up, transforming a centuries old common into a modern industrial site. The proposal to build another 'new town' in the Llantrisant area has recently been rejected. Nevertheless, the degree of change which has taken place in this once delightful countryside is a further illustration of the current trend in the movement of population downwards from the valleys of South Wales to the lowlands and its coastal regions.

Of the many new architectural features which have appeared in the new and, indeed, the old urban landscapes of South Wales during the post-Second-World-War period, perhaps the most conspicuous are the multi-storey buildings —flats, offices, hotels, prestige buildings, etc.—which dominate their respective skylines. These often overshadow the old traditional landmarks such as the church towers or spires whose elegance has become blurred in the welter of modern structures.

The various facets of the South Wales landscape we have now discussed represent some of the visible memorials of man's individual and corporate efforts through the ages to exploit the natural resources of the region for the satisfaction of his material and non-material needs and aspirations. His progress from time immemorial has been dictated mainly by the character of the local soils, topography and climate, that is, the liberality or niggardliness of nature. The resultant human landscape, however, does not only show the effects of the uneven distribution of these natural resources on the pattern of human settlement in the uplands and lowlands; it also shows the results of the interplay of those human factors which arose out of the inequalities of individual chances and opportunities that prevailed throughout the ages in relation to the ownership of land and other forms of wealth. Thus the rather mean little churches, farmhouses and cottages which still dot the South Wales landscape, more especially in the rural areas, reflect the historic poverty of the countryside as compared with England. This was a feature which commanded the attention of many of the 'tourists' in the late eighteenth and early nineteenth century, particularly in those areas where mineral wealth was being exploited by English financiers who, more often than not, directed the money they made in Wales away from Wales, leaving behind much unrelieved ugliness which has characterised the face of South Wales to this day.

It has been estimated that Wales has upwards of 29,000 acres of derelict land, more than half of which is to be found in Glamorgan and Monmouthshire alone. Despite the praise-worthy reclamation work that is proceeding in such places as Merthyr Tudful, Gilfach Goch, the Ogmore and Swansea Valleys, new land is continually being brought into industrial use, and where the tipping of waste is a necessary operation, the area of land 'rendered incapable of beneficial use without treatment' is likely to be still increasing rather than decreasing.

Notwithstanding the large scale devastation that has been left behind, mostly during the last two hundred years, there remain considerable tracts of unexplored and unspoiled country to be enjoyed and studied. For instance, in the Pumlumon, Brecon Beacons and Radnorshire hills, the Presely Mountains in Pembrokeshire, on the outskirts of Allt-yr-yn and the upper reaches of the Usk Valley and the Wye Valley in Monmouthshire are many picturesque and romantic scenes to be admired, where the poet and musician might still be inspired to sing the praises of the streams, the heather, and the birds upon the wing, and, indeed, of the hills themselves.

Fortunately, many of these idyllic landscapes lie within the boundaries of the two National Parks located in South Wales, and come, therefore, under the protective care of the National Parks Commission (now the Countryside Commission) which will ensure the preservation and enhancement of their natural beauty for public enjoyment. The area so protected encompasses about 750 square miles of mountain, moor and coastal scenery, ranging from the vast stretches of unspoilt coastline of Pembrokeshire with its impressive cliffs, secluded coves and sandy bays to the colourful mountain moorland centred on the Brecon Beacons, bounded by the Black Mountains above Abergafenni in the east, and the Black Mountains of Carmarthenshire in the west. The commendable work of the Countryside Commission and allied bodies displays a keen awareness of our landscape heritage in the face of disorderly industrial development and encroachment.

In the more familiar and intimate surroundings, however, no matter in what direction we cast our eyes, we shall find the 'traditional' landscape being subjected to a continuous

The Making of the South Wales Landscape

and relentless modification by modern man in an irrepressible pursuit of his aspirations. Indeed the 'personality' of both town and country is changing rapidly, making each return journey to 'old familiar places' an experience similar, in many ways, to that expressed in a dialogue by Dylan Thomas on revisiting a Swansea Hostelry after the war:

> Narrator: What's the Three Lamps like now?
> Customer: It isn't like anything. It isn't there.
> It's nothing mun . . .[5]

SELECT BIBLIOGRAPHY

Crowe, Sylvia, *Tomorrow's Landscape* (London, Architectural Press, 1956).

Cwmbran New Town: Its Purpose and Development (Cwmbran Development Corporation, 1972).

Davies, Margaret, *Looking at Wales* (London, 1968).

Fairbrother, Nan, *New Lives and New Landscapes* (London: Architectural Press, 1970).

Hallett, Graham and Randall, Peter, *Maritime Industry and Port Developments in South Wales* (Department of Economics, University College, Cardiff, 1970, 1972).

Wales: The Way Ahead (Cardiff, H.M.S.O., 1967).

[5] *Quite Early One Morning* (London, 1957), p. 77.

Index

Aberaeron, 241; planned town, 211–12

Aberafan, 81, 188, 227; bridge, 204

Aberarth (Cards.), creek, 72

Aberdâr (Aberdare), 126, 224

Abergafenni, 36, 144; canal, 196; early Grammar School, 125

Abergwili, 101, 187

Abertawe, see Swansea

Aberthaw, 97; port of, 106, 107, 108; power station at, 259; sea walls of, 108; shipbuilding at, 108

Aberystwyth, 209, 211, 238–41; harbour of, 240; pier, 245; University College, 179

Act of Uniformity, 1662, 163

Act of Union, 1536, 25, 94, 124, 184

Afan, River, 73

afforestation, see forests

Agricultural Societies, 99, 145–7

agriculture, 29, 31, 59, 96, 129

airfields, 256

air photography, 87

Aissa, see Monknash

alms houses, 126

Angle (Pembs.), windmill, 154

aqueducts, 38, 196

Assarts, 69

Aubrey, Sir John, 120, 125

Bagendon (Glos.), 102

Baglan, early coal prospecting in, 190

Barallier, Louis, of Toulon, 213

Barnsley (Glos.), 102

Barry, 89, 97, 106, 107, 109, 227, 242; manor of, 132; population of, 200; railways, 200

Beaupré, 108

Beche, Sir Henry de la, 220

Betws, bridge, 203

Black Mountains (Brecs.), 28, 263

Blaen Cwm-bach, see Roman camps

Blaenau Morgannwg, 58, 119, 158

Blaenavon, 185

Board of Agriculture, the, 157

Bonvilston, 84

Boverton, windmill, 154

Bowen, Prof. E. G., 68

Brecon, 25, 57, 136, 263; canal, 196; Christ College, 124–5; priory of, 114

Brecon Beacons (Y Bannau), 25, 263

Breconshire, 33, 132; Agricultural Society, 145, 146, 174; houses in, 122

Bridgend, 81

Bridgwater, 108

Bristol, 108; Channel, 61; Welsh Back, 104

British and Foreign Society Schools, no. of, 178

Briton Ferry, 70, 196, 227; early coalmining at, 190

Briwnant, monastic grange, 187

Bro Morgannwg see Vale of Glamorgan

Brogden, family, 244

Bronze Age, 31, 32, 33

Brycheiniog, see Breconshire

Bryn Mawr, 176

Brynmill, 64

Buckland, old mill, 153

Buckland, William (geologist), 26

Builth (Buellt), 51, 230

Builth Wells, 46

Burgess, Dr Thomas, 178

Burry Holms, 52

Bute, 2nd Marquis, see Stuart, John Crichton

Butetown, growth of, 231

Bwlwarcau (bulwarks), Llangynwyd, 50, 60

Caerffili, 111; castle, 60

Caerleon, 36; castle, 57; Cistercian abbey, see Llantarnam

Caerwent, 37–8, 208

cairns, 32

265

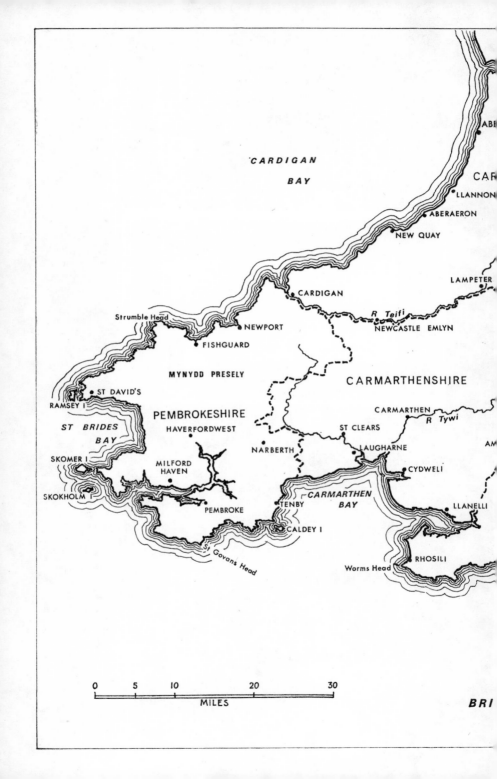